"With a firm conviction that today being religious must be being interreligious, Fabrice Blée offers us a rich account of how monastic interreligious dialogue has made an indispensable contribution not only to Christian renewal but also to world peace through the sharing of religious experiences. The 'third desert,' of which Blée speaks so eloquently and masterfully, is the space of silence in which one listens to the other to discern both similarities and differences. It is the 'désert de l'altérité'—to quote the original title of the book—that is becoming the dwelling-place of Christianity in its third millennium. The English translation has faithfully rendered the clarity and elegance of the French original. A book that is to be read and pondered over by those interested in interreligious dialogue and spirituality."

> —Dr. Peter C. Phan
> The Ignacio Ellacuría Chair of Catholic Social Thought
> Theology Department
> Georgetown University
> Washington, DC

"Here we have the first ever slow-motion replay of the humble ongoing movement of Christian monks, who—through their relentless struggle (never given up despite many setbacks) to establish and perpetuate an incessant conversation with their non-Christian counterparts in an atmosphere that alternates speech with silence—had proved to the post–Vatican II church that the new world that it dreamt of as our common future can begin to become a reality only when religious persons who have given up the world in order to take up its cause accept themselves as partners in a common mission rather than rivals in a conversion race. This is a facet of contemporary church history little known and scarcely mentioned."

> —Aloysius Pieris, SJ
> Tulana Research Centre
> Gonawala-Kelaniya, Sri Lanka

MONASTIC INTERRELIGIOUS DIALOGUE SERIES

The Third Desert

*The Story of
Monastic Interreligious Dialogue*

Fabrice Blée

Translated by William Skudlarek
with Mary Grady

LITURGICAL PRESS
Collegeville, Minnesota

www.litpress.org

This work was originally published in French under the title *Le désert de l'altérité*. © 2004 by Médiaspaul, Quebec, Canada.

Cover design by David Manahan, OSB.

Interior photographs used by permission of Alliance of International Monasticism (AIM).

© 2011 by Order of Saint Benedict, Collegeville, Minnesota. All rights reserved. No part of this book may be reproduced in any form, by print, microfilm, microfiche, mechanical recording, photocopying, translation, or by any other means, known or yet unknown, for any purpose except brief quotations in reviews, without the previous written permission of Liturgical Press, Saint John's Abbey, PO Box 7500, Collegeville, Minnesota 56321-7500. Printed in the United States of America.

Library of Congress Cataloging-in-Publication Data

Blée, Fabrice, 1968–
 [Désert de l'altérité. English]
 The third desert : the story of monastic interreligious dialogue / Fabrice Blée ; translated by William Skudlarek with Mary Grady.
     p.   cm. — (Monastic interreligious dialogue series)
 "This work was originally published in French under the title Le désert de l'altérité"—T.p. verso.
 Includes bibliographical references.
 ISBN 978-0-8146-3357-1 — ISBN 978-0-8146-3949-8 (e-book)
 1. Benedictines—History.   2. Catholic Church—Relations.   3. Meditation—Catholic Church—History.   4. Monastic and religious life—Asia—History.   5. Asia—Relegous life and customs.   6. Meditation—Asia—History.   I. Skudlarek, William.   II. Grady, Mary.   III. Title.

BX3006.3.B6413   2011
201'.5—dc22   2010031157

*To Richard Bergeron,
with gratitude and friendship.*

*To all the artisans of monastic interreligious dialogue
who, by their dedication and perseverance,
have opened the church
to the treasures of the Third Desert.*

*Then people will come
from east and west,
from north and south,
and will eat
in the kingdom of God.*

Luke 13:29

Contents

Foreword   ix

Preface   xiii

Introduction   1

Chapter 1
No Mission without Dialogue   13

Chapter 2
Dialogue for a Changing World   50

Photos   93

Chapter 3
Autonomy and Assessment   101

Chapter 4
Developing a Spirituality of Dialogue   136

Notes   205

Bibliography   211

Index   220

Foreword

In a 1968 speech about the relationship between dialogue and mission, Cardinal Marella, President of the Secretariat for Non-Christians, said, "Dialogue! That is the great and awe-inspiring word of our time" (Comby [1992], 295). Taking interreligious dialogue to its logical conclusion means reexamining the grand themes of the Christian faith and confronting once again the questions addressed by the earliest theologians. According to Karl Rahner, the challenge is of such magnitude that it will be difficult to recognize the church of the future. The dialogue that currently engages the Benedictine and Cistercian monks appears especially promising because they courageously and wholeheartedly accept all that is implied by receiving another religious experience with reverence. This book, written from a monastic and Christian perspective, is intended to introduce us to that form of dialogue.

My intention is not to provide a synthesis of monastic expressions of dialogue. Given the number and the multifaceted nature of the events that have been held over the course of years, that would be a colossal task indeed. What I can offer is an interpretation of monastic interreligious dialogue. By looking at its history, its leading figures, and its principal writings, we can show how it has developed and what it means. While this book does not go into a detailed description of the movement, it does attempt to provide a general description of one of the most demanding, little known, and often misunderstood expressions of dialogue.

This work is the fruit of a study of American and European monks[1] engaged in dialogue that I began about fifteen years ago. Since so little had been written, I began a research project that involved conducting interviews, collecting unpublished reports, and engaging in personal correspondence. Taken together, these materials have given me a better grasp of the inner logic and the challenges of this multifaceted form of dialogue that is taking place on several continents. Rather than pretending to provide an exhaustive report on everything that has been said and done by monks involved in dialogue, I have preferred to let those who have an interest in the cause and are sympathetic to it clarify the meaning and prospects of the experience of dialogue described in this book. I am grateful to Médiaspaul for making possible the publication not only of the original French version, entitled *Le désert de l'altérité* (The Desert of Otherness), but also of a series devoted to "Spiritualities in Dialogue." It was my contact with intermonastic dialogue that inspired the idea to launch a series of volumes devoted to the specifically spiritual dimension of inter-religious encounter. While monks are by no means the only ones involved in this type of dialogue, they certainly have pointed the way by their special charism, their long experience, and their gift of discernment. I would also like to thank the Woodstock Theological Center and Georgetown University for providing the conditions needed for the writing of this work. Thanks are also due to the International Thomas Merton Society for a Shannon research grant. Finally, I wish to express my profound gratitude to all who offered encouragement and valuable comments on the whole or a part of this book: Richard Bergeron of the University of Montreal; Bertrand Roy MEQ of the University of Saint Paul, Ottawa; Brother Sylvain OCSO of the Abbaye Val Notre-Dame, Saint-Jean-de-Matha (formerly at Oka), Quebec; Pierre de Béthune OSB of Clerlande, Belgium; Mayeul de Dreuille OSB of La Pierre-qui-vire, France; Bettina Bäumer of the University of Vienna; and James Redington SJ of the University of California, Berkeley.

Since the appearance of *Le désert de l'altérité* in 2004, the dialogue engaged in by monks has continued to attract attention in interreligious circles. One sign of this interest is the fact that the book has been published in Italian—*Il deserto dell'alterità* (Citadella, 2006) and is now appearing in English. I am grateful to Liturgical Press for making *The Third Desert* available in the English-speaking word, and to William Skudlarek for his accurate and sensitive translation.

Fabrice Blée

Preface

This book is welcome indeed because it treats a subject that has rarely been addressed. Interreligious dialogue is, of course, well known, and numerous works have appeared on the subject. They often make reference to the dialogue Christian monks began with monks of other religions, presenting it as an expression of dialogue in depth, but very few works have given much attention to the paradox of dialogue engaged in by people dedicated to silence.

Fabrice Blée sensed that this monastic way of entering into dialogue was something more than a unique undertaking limited to a specific group of individuals. He understood that a study of monastic interreligious dialogue could open up a new way of approaching the challenge and demands of all forms of interreligious dialogue, and he therefore embarked on a extended study of this phenomenon. Monastic interreligious dialogue was the subject of his doctoral dissertation, and after defending it in 1999 he decided to continue his research by establishing other contacts and by visiting various monastic settings for long periods of time, not only in America and Europe, but also in India and Japan.

This book, then, is the fruit of much research and reflection. The historical data and ample bibliography attest to its academic rigor. But it is also the fruit of his personal reflection on the implications of this type of dialogue.

It is extremely important to have such a description of how the dialogue of religious experience first began and how it developed within the church. It is possible to find some traces of this kind of dialogue in the history of past centuries, but an openhearted acceptance of other spiritual traditions has only been intentionally pursued since the middle of the twentieth century, first of all by the Benedictine monk Henri Le Saux, who was soon joined by other pioneers. Even though this initiative came out of the great missionary tradition of the church, it was such a daring innovation that it merits special study.

In 1978, only fifteen years after the death of Father Le Saux, his intuition was validated by the creation of commissions for monastic interreligious dialogue. These attempts to institutionalize monastic dialogue have had some degree of success and acceptance. It is revealing to study the ups and downs of the past thirty years, for the early history of the movement gives us a much clearer insight into its present position.

One of the reasons a book like this is so valuable is that there was a frequent turnover in leadership roles, especially in the United States, and it was not always possible to pass on the lessons learned. An outside perspective was needed to find an overview and to draw some conclusions from it.

Finally, this global historical treatment of the monastic movement for dialogue makes it possible to situate it in the more general movement for dialogue initiated by the Second Vatican Council in 1965. For all these reasons Fabrice Blée's work is extremely valuable for whoever is interested in the evolution—perhaps it would be better to say conversion—of the Christian frame of mind.

Guided by these historical markers, a theological reflection can ascertain the significance of the movement for dialogue that is developing in monastic circles. But first of all a question needs to be asked: What is a monk? What is this monastic tradition that is spoken of throughout the book? And even more important, what is the specific contribution these solitary, silent ones make to encounter and dialogue? I will begin by recalling that monks, male and female, are indeed people of solitude, as the etymology of the word "monk" indicates. However, their solitude is not so much a peaceful haven as their place of spiritual combat, a place that must always be kept free of encroaching complacency in order that the Presence may be discerned there.

Monastic solitude is a place of listening—"Listen!" is the first word of the Rule of Saint Benedict. The monk strives to listen to the call of God mediated through all of existence. When monks exercise this developed faculty of listening by applying it to other spiritualities, they become acutely aware of how beautiful and fascinating they are. This awareness presents itself at the very center of their religious quest, and openness to these spiritualities often gives rise to tensions, possibly even rupture, between the demands of their exclusive attachment to Christ and those of unconditional acceptance of the other in his name. But it is precisely at this level that one experiences *intra*-religious dialogue, a dialogue that involves all the energy at play in the religious vocation. Equally as much energy is needed to meet the challenge of interreligious dialogue, because it is clear that if little is invested, nothing is gained.

If it seems paradoxical to think that monks have a special role to play in the history of dialogue, we need to remember that all dialogue is paradoxical. It always involves an unwavering openness to the other. Meeting someone from another religion, especially when that person is a monk like oneself, is often an enriching and pleasant experience, an experience of spiritual friendship. However, if this satisfying encounter is taken to a deeper level it becomes clear that the other is also very different, unchangeable, and inaccessible, even—dare we say it?—an enemy. The paradox exists at the very heart of dialogue: concord and conflict are very close to one another, and we can honestly say that today dialogue is both indispensable and impossible.

This is the context for understanding the original title of this book: *The Desert of Otherness*. In fact, when we find ourselves before the other we see someone we recognize, someone in whom we discover a fundamental similarity. But sooner or later, inevitably, we become conscious of what separates and isolates us. That too is part of the experience of dialogue. The necessity of respecting the otherness of the one we encounter is an asceticism even more demanding than the penitential practices of ancient monasticism.

This desert and this emptiness can become even heavier to bear when this spiritual experience is subjected to the most rigorous testing. The other can be received as a guest, as someone sent by God. But the other can also turn out to be a "Trojan horse" who threatens to tear down our faith. Our loss of interior guideposts becomes an experience of extreme poverty or a dark night of faith.

This book marks a significant stage in the history of monastic interreligious dialogue because it offers a view of the whole. It takes stock of the situation and initiates reflection on this new, unusual, risky form of dialogue—indeed, on dialogue in all its manifestations.

Because of all the risks involved, there are many today who express hesitation about the work of dialogue, and at times their fear leads to a certain paralysis. This book is an invitation to have no fear and to go forward, because the history of dialogue, as short as it is, has already revealed its treasures. Looking at all that has already taken place allows us to hope that there will be still more to discover as we continue this way of putting the Gospel into practice.

Pierre de Béthune OSB
Secretary General of the Commissions
for Monastic Interreligious Dialogue
Clerlande, Belgium, August 2004

Introduction

To be religious is to be interreligious! This maxim represents one of the great discoveries of the last century and will affect the way we relate to the sacred for generations to come. It summons us to enter into dialogue with other believers in virtue of our relation to God, a dialogue that has become in our time a providential means of divine self-revelation. Now, for the first time in history, there are countless Christians whose spiritual lives are being fashioned by a respectful and open relationship to other religions.

The above maxim appeared for the first time at the thirteenth annual congress of the Theological Association of India, which was held in 1989 in Tiruchirapalli in the state of Tamil Nadu. It then reappeared in an official statement issued by the thirty-fourth General Congress of the Jesuits in Rome. This openness to religions has special significance for the Christians in Asia, but it is also of major interest—as well as concern—to the church in the West.

Following the Second World War humankind entered the new era of globalization, characterized by a pronounced feeling of interdependence and coupled with the affirmation of ethnic identities. Pluralism became an unquestionable reality that had to be contended with, for it demanded that all sectors of society think differently about their relation to the individual, the collectivity, and the world. Religions were not spared, and today there are many theologians who hold that Christianity can no longer think of itself in isolation from other religious experiences without the risk of succumbing to fundamentalism and thereby betraying its most cherished values.

If the shock of cultures reinforces identity politics in the area of religion, it is also responsible for the many expressions of a movement toward dialogue. While this movement is not well covered by the media, it is still very influential. On every continent the number of local, national, and international interreligious encounters continues to grow. Over the span of years, partners in dialogue have become familiar with one another and have banded together against injustice. Their frequent contact with one another has helped to reduce the harmful effects of prejudices and fears vis-à-vis other religions. All this takes place because these individuals, engaged in dialogue, have been able to identify common values while respecting what is specific to each of their traditions. Together they have discovered the necessity—indeed, the urgency—of understanding one another in order to lay the foundations of a peaceful world while becoming themselves more open to the unlimited horizons of the divine reality, a mystery that can be neither exhausted nor monopolized by any one theological or philosophical system. These endeavors are only the first step of a long-term course of action, and the future is uncertain. Still, that future rests on a solid foundation, namely, the realization that interreligious dialogue is the vocation of all the baptized. In his allocution to the Secretariat for Non-Christian Religions in 1984, Pope John Paul II declared: "All Christians are called to dialogue. While it is important that certain individuals have specialized training in this area, others also have an important contribution to make. I am thinking in particular of the intermonastic dialogue and that of other movements, groups, and institutions."[2] Later, in his encyclical On the Permanent Validity of the Church's Missionary Mandate (*Redemptoris Missio*) he reiterated the fact that "Inter-religious dialogue is a part of the Church's evangelizing mission" (RM 55).

Within the space of several decades the dominant Catholic attitude toward other religions has progressed from an exclusivist regard, captured in the saying "outside the church, no salvation," to an expression of welcoming and openness in response to the plea of John XXIII and the Second Vatican Council to see in cultural and religious pluralism a sign of the times (*kairos*), the locus of an invitation to humanity to be reconciled to the divine mystery. An encounter with other religions is not a luxury, an optional or insignificant activity, or even less a fad. This encounter is as fundamental a dimension of Christian action and salvation as evangelization or the preferential option for the poor. Rather than being a narrow field of activity for a particular local church seeking to become inculturated, it is the fertile soil in which the entire church can plant the seed of renewal for the benefit of all.

For Christians, the vocation to enter into relationship with other religions takes several forms. The Pontifical Council for Interreligious Dialogue[3] has identified four: the dialogue of life, of works, of theological discussion, and of religious experience.[4] The dialogue of life takes place in daily life through informal meetings in one's neighborhood, at work, or in some other activity. The dialogue of works brings together members of different groups who share a common desire to work for a just and humanitarian cause. The dialogue of theological discussion has as its purpose the understanding of the doctrines of each religion in an effort to determine what they have in common and where they differ. It is easy to remember these first three types of dialogue, and their meaning is clear. But the last one, the dialogue of religious experience, can easily be overlooked. Some think it is simply not all that relevant, given the huge challenges of injustice, poverty, or doctrinal and political discord. Nonetheless, this fourth form of dialogue—the subject of this book—is extremely important. More than that, it is essential for the development of dialogue in all its dimensions.

In order to comprehend the dialogue of experience one must first know just what it refers to. The pontifical document *Dialogue and Proclamation* (Reflection and Orientations on Interreligious Dialogue and the Proclamation of the Gospel of Jesus Christ, 1991) defines the dialogue of religious experience as one "where persons, rooted in their own religious traditions, share their spiritual riches, for instance with regard to prayer and contemplation, faith and ways of searching for God or the Absolute"

(DP 42). This formulation describes a type of dialogue that goes beyond speaking of one's spiritual journey or listening to that of the other, much less simply studying the beliefs of someone else in a purely intellectual way. It implies entering into the religious experience of the other, or, to put it in other words, offering the other a space within oneself. How can we hope to comprehend the spiritual journey of someone else, their way of living in relation to the sacred, if we do not go beyond words and different interpretations and allow ourselves to be converted to that way, at least to some degree? The dialogue of religious experience is more than a discussion of some particular theme. Above all it is a *praxis*, a practice and a process built on internalizing our relationship to the other, who is welcomed along with everything that makes the other different from a spiritual and religious point of view.[5] By its very nature such a relationship raises existential questions and makes dialogue a rich spiritual act founded on an expression of hospitality that affects the very existence of those who engage in it.

This kind of dialogue—following Panikkar (Blée [1966a]), we can refer to it as inner- or intrareligious dialogue—is especially challenging because it demands that we allow our deepest faith to be questioned by another religious truth we have come to know and admire. Internal dialogue not only requires that we have a good knowledge of our own tradition; it demands that we be nourished by another way of thinking, feeling, and praying. In the last analysis that is the only way to attain a true understanding of what makes the other "other"; it is the only way to avoid making dialogue some kind of strategy or reducing it to a comparative study of religions. With regard to other forms of dialogue, internal dialogue requires that we cannot give in to indifference but rather should unite ourselves with other believers to share in their humanity and their deepest aspirations. To repeat, internal dialogue does not designate a purely verbal exchange centered on the religious experiences of each person involved. It is a religious experience in itself in which relationship to the other is what prompts a renewed relationship to the divine.

The dialogue of spiritual experience is not a higher form of dialogue, an esoteric activity for a spiritual elite. It would be wrong to thus limit its importance by saying that it has little to do with social and practical concerns. The four kinds of dialogue mentioned above are not separate forms of dialogue in the sense that you can choose the one that appeals to you and exclude the rest. Rather, they are different dimensions of one and the same dialogue. The only reason to distinguish them is so that the potential of each can be developed more fully.

In fact, the dialogue of religious experience is open to everyone. Among Christians many and wide-ranging groups of individuals are involved: laypeople, priests, religious and contemplatives of various orders. It takes place in many different settings and at different levels; all that is needed is respect for otherness. There are many ways to be open and receptive to another religious truth: reading the sacred texts of other traditions; growing up in or moving into another religious culture, taking part in its rituals, feasts, or pilgrimages; marrying someone from a different faith or being the child of an interfaith marriage; contemplating the religious works of art of another tradition; or adopting, as a Christian, the meditation practices of a Buddhist, Hindu, or Sufi.

This book focuses on the experience of Christian contemplatives of the Benedictine and Cistercian orders. If one looks at the various forms of dialogue that have developed within the church over the past forty years, one sees that Benedictine monks, men and women, have given especially strong and ongoing witness to the fourth kind of dialogue. Monks have a special affinity for the dialogue of experience. It was, in fact, after the 1983 Spiritual Exchange program, in which European Benedictine monks offered hospitality to Japanese Zen monks, that the dialogue of experience was added to the three other types in the pontifical document *The Attitude of the Church toward the Followers of Other Religions: Reflections and Orientations on Dialogue and Mission*, which was published the following year. While the spiritual dialogue mentioned here refers to monastic experience without identifying it as such, it cannot be limited to monasticism nor does it diminish the quality and relevance of other experiences of dialogue. I should add that while—in theory, at least—monks are receptive to dialogue with all religions, in practice they have developed a close relationship with Eastern spiritualities, especially Buddhism. This being the case, it is correct to say that "today they are the farthest along on the road of dialogue with Buddhists " (Gira [1991], 104). Dialogue with Islam and Judaism may be more developed, but if one takes into account the level of communion between the partners in dialogue, the exchange of hospitality, the continuity of their exchanges, and the overall organization of this encounter, monastic interreligious encounter is among the richest and most promising experiences of dialogue. We should not forget to mention that it has always benefited from the support of monastic and church authorities. No other group within the Catholic Church has been engaged in such in-depth dialogue of contemplative experience, in such an organized way, at the international level, and over such a long period of time.

Some may wonder if the aura surrounding this kind of dialogue might not be exaggerated, given the fact that a secular society like ours, which gives priority to social action, does not have much time for monks. Can anything good come from monasteries, those havens of archaism?

Moreover, since what is characteristic of the monk is silence and retreat from the world rather than conversation and social engagement (Blée [1999a]), it would be legitimate to wonder if it is not simply a contradiction in terms to speak about monastic dialogue. It might also be pointed out that this kind of dialogue only concerns a small group within the larger Benedictine family. If monks represent a marginal group within society, that is doubly true of monks involved in dialogue! And yet one can believe that monastic dialogue has a prophetic role to play in contemporary society. In order to understand why, we have to look briefly at the *raison d'être* of monastic life and its influence on the development of the church.

The *monachos* is someone who retires into solitude and silence, leaving behind worldly obligations in order to be fully dedicated to the search for the divine. The monk is drawn by a sense of the urgency of returning to the essential, expressed by a deliberate stripping away of all that is ephemeral and makes for a divided heart. The nature of the monastic vocation is twofold: nonconformity coupled with the safeguarding of the highest human values. For this reason, monks have their place at both the margins and the center of the established order, a position that makes them powerful agents of transformation not only on the individual but on the social level as well. Their role is especially critical in times of great crisis. This was particularly evident in the primitive church when monks filled the deserts of Egypt and Syria in reaction to the decline of Roman civilization and to a church that was often becoming lax. That is where Christian monasticism was born. Later it spread throughout Europe and laid the foundations of a new civilization. Today, when the church and Western societies are being put to the test on all fronts, Benedictine and Cistercian monks are once again surprising us by their response to the contemporary cultural and religious crisis.

Starting in the 1960s, numerous monastic foundations were made in Africa, South America, and Asia. At the end of the 1970s a structure to support interreligious dialogue was set up, first in Europe and the United States, then in Australia and India/Sri Lanka. In the past the followers of Saint Benedict played a major role in the evangelization of Europe and contributed to the shaping of Christianity in the West. Now they turned their attention to the rest of the world and, as Christian monasticism was becoming (and continues to become) less and less Western, became the promoters of spiritual dialogue with other religions. This turnaround bears witness to a new way for Christianity to be present in the world. Instead of a European—or, more broadly speaking, Western—church, based on a centralized administrative structure, what is emerging is a pluralistic church that builds on an integrated experience of the Mystery. The German theologian Karl Rahner spoke of the necessity of a global Christianity and predicted that the Christian religion would only survive in the twenty-first century if it were mystical. Perhaps monks involved in dialogue are proving him right. Monks are once again putting aside the *status quo* in order to open new spiritual paths in accord with the interior laws of the Spirit. By doing so they offer hope for a better future to men and women who, now more than ever, feel confused and abandoned.

I do not believing in clinging to a romantic and idealized vision of the monastic life. Monastic dialogue is itself a critique of a monastic way of life that reels under the weight of administrative tasks, activism, and routine, all of which often leave little time for contemplation, the primary vocation of the monk. Thomas Merton (Merton [1972]) gave eloquent, if at times harsh, expression to such criticism. My intention is simply to recall the decisive, though not exclusive, role played by monks as artisans of civilization, and to point to monastic dialogue as one more element in the history of religious changes that has emerged from the silence of monasteries. We can think, for example, of the Crusades with Saint Bernard, the Reformation with Martin Luther, a member of the Augustinian order, the patristic studies undertaken by the Maurists in the seventeenth and eighteenth centuries, or the liturgical reforms of the twentieth century.

We need, therefore, to pay attention to this recent movement within Catholic monasticism that flows from the conviction that to be religious is to be interreligious.[6] As unobtrusive and small as it is, it could very well have an enormous impact on religious conduct in the future. Stephen Batchelor expresses that same opinion when he writes that this monastic movement for dialogue is "a much quieter movement within the Church working towards a closer understanding of Buddhism, that in the long term may bear the most fruit" (Batchelor [1994], 219). I do not want to overstate the importance of monastic interreligious dialogue, but I do see it as the symbol or archetype of a Christian attitude that rests on two pillars: the search for the divine in each person and love for those whose beliefs are different from ours. It is precisely for this reason that such an enterprise cannot and should not be limited to a small group of monks. In fact, it has spread out from monasteries by offering hope for a return to the essence of the Christian vocation in response to the challenges of the present time. Monasticism has demonstrated that it is capable of showing the way to a spirituality that is applicable to all because it is open to all the ways that lead to God and to the multiple manifestations of the Spirit.

If that is the case, we can put to rest the widespread belief—actually a reproach—that monks have isolated themselves from the world for the sake of an individualistic search for the divine. Exile is undoubtedly a part of the monastic ideal. Monks set out to reach the place where they can engage in the struggle for unity and simplicity, a place that cannot be reached without the renunciation of familiar landmarks. Initially the desert was that privileged place. Later, in Europe, it took the form of a monastery in the forest, on a mountaintop, or in a valley. Today the desert is not a geographical place or a structure. The monk engaged in dialogue withdraws into the heart of religious otherness. After the desert of sand and the desert of stones, we come to the third desert. Today more than ever, a relationship with other believers becomes this deserted place that is filled with trials, temptations, and union with the divine. This desert has no particular form and does not separate the monk from human activities. It is, quite simply, the axis of the kingdom to come, that reality where all communication becomes communion. What is taking place within contemporary monasticism is an exceptionally creative development that owes its existence to an unusual alliance between dialogue and silence, openness to the other and interiority.

The principal, most direct, and also most narrow gate that gives monks access to the place of dialogue we are calling the third desert is the adoption of non-Christian practices of meditation, especially Zen, Vipassana, or yoga. In this way monastic dialogue contributes to bringing together the spiritual treasures of Asia and those of Christian monasticism, a process that has really just begun. According to pioneers like Henri Le Saux, Bede Griffiths, or William Johnston, this coming together of Eastern and Western spiritual practices could be just as significant for the development of the church as was the coming together of primitive Christianity and Greek philosophies two thousand years ago. Even though the adoption of such meditation practices has not become the norm, or something all monks are involved in, it is still at the heart of their dialogue, an indispensable element for understanding its development and the challenges it faces.

This book, then, offers an interpretation of monastic dialogue by giving special attention to the part played by Eastern meditation practices. Without going into great historical detail, I want to bring to light the genesis of a new Christian consciousness that is anchored in the twofold need to rediscover the meaning of interiority and to bring about peaceful coexistence among the peoples of the world. I would like to familiarize the reader with this rich but modest intrareligious[7] experience in order to uncover its motivations, its challenges, and its promise. To achieve that end I will limit myself to presenting several key periods in the history of this monastic dialogue. Better, I will describe the distinctive attitudes monks bring to an encounter with other religions, attitudes that demonstrate the spirit of the dialogue of spiritual experience in various times and places. Names and dates are included to show the development of these attitudes and not to give the impression of an exhaustive study.

This work is composed of four chapters. Each of the first three deals with a specific way of engaging in intrareligious dialogue and highlights the crucial role played by the adoption of a way of meditation developed in another tradition. Each of these ways is related to an important period in the history of monastic dialogue during which its basic orientation was shaped by a particular vision and institutional structure. It should be said, however, that if a particular orientation of internal or intrareligious dialogue is stressed in a given period, it is not limited to that period, but can be found in all the other periods to a lesser degree or in a more underground fashion.

The thesis of the first chapter is that dialogue lived out at the level of religious experience—that is to say, at the level of faith and of the intimate relationship of the believer to the divine— emerged from a concern that Western monasticism become inculturated, especially in Asia. Interreligious dialogue grew out of the missionary renewal undertaken by the followers of Saint Benedict in the early 1960s and was identified with this setting until the end of the 1970s. The work of the pioneers showed that dialogue flowed from the necessity of having a hands-on knowledge of Eastern religions and of making monastic life less Western. The interest in meditation practices such as Zen or yoga quickly became a determining factor in this effort.

The second chapter examines intrareligious dialogue at the service of a cause that now goes beyond the missionary concerns of the church in the West. After receiving its own institutional structure, monastic dialogue continued to develop from the end of the 1970s to the mid 1980s in response to the importance of contributing to world peace by setting down the spiritual foundations of a global culture. This involved searching for a way to bring East and West together within oneself so that a new consciousness of the divine mystery could come to birth in the human heart and be the guarantee of peaceful coexistence. What gave rise to this approach was the monks' recognition that they needed to become involved in a pastoral ministry focused on contemplation and offered to those Christians who had had a significant religious experience through contact with Buddhism, Hinduism, or a new religious movement related to Eastern spirituality, and were now coming to monasteries to seek spiritual direction.

The third chapter calls attention to interior dialogue as the place where a new way of being a Christian in the world was emerging. From the middle of the 1980s to the end of the 1990s monks involved in dialogue, because of various criticisms and suspicions directed at them, made an effort to find their place in their respective communities. They promoted the organizational independence of dialogue and strove to formulate a clear statement of its particularity. The foundations and conditions of the intrareligious experience having been defined, what was emphasized now was the development of a spirituality of dialogue. The work has just begun and calls for the continued attention of contemplatives.

The last chapter does not pretend to give a full picture of the fourth stage in the history of intrareligious dialogue, since such a treatment demands the perspective afforded by greater distance. Instead, what I want to do in this chapter is to make known the meaning and challenges of a spirituality of dialogue. An overview of this monastic interreligious venture allows us to appreciate what makes it unique, the conditions that make it possible, and its meaning for Christian life.

I offer this book to everyone who wants to become involved, or is already involved, in these new spiritual ventures at the crossroads of different religions. We can be assured that such an undertaking is not marginal to the Christian tradition and that we do not have to start from zero. Much has already been accomplished, and that can be a source of inspiration for all of us.

Chapter **1**

No Mission without Dialogue

The attitude of Benedictine monks toward other religions was initially shaped by the missionary ventures undertaken by Benedictines, especially during the decades of the sixties and seventies. It may seem surprising that missionaries fostered dialogue with other religions since they so often simply rejected the beliefs and practices of the people they were evangelizing. True as that may be, we should also remember that during the centuries Europeans were discovering new lands, missionary activity was responsible for gradually bringing Christians to accept religious diversity as the missionaries themselves strove to understand how other religions might fit into their overall understanding of salvation.

What may be especially surprising is that there is a connection between monasticism and mission. Insofar as monks give primacy of place to seclusion and silence, there would seem to be a certain contradiction between these two ways of life. How can a monk reconcile a life of interiority and stability with the skills and mobility required by missionary work? Simply raising these questions leads us to recall that the evangelization of Europe was in large part the work of monks, not only of the sons of Saint Benedict but of other monastic movements as well, for example, the Irish monks who were followers of Saint Columban. What is actually most surprising is not the simple fact that monks were and are missionaries, but that they always brought something essentially and uniquely monastic to this work, even after the apostolic orders replaced them and left little room for their involvement in spreading the Gospel.

Following the two World Wars there was a renewal of missionary activity on the part of Benedictines and Cistercians. One of the principal reasons for this was recognition of the importance of engaging in a profound dialogue with non-Christian spiritualities. This form of dialogue is grounded in hospitality and culminates in the adoption of methods of meditation that have been developed in other religions. Adopting a meditation practice that is the cornerstone of another religious tradition is what makes possible a deep and meaningful relationship with that tradition. Dialogue and mission, in effect, are two inseparable and interrelated realities. It would be impossible to grasp the origin and concerns of the monastic interreligious experience without first looking at monastic mission. The point is not to compile a history of monastic missionary activity but to understand what motivates it and what it demands.

What inspires the missionary monk to enter into spiritual dialogue with other religions? Three points have to be taken into consideration. The first is the fundamental orientation that undergirds monastic mission, namely, the desire to understand the cultural and religious distinctiveness of the peoples who will receive the Gospel. Next we have to look at this desire in an Asian context, because it is there that it will face its greatest challenge and, at the same time, find conditions especially favorable to dialogue. Finally, dialogue develops, thanks especially to a study of the ascetic methods of Hinduism and Buddhism. Such study is essential for the implementation of a mission that will only succeed through a willingness to become acquainted with the other, even before the other is able to know you.

Knowing in Order to Be Known

The renewal of monastic mission began rather timidly at the end of the nineteenth century. After having experienced pronounced hostility in post-Reformation Europe, monasticism there enjoyed a rebirth during the Romantic period, which gave rise to new vitality in the areas of liturgy, institutions, contemplation, and also mission. It was during this period that the Trappists founded several monasteries outside Europe, especially in Africa. Pope Pius XI encouraged the missionary expansion of this newly revived monasticism in his 1923 apostolic letter *Umbratilem* and then in his 1926 encyclical On Catholic Missions (*Rerum Ecclesiae*), in which he called for the setting up of contemplative monastic communities in the countries where the church was being established.

But it was only in the second half of the twentieth century that monastic mission flourished and made dialogue one of its major activities. The person most responsible for this development was Cornelius Tholens, a Dutch Benedictine who opened the way for monasticism to become actively involved in the creation of a better world. He encouraged his confreres to learn about and be concerned with the world around them, thus offering it the hope that people could become reconciled with God and with one another.

To arrive at this end he proposed the creation of an organization that could help remedy the fact that Benedictine monasticism was almost unknown outside the West. This organization would be a center for aid and information, and its goal would be to establish monastic communities in mission lands and to provide essential resources to those willing to be part of this venture. In 1959 Tholens came to the congress of Benedictine abbots that was being held at the international Benedictine college of Sant' Anselmo in Rome and proposed the founding of a Secretariat for the implantation of Christian monasticism in mission lands. Even though Tholens was not the only one to propose this idea, and though others played a significant role in implementing the proposal, he and his vision and work are primarily responsible for bringing the Secretariat to realization. At first there was hesitation on the part of some abbots who thought an organization at the level of the confederation might threaten the juridical independence of their monasteries. But thanks to his perseverance and reasoned responses, Tholens convinced the assembled abbots that the proposal merited their support, and they responded by voting unanimously to create a new Secretariat. It was given the name "Aide à l'implantation monastique" (AIM), and one year later its office was set up in Vanves, on the outskirts of Paris. It quickly became a center that supported the development of serious dialogue with other religions.

Renewal Through Mission

The involvement of monks in the missionary activity of the church enables us to see that while the church enters history through mission, mission also calls it to a process of self-examination that often leads to a new way of understanding itself and its calling. In the beginning AIM was a way of responding to the call to mission given by Pope Pius XII in his 1957 encyclical On the Present Condition of the Catholic Missions, Especially in Africa (*Fidei Donum*). At the same time monks entered mission in reaction to a certain number of situations that in the postwar period affected the church and its expansion.

The decline of the European powers and the large number of former colonies that became independent countries brought the church into a "postcolonial" world shaped by new borders and open to new ways of thinking. The church had to deal with the spread of atheism and religious pluralism. In Africa especially, countries that had recently become independent were subject to secular, political, and religious influences that the encyclical judged to be at odds with the message of Christ. Added to this was a sense of panic in the face of possible annihilation. After the two most devastating wars in history, the threat of a nuclear holocaust led some to think that the end of the world was imminent and others to doubts about the existence of a God judged to be indifferent to intolerable suffering. It became clear that, in a world where all nations and cultures are bound together more than ever before, the beliefs that had always been considered contrary to the Christian faith were now able to be spread to the four corners of the earth in a relatively short period of time.

In this state of instability and rapid change Pope Pius XII issued an encyclical to all Catholics urging them to work for the establishment of the church in mission lands, above all in Africa. This was the first time a pope had called on all the faithful to devote themselves to the spread of the faith, an appeal that gave evidence of the precarious situation of the church vis-à-vis the emerging new world. Tholens' sensitivity to the current state of affairs led him to interpret one passage of the encyclical in a typically monastic way. That passage reads: "A man is no true member of the Church unless he is likewise a true member of the entire body of Christian believers and is filled with an ardent desire to see her take root and flourish in every land" (FD 44). Tholens' paraphrase of this passage set the course for the future missionary activities of the Benedictine family. "Monks understand that *Fidei donum* is especially addressed to them; they do not belong to Christ if they are not totally devoted to the cause of the Church's universality, if they do not ardently desire that it take root and flourish throughout the entire world" (Leclercq [1986], 8). While Tholens was convinced that there had to be a renewal of the missionary spirit at the heart of monasticism, his understanding of mission was different from that of the encyclical, which, in his mind, was based on outmoded ideas.

Rather than getting behind the encyclical's call to propagate the "true faith" in opposition to other religions, Tholens held that "before anything else, abbots must recognize that monks of the Benedictine Order have the duty, to go out in the name of the Order to encounter other peoples, other races, other religions" (ibid.). Unlike Pius XII, Tholens grounded mission in the act of listening to non-Christian religious traditions, convinced that the only way Christianity could become universal was through dialogue with other traditions. The pope, on the other hand, adopted an exclusivist approach, not only calling on Catholics to oppose atheists ("enemies of God's name"), but also to confront the "pagan beliefs" that affect millions of Africans and to go up against Islam—though he does not mention it by name—which had been spreading rapidly throughout Africa since the beginning of the twentieth century. Pius XII evoked a sense of urgency: Act now or it will be too late. Act now before Africa becomes impervious to the one true faith. In so doing he confirmed the expansionist ideal of the church of an earlier age: "We should spare no efforts in order that the Cross of Christ in which is our salvation and life might cast its shadow over even the most distant quarters of the universe" (FD 8). Tholens, on the other hand, preferred a constructive approach to other religions, which he regarded not as an obstacle to the Christian faith but as a way of deepening it.

A Favorable Social and Theological Context

Tholens' non-traditional understanding of mission was not idiosyncratic; it was favored by a worldview shaped by social and theological developments that took place after the Second World War. At that time the world witnessed the resurgence of a sense of national and religious identities, while the institutional church was losing its influence not only on the world stage but among its own faithful. These two phenomena were leading Christians to accept the fact that converting the whole world was a dream they would never see fulfilled. Moreover, informal exchanges on the local level between adherents of different religions became more and more common, especially in the 1970s (Basset [1996]). The friendships born from these exchanges made it possible for people to move beyond their ignorance, fears, and prejudices. In this new social context—which was also marked by a rise of different forms of fundamentalism—dialogue with other religions was judged preferable to condemnation if the church was to maintain and strengthen its presence in the world and thus be able to devote itself to the cause of justice and peace.

A readiness for dialogue was also encouraged by inclusivist theologians of the 1950s and 1960s such as Karl Rahner, Henri de Lubac, and Yves Congar, who affirmed that Christ was actively present in other religions even though their followers were unaware of it. Taken up by the Second Vatican Council and inspired by the fathers of the church, this view of other religions granted other believers the possibility of salvation outside the church, while continuing to maintain that the ultimate role of

Christianity was to lead all other religions to their full realization. Such an understanding of other religions inevitably opened the door to dialogue.

This theological orientation provided the context for monastic mission. Indeed, monastic mission contributed to the development of fulfillment theology. One has only to think of the friendly yet thoughtful correspondence between Henri de Lubac and Jules Monchanin. The latter, together with Henri Le Saux, was the founder of the Christian ashram known as Shantivanam (Gadille [1983], 35).

One should also mention the contribution of Asian and especially Indian theology to the development of an interreligious consciousness. In 1950, right after independence, India's first plenary council recognized that there was goodness and truth outside Christianity. In 1957, 1958, and 1960 there were conferences at Shantivanam to consider mystical experience in Christianity and Hinduism, and between the years 1961 and 1964 Jacques-Albert Cuttat brought together a group that included Henri Le Saux, Murray Rogers, and James Stuart to consider the question of spiritual dialogue between Hindus and Christians. These latter meetings, taking place at the same time the Second Vatican Council was in session, gave rise to the conviction that the more one enters deeply into one's own religion the more one is able to go to the heart of other religious traditions. This insight opened the way to a spirituality of dialogue by insisting that true encounter is grounded in spirituality, and that internal dialogue, that is, experiencing another's faith while entering more deeply into one's own, must precede all interaction with adherents of other religious traditions (Kuttianimattathil [1995]).

If monks in mission contributed to the theological openness that was developing even before the beginning of the Second Vatican Council, they were even more involved in putting this openness into practice. At the same time these monks continued to examine their own motivation and intentions in order to be sure that their relationship with people of other religions was always honest and respectful. They were convinced that if one wanted to be known by someone else one first of all had to make an effort to know the other. This desire to know and be known is dialogue's *raison d'être*. After creating the Secretariat for Non-Christians in 1964, Paul VI described its purpose and mission in his 1967 constitution *Regimini Ecclesiae universae*: "This Secretariat is responsible for research into the ways and means that will make it possible to engage in dialogue with non-Christians. It will take special care to insure that Christians become familiar with and have high regard for non-Christians, and that non-Christians do the same with regard to Christian life and teaching" (99). Monks involved in missionary activity follow this approach, especially when their dialogue with other religious adherents gives rise to an internal spiritual dialogue.

One might ask why monks in particular developed such deep respect for interreligious otherness. After all, the methodology of "knowing in order to be known" had marked Christian missionary activity for a long time without necessarily giving rise to true dialogue, dialogue that recognizes and accepts the other as incontrovertibly different. Thanks to their wide-ranging knowledge of the Greek philosophers and the religions of their time—a knowledge that was experiential and not simply acquired through study—the fathers of the church were able to expound the Christian revelation to a "pagan" society. The seventeenth-century Jesuits Matteo Ricci in China, Roberto de Nobili in India, and Ippolito Desideri in Tibet and India operated in much the same way. These missionaries did their utmost to become familiar with the traditions of the local religious culture. At the same time, their efforts were directed toward the conversion of souls and they rarely concerned themselves with developing a mutual relationship of equal to equal. Despite their sincere attempts at adaptation—one thinks especially of Roberto de Nobili—they left little room for the kind of dialogue that seeks to understand others as they themselves want to be understood. Acquiring knowledge of another religion can be done in order to forge a weapon to use against it. Friendship can become a means to make another more like oneself. The intention behind the desire to know another and to be known is all-important. It can be a strategy for demonstrating the superiority of one's own faith.

Mastering others' language and adopting their customs does not necessarily mean that one respects them in their difference. The renewal of monastic missionary activity shows the value of emphasizing respect for others and their deepest longings without any intention of winning them over or pointing out their faults. What is apparent in the attitude of monks toward dialogue is the idea developed by Raimon Panikkar, namely that it is impossible to understand other believers as they understand themselves without sharing their view of the world and to some degree, at least, making their view one's own and finding something of value in it. To say that one understands someone else's vision of the world and then to say that it is false is a contradiction. As Panikkar says, "to understand means to be converted to the truth that one understands" (Panikkar [1999], 59). There is a way of being honest in our dealings with others that leads us beyond what we could ever have imagined. Honesty of this kind brought Monchanin to the painful conclusion that it was impossible to reconcile Hinduism and Christianity. The same honesty led Le Saux to experience the suffering brought about by engaging in dialogue at the deepest level. Monastic dialogue witnesses to the appropriateness of applying the phrase "to know in order to be known" to intrareligious dialogue, described by Panikkar as "an inner dialogue within myself, an encounter in the depth of my personal religiousness, having met another religious experience on that intimate level" (Panikkar [1999], 73–74).

Contemplative Life as a Catalyst

What gives rise to this internal dialogue, and why do monks play such a key role in developing it? The answer is to be found, in part, by considering the place of contemplation in their way of life. This is not to say that the contemplative life guarantees openness to the other. However, when it is grounded in good theological reflection and pastoral practice, contemplation makes possible the deepest expression of this openness.

What is specific to monastic mission is that it responds to the growing number of vocations, especially in Africa, by offering a way of life devoted to prayer and silence. What the church asks of missionary monks is that they highlight the contemplative life. Even if the conciliar documents make little mention of contemplative religious orders, the contemplative dimension of Christian life is recognized as an essential element of successful evangelization.

It is all the more difficult to isolate those passages that directly concern monks because the documents usually speak of "religious institutes" or the "religious life," generic expressions for both apostolic and contemplative religious orders. The decree of Vatican II on the Mission Activity of the Church (*Ad Gentes*) emphasizes that "Religious institutes of the contemplative and of the active life have so far played, and still do play, the main role in the evangelization of the world" (AG 40). It makes reference to the progress and exemplary role of monks, whose primary vocation is contemplation:

> Worthy of special mention are the various projects for causing the contemplative life to take root. There are those who in such an attempt have kept the essential element of a monastic institution, and are bent on implanting the rich tradition of their order; there are others again who are returning to the simpler forms of ancient monasticism. But all are studiously looking for a genuine adaptation to local conditions. Since the contemplative life belongs to the fullness of the Church's presence, let it be put into effect everywhere. (AG 18)

The decree goes on to invite these institutes "to found houses in mission areas, as not a few of them have already done, so that there, living out their lives in a way accommodated to the truly religious traditions of the people, they can bear excellent witness among non-Christians to the majesty and love of God, as well as to our union in Christ" (AG 40).

The conciliar document emphasizes that the principal work of contemplatives in mission is related to the deepest spiritual longings and dreams of peoples, while giving less attention to the way in which the monastic life—a life centered on deepening a direct relationship with God—will affect the growth of the church. In point of fact, the contemplative life makes missionary activity more fruitful by giving birth to a profound spiritual dialogue within the human heart. From the Christian point of view contemplatives are those who, in a spirit of interior recollection, prepare themselves to listen to the divine Spirit and, with the help of God's grace, offer themselves completely to the transforming work of the Spirit that leads to perfect union. Consequently, the establishment of the contemplative life in accord with the law of "knowing in order to be known" necessarily involves listening to the Spirit manifested in other religious and cultural settings. This, in turn, inevitably leads to a challenging internal dialogue. Dialogue of this kind demands a great deal: knowing one's own contemplative tradition, both in theory and practice; allowing oneself to be affected by a different experience of the divine; and not interpreting that experience in Christian categories. On the other hand, this dialogue also demands not diluting the Trinitarian experience proper to Christianity with a vague, formless, and "universal" experience of the divine. The silence, patience, and discernment proper to those who follow the Rule of Benedict are valuable resources for engaging in this out-of-the-ordinary form of dialogue. This is all the more true in relation to the spiritualities of Asia with their highly developed contemplative sensitivity.

The Challenge of Asia

The Benedictine Cornelius Tholens was successful in helping monks recognize early that interreligious dialogue was an essential element of missionary activity, but it was in Asia that monks really became conscious of its necessity. At first the attention of monks was directed toward Africa. As we have seen, the creation of a Secretariat for mission (*Aide a l'implantation Monastique*/ AIM) came in response to the encyclical *Fidei Donum*, which, in turn, was issued out of a concern for the future of Africa. The first congresses organized by AIM, those of Bouaké in 1964 and Rome in 1966, addressed issues specifically related to Africa.

Moreover, the bulletin of AIM was originally called *Bulletin de liaison des monastères d'Afrique* (Contact Bulletin for Monasteries in Africa). It was only later, in 1968, that its name was changed to "AIM Bulletin," a change that took place after the 1966 congress of Benedictine abbots, at which a request was made that the Secretariat also direct its attention to Asia and Latin America. As Jean Leclercq, a monk of Clervaux, noted,

> The attention of monks and indeed of the whole Church was first directed to Africa, but Asia soon gained in importance. Without giving it a priority that would have worked to the detriment of other continents, it was imperative to look closely at the problems that had to be faced, not only in the countries that made up this continent, but in Western societies as well. (Leclercq [1986], 123)

Two Foundational Events

One way for AIM to come to the aid of developing countries (long considered "mission lands") was to organize continental congresses at which participants could share the experiences and problems that arose in a particular setting, and then reflect together—Westerners and "natives"—on how to respond. It was at congresses in Bangkok (1968) and Bangalore (1973) that monks came to a better understanding of the principle that there cannot be mission without dialogue with other religions, in particular with Buddhism and Hinduism. They already knew this in theory, but now it was becoming an existential necessity. To gain a better understanding of the role these congresses played in the genesis of monastic dialogue it is important to look at them together, seeing the second as a way of giving flesh to the hopes expressed in the first.

The Bangkok congress brought together Benedictine and Cistercian monks from Asia and the West. This was a pioneering event in monastic dialogue, and it had an enormous impact. At the Bangkok congress, for the first time, the members of the AIM Secretariat made contact with Eastern spirituality *in situ* and became experientially conscious of the fact that monasticism was not just a Christian phenomenon. For many, like Mayeul de Dreuille, a member of the congress of Benedictine abbots, this was their first contact with Buddhism. According to John Moffitt, who wrote the *Acts* of the congress, "no other meeting between Christians and adherents of other religions enabled the participants to come to such a clear awareness of the work of the Holy Spirit outside Christianity" (Moffitt [1979], 7).

In the subsequent meeting in Bangalore the participants came from a wider background. They included Christian monks and nuns, specialists, observers, Hindu and Buddhist monks, hippies, and Western laypeople who lived in community (ashrams). It made less of a splash than Bangkok, but by giving its participants a concrete opportunity to engage in dialogue and contemplative practice it took a step forward in the encounter between different monastic traditions. Christian monks were able to listen to non-Christian spiritual teachers and be initiated into their respective meditation practices. This coming together of different voices from throughout Asia inspired Tholens to describe the Bangalore congress as "the Pentecost of the monastic world." At Bangkok and Bangalore monks discovered that what especially characterized the continent of Asia was its spirituality and its pluralism. They became conscious of how great a challenge it would be to implant Christian monasticism in this part of the world and make it a truly Asian institution.

Difficulties to be Overcome

The challenge to Christian monasticism in Asia is fourfold. First of all, the presence of Christianity in Asia is extremely weak, as those who took part in the 1968 congress saw at first hand. Thailand was chosen as the location for this meeting because this country, with its myriad Buddhist monasteries and complete absence of Christian monasticism, typified what one could find throughout the continent. With the exception of the Philippines, and in spite of a missionary presence that spanned five centuries, the message of the Gospel encountered such strong resistance in Asia that Christians still make up only a small minority of its population.

The second challenge is the fact that many Asians regard Christianity as a foreign religion, a hangover from colonial times that would best be done away with. That judgment certainly puts Christianity in a precarious situation, but the situation is even more complex than at first appears. Some native Christians actually want to preserve the foreign trappings of their religion. In India, for example, the obviously foreign features that are characteristic of Catholicism, especially in the south, are often regarded by its members as a guarantee of their identity in the face of Hinduism's powerful ability to assimilate other religions, and also of their liberty vis-à-vis a caste system legitimated by the dominant religion. Christians therefore find themselves in a delicate situation, since their attempts to maintain the integrity of their faith are not conducive to making progress in the area of inculturation.

In the third place, there is a long and widespread sense among Hindus and Buddhists that Christianity lacks spiritual depth. Christians certainly exhibit a high degree of charity, but when it comes to self-knowledge or an experience of God that goes beyond words and doctrines, they fall short. At the congress in Bangalore Bishop Patrick D'Souza spoke quite eloquently on this subject when he said: "We have been for the inhabitants of this country a sign of love for our neighbor, but we have not succeeded in being signs of the presence of God in us and around us" (Leclercq [1986], 111). We should add that sometimes even Christian love is regarded with suspicion as a trap to capture and convert its unsuspecting recipients (Gregorios [2000], 220).

Finally, there is the strong bond between culture and religion, so strong that in India "being Indian can be confused with being Hindu" (Amaladoss [1997], 25). It is impossible to know a culture without taking into account the religion that is found in it, or better, the religion that sustains it and is at its very heart. Missionaries to Asia were especially conscious of the close relationship between religion and culture—monks even more so, because it was at the heart of Hinduism and Buddhism that they found the most evolved forms of monasticism. In order to understand the cultures of Asia, one has to take into account the contemplative dimension that is central to them. Paying close attention to this contemplative dimension makes it possible for Christians and scholars of Eastern spiritualities to participate in their most profound intuitions. Coming into contact with what is most spiritual and central to Eastern religions allows Christians to discover a greater resonance with the Asian soul.

The Bangkok congress made dialogue a point of no return. First of all, there was the official encouragement of Catholic and Buddhist authorities. The Vatican Secretary of State, Cardinal Amleto Giovanni Cicognani, forwarded a telegram from Pope Paul VI to the superiors of Benedictine communities stressing the importance of dialogue with the religions of Asia as promoted by the Second Vatican Council. The message reads as follows:

> His Holiness offers paternal encouragement to monastic superiors gathered in Bangkok to study the situation of Far Eastern monasticism, regards favorably this opportunity to establish or deepen contacts with non-Christian monasticism in the spirit of recent conciliar documents, and gladly imparts his apostolic benediction to the Benedictine abbots and all participants for a successful outcome of their labors. (Leclercq [1986], 77)

The Supreme Patriarch of the Thai Buddhists, Somdet Phra Ariavong Sankarat, also expressed his support for a closer relationship with Christian monks. Invited to give the opening speech, he affirmed that the adherents of all religions are people of peace. He made these comments publicly, at the national level, and did so while the Vietnam war was raging.

One of the main reasons the congress of 1968 became known outside monastic circles as an important event for interreligious dialogue was the presence and, even more, the untimely death of Thomas Merton, who had appealed to his confreres to devote themselves to serious engagement with the spiritual riches of the East. The impact of the congress can be seen in the title given to its *Acts*—"A New Charter for Monasticism"—in which monks were given the task of finding ways to promote mutual enrichment between Christianity and the mystical traditions of Asia. Bangkok marked a decisive step in the development of monastic dialogue. "In the resolutions adopted in Bangkok, one can already see the beginnings of what would soon emerge from AIM, namely DIM [now DIMMID: *Dialogue Interreligieux Monastique* • Monastic Interreligious Dialogue]—dialogue between monasticisms and religions" (Leclercq [1986], 83).

In spite of its success, the first pan-Asiatic congress had its limits. The concern for dialogue was quite weak and still theoretical. In response to the encouragement it had received from on high there were informal discussions throughout the course of the congress, but overall this was but the first step in raising the consciousness of Christian monks to the question of dialogue. Bangkok's main contribution was to provide intellectual preparation for the actual practice of dialogue, such as would take place five years later in the south of India. At Bangalore monks were invited to enter into contact with different religious traditions, and it was there above all that they realized how important it was to rediscover the essence of their vocation if they were to maximize the chances for Christian monasticism to take root in Asian soil.

Rediscovering the Essence of Monasticism

Benedictine and Cistercian monastic customs were too Western in character to be appreciated in an Asian milieu. Missionary monks saw that, in order to make their way of life intelligible to Buddhist and Hindu monks, they would have to identify the essence of monasticism and highlight what was essential to monasticism everywhere. This would be the only way to make Christian monasticism understandable and appreciated in Asia. These fundamental elements are essentially to be understood in terms of experience. In his *Asian Journal,* Merton insists that what is essential to the monastic way of life is not the cloister, or the habit, or even the monastic rule. The essential is to be found in something that goes much deeper, namely, a total interior transformation. Everything else is there only to contribute to this end (Merton [1975]). Bede Griffiths proposed going beyond historical structures and returning to the original myth of Christianity (Griffiths [1982]). Whatever shape it takes, Christian monasticism has to recognize the centrality of the experience of God in the monastic endeavor, and the necessity of making this experience a priority, especially in those mission countries where interiority is highly regarded and developed.

In dialogue with Hindus or Buddhists, Christians are often called on to speak about their own religious experience. On such occasions they have to ask themselves if their words about the great themes of the Christian faith spring from their practice and their own intimate relationship with the divine, or if they are simply a repetition of formulas they have learned and more or less made their own. Situations such as these can provide an opportunity for returning to essentials, but they can also lead to a certain crisis of faith by revealing the superficiality of words that do not flow out of experience, words that have not been tested and validated by those who create them or repeat them.

It is simply wrong to think that the proclamation of the Gospel is weakened when it is not put into words or supported by good arguments. If one can believe Saint Gregory, just the opposite is true. As he put it, grace is not given to those who speak about their faith, but to those who live it. The Dalai Lama says that he best understands who Christ is through the example and deeds of people who live as he lived. "I have read the Bible; it has been translated into Tibetan. But the way I have understood the message of Christ is through the acts of certain people who live it. People like Mother Theresa, Thomas Merton, Bede Griffiths . . . are living Gospels. In such individuals I have found many similarities to the Buddhist approach to the religious life."[8] Mahatma Gandhi loved to say to Christian missionaries, "May your life be an open book." These comments highlight the challenges that face monks in India—to reconnect with the inner laws of the Spirit, which is the only way to witness to an authentic spirituality. The Gospel is communicated much more effectively by concrete action and silent witness than by rhetorical flourishes and precise doctrinal formulations. Monks are particularly conscious of the fact that the Gospel must be proclaimed through deeds. John Moffitt recalls that Merton would insist that we are called "not so much to speak about Christ as to let him live in us so that others can come to know him through our lives" (Moffitt [1979], 73).

Recovering the essence of monasticism was one of the principal concerns of the congress in Bangalore. Bangkok opened the way by insisting that monasticism had to put aside its Western trappings, but how to go about doing that was still not clear. Greater clarity came in 1973 when "the experience of God" was chosen as the theme of the Bangalore congress. Panikkar, one of the most notable participants at that gathering, described the experience of God as immediate consciousness of ultimate reality. What are the paths that lead to such an experience? What place does it have in the life and prayer of the community? How is it related to our responsibility for the world we live in? All these questions directed the attention of the participants to interiority, mysticism, and the poverty that flows from it—the last then chosen as the topic of the third pan-Asiatic congress held in Kandy (Sri Lanka) in 1980.

Generally speaking, Asia was the occasion for the missionaries of Saint Benedict to return to their monastic sources by recognizing the primacy of the contemplative dimension of their vocation. In so doing they were called to play a role the active orders found difficult to fill in settings where indigenous religions emphasized a mystical approach to the sacred.

It is interesting to note that it was far from easy for the monks themselves to accept the idea that the essence of monasticism consisted in the search for wisdom and the knowledge of God. A proposal to that effect was not unanimously accepted at Bangkok (Leclercq [1986]), even though it seems perfectly obvious that from the very beginning monasticism presented itself as a way of life centered on the contemplative experience of the divine. It appears that it was in the context of the postwar missionary movement that monks rediscovered this truth. If prior to the congress in Bangalore monks had a difficult time understanding the place of contemplation in the monastic life, the reason may be that they were part of Western Christianity, which, over the course of several centuries, had neglected the contemplative dimension of the faith. The recent reappropriation of this dimension as a central element of monasticism took place, in part, in the context of an in-depth relationship with Eastern spiritualities.

Ridding Monasticism of Western Accretions

By placing the experience of God at the center of the monastic endeavor the members of AIM provided a rationale for ridding monasticism of Western accretions that were nonessential or—even worse—got in the way of experiencing and expressing the divine mystery. Rediscovering the essence of monasticism led to a program of de-Westernization. At Bangkok Jean Leclercq especially defended this plan by often pointing out the degree to which Christian monasticism had become culturally Western. He spoke of the need to "dehellenize" Western monasticism, arguing that the influence of ancient Greek culture made it extremely difficult to establish a meaningful relationship between Christian monasticism and the traditional cultures of Asia. Leclercq became a passionate defender of a Christianity that did not identify itself with European cultures but embraced all cultures of the world. Recalling that Saint Benedict had been declared patron of Europe, he went so far as to propose that Christian monasticism be "de-Benedictinized" in order for it to become truly Asian, and not just something Western in Asia. In saying this Leclercq was not turning his back on the church. On the contrary, he was identifying the source of its vitality in much the same way that Paul VI did when he said:

> The renewal envisioned by the council does not consist in doing away with the present life of the Church, nor in a break with the essential and revered elements of its tradition. In fact, it gives homage to this tradition when it strives to rid it of what has become outmoded and deficient and in this way make it authentic and fruitful. (Paul VI [1963], 643)

In his speech opening the Bangkok Congress, Rembert Weakland, the Abbot Primate of the Benedictines, stressed the importance of establishing a "pancultural" monasticism that would have distinctive features in different parts of the world. He insisted that Christian monasticism must never be spread in a spirit of conquest. "We are here not to civilize, nor to conquer, nor to convert, but to live. We hope that by being here we will come to a fuller understanding of who we are, and that by our contacts with representatives of a tradition different from ours, we will grow in our own monastic vocation. At the same time, we have not come empty handed" (Leclercq [1986], 73). The intention was clear, even if changes did not come about as quickly as one might have hoped. At the conclusion of the second pan-Asiatic congress Weakland expressed his disappointment over how little progress had been made: "We did not hear the voice of universal monasticism at Bangalore, only that of Western monasticism" (Leclercq [1986], 113).

Much remained to be done if the Christian message was to be freed of every form of cultural domination, but at least monks had been made aware of the task ahead. These two congresses brought an important insight, namely, that it is impossible to attend to the double demand of going back to the foundational experience of monasticism and freeing it from its cultural trappings without at the same time knowing and admiring the spiritual yearnings that shape the religious practices of the people you are communicating with. In other words, you can only understand your own sources and the essential elements of your religious vocation by being in relation with other forms of spirituality. In Asia and in dialogue with Buddhist and Hindu forms of monasticism, Christian monks found the motivation and the method for reappropriating what is central to their own tradition. This is not to say that the East makes up for what is lacking in Christianity. Rather, these contacts provided the occasion for Christians to affirm their own mystical and contemplative tradition, which had been become atrophied over the course of centuries but was now being recognized as an essential element in the authentic reception of the Christian message in a missionary setting, especially during the second half of the twentieth century.

It should be noted that while there was much talk of "adaptation" in the 1960s and 1970s, missionary monasticism from the very beginning looked for ways to inculturate monasticism rather than simply to adapt it to different cultures and societies. It went far beyond a strategy that risked reducing evangelization to its external forms. If the Gospel was to take root and bear fruit it would have to speak to the religious yearning in the heart of every individual and every community. Doing this meant refusing the superficial approach of grafting the faith onto a given culture. Rather, the faith must come to expression as a constituent and natural element of the culture. The culture that brings the message must not present itself as the evangelizer. It has to cancel itself out, so to speak, so that the faith can develop with the characteristics of the culture that has received the Gospel. At the congresses of Bangkok and Bangalore charismatic and experienced pioneers of dialogue from throughout Asia embodied this imperative and demonstrated the kind of monasticism that needed to be established.

The Fathers of Dialogue

The first period of monastic dialogue belongs to the pioneers. At Bangkok and Bangalore the realization that the West had been blinded by its sense of self-sufficiency was balanced by the presence of individuals from different backgrounds whose example and message indicated new ways for the message of the Gospel to enter into a profound relationship with local cultures and religions. Among these individuals were the Jesuits William Johnston and Hugo M. Enomiya-Lassalle, the Dominican Shigeto Oshida, the Cistercian Francis Mahieu (Acharya), and the layman John Moffitt. All of them bore witness to the possibility of remaining fully Christian while at the same time being genuinely hospitable toward a different religion. Those whose influence was most decisive in what can properly be considered monastic dialogue were the Cistercian Thomas Merton and the Benedictines Henri Le Saux (Abhishiktananda) and Bede Griffiths. They were at one and the same time pioneers of dialogue and renowned mystics. Today they are recognized as veritable symbols of spiritual dialogue.

The lives of these individuals, as well as their teaching, took monastic dialogue out of the realm of theory and put it into practice, inspiring others to follow in their footsteps and continue the journey. In 1993, the twenty-fifth anniversary of the death of Merton, the twentieth of Le Saux, and the year of Griffith's death, the North American Commission of Monastic Interreligious Dialogue singled out these three monks as inspiring, if perhaps unattainable, models of monastic dialogue. Their photos appear on the cover of *Bulletin 48* under the heading "Three Monastic Prophets."[9]

The influence of these three pioneers is so great that I do not hesitate to call them "fathers of monastic dialogue," understanding "monastic" to include all forms of dialogue at the level of spirituality. The term "father" is not used lightly. It certainly is not meant to minimize the role of women in monastic dialogue. Their contribution is significant, as I will point out below. Rather, the term is symbolic, expressing my conviction that these pioneers, along with others, were responsible for getting Christians to think dialogically and would thereby give direction to Christian practice for generations to come. In the same way that the fathers of the church, the fathers of the desert, the fathers of Citeaux, or the fathers of the Second Vatican Council changed the course of history and gave a push that was needed for the evolution of the church, these pioneers of dialogue, I believe, will also be recognized as standing at the head of a movement that brought about major changes in thought and behavior. The fact that they believed Hindu and Buddhist ways of meditation are an especially apt way to become familiar with these religions and enter into profound dialogue with them is yet another reason why it is right to consider them pioneers.

The Adoption of Eastern Forms of Meditation

Monks often found themselves in dialogue with Eastern religions after having practiced various kinds of meditation that had been developed within these religions. This was true at the beginning of monastic dialogue as well as later on. This is not to say that all monks involved in dialogue feel comfortable with these practices and engage in them, nor that all adopt them with the same understanding. Nonetheless, practicing one or the other form of Eastern meditation is widespread among monks engaged in dialogue and not just typical of a few "enlightened" ones. Meditation is seen as an ideal and appropriate way of getting to know the Buddhist and Hindu traditions from the inside. At the Bangkok congress Marie-Robert de Floris, the then-president of AIM, expressed the hope that all missionary activity in Asia would bring about the transformation of the Christian deposit of faith through its contact with Buddhism and Hinduism. Engaging in the practice of an Eastern form of meditation is one way of responding to that hope.

In Bangkok, Merton encouraged his colleagues to adopt Eastern ascetic practices. But it was in Bangalore that the issue was addressed more formally. There were discussions on the place of Zen and yoga in Christian spirituality, and participants were given an opportunity to engage in these practices. From one congress to the other, interest in Eastern meditation practices grew considerably. There were two reasons for this. First of all, these practices are at the heart of Asian monasticism: various kinds of *yoga* in Hinduism; *zazen* in Zen Buddhism; *vipassana* in Theravada Buddhism; *shi'nay* in Tibetan Buddhism, and *dzochen* in the Nyimgmapa tradition.

While it is true that meditation is practiced by a minority within Buddhism and Hinduism—the majority of their adherents engage in more devotional forms of religious practice—the fact remains that meditation offers a unique entrée to the Asian soul and allows one to discover the jewels of its two principal religions: the Hindu experience of non-duality (*advaita*) and the Buddhist experience of emptiness (*sunyata*).

Moreover, the different ways of meditating offer a certain common ground of understanding where monks of all traditions immediately feel that they are part of the same family in spite of their doctrinal difference. Meditation is a space that offers the conditions in which dialogue can develop and bear fruit. In Bangalore it was said that the goal of every spiritual method, Christian or other, is finally the same—namely, to draw close to or to be united with the absolute. The contemplative prayer of some Christians is similar in many ways to yoga or other forms of meditation when it involves placing oneself completely at the disposition of the mystery that is within and thus being able to perceive the fundamental reality of things in an experience that transcends meaning and words, and where silence, light, or even "intoxication" are some of the most appropriate ways to describe this experience. When Christian monks become seriously interested in Eastern forms of meditation they enter into contact with the religions of Asia and provide themselves with the means to know these religions not just intellectually but in their bones. This gives them a clear advantage in the work of inculturating Christianity. Without succumbing to the relativism that says everything has equal value and without pretending that they have completely grasped the deepest spiritual longings of the East, they echo those longings, and in that act they look upon their own spiritual yearnings with fresh eyes, making it possible, in turn, for their own yearnings to strike a chord in the heart of the other. It is no wonder that the fathers of the Second Vatican Council encouraged the exploration of contemplative ways that had been developed in other religions.

The Encouragement of the Council

The conciliar Decree on the Mission Activity of the Church (*Ad Gentes*) stresses the importance of the contemplative life in the work of evangelization because it "clearly manifests and signifies the inner nature of the Christian calling." The decree goes on to say: "Religious institutes, working to plant the Church, and thoroughly imbued with mystic treasures with which the Church's religious tradition is adorned, should strive to give expression to them and to hand them on, according to the nature and the genius of each nation" (AG 18). To accomplish this the document invites religious to "reflect attentively on how

Christian religious life might be able to assimilate the ascetic and contemplative traditions, whose seeds were sometimes planted by God in ancient cultures already prior to the preaching of the Gospel" (ibid.). This proposal grants a certain legitimacy to the adoption of non-Christian forms of meditation in the service of the Gospel, thereby upholding the courageous practice of monastic dialogue. As Eugene D'Souza wrote in the preface to Henri Le Saux's *La rencontre de l'hindouisme et du christianisme*, published in 1965, "A book like this could not have been written in any age previous to ours" (Le Saux [1965], 13).

Vatican II was so important for monks because it laid the foundation for interreligious dialogue and also because it suggested they could explore the furthest reaches of dialogue by seriously studying other meditation practices, especially those of Asia. The editor of the North American MID *Bulletin*, Sister Pacaline Coff, made the appeal of the Council's Decree on the Mission Activity of the Church the theme and goal of monastic dialogue by printing the appeal on the first page of the *Bulletin* during the first four years of its existence, from 1978 to 1982. Alongside the Decree on the Mission Activity of the Church, the Constitution on the Church in the Modern World (*Gaudium et Spes*) also directed monks toward an experiential knowledge of Eastern meditation practices when it exhorted all the baptized to "work in close conjunction with their contemporaries and try to get to know their ways of thinking and feeling, as they find them expressed in current culture" (GS 62). Without directly addressing the topic of meditation, this directive opened the door to the adoption of meditation practices of other religions, in the knowledge that doing so becomes all the more meaningful as it gives concrete expression of the idea that "the more deeply we come to understand their ways of thinking through kindness and love, the more easily will we be able to enter into dialogue with them" (GS 28). The truth of this statement can be found in the example of the fathers of dialogue, each of whom in his own way and according to his own gifts contributed to an exploration of the ascetic practices of the East and inspired others to do the same.

We are not speaking here of something marginal or idiosyncratic. Those who engaged in other meditation practices looked to the encouragement of the official authority of the council for justification, and also to the spiritual authority of the fathers of dialogue: Merton, Le Saux, and Griffiths. As can be seen from their lives and their writings, their search for the divine went hand in hand with the practice of other methods of meditation that allowed them to be receptive to universal truth, truth that was not defined in Christian or any other particular religious categories. While it may be harder to verify the existence of such practices in Merton's life, he was without doubt the person who was most explicit about encouraging other monks to walk this path. In what follows my intention is not to give short biographies of these pioneers, but briefly to describe their relationship to Eastern forms of meditation.

Thomas Merton and Zen

Just hours before his death, at the conclusion of his public talk in Bangkok, Thomas Merton[10] made the following statement in the presence of the members of AIM:

> And I believe that by openness to Buddhism, to Hinduism, and to these great Asian traditions, we stand a wonderful chance of learning more about the potentiality of our own traditions. . . . The combination of natural techniques and the graces and the other things that have been manifested in Asia and the Christian liberty of the gospel should bring us all at last to that full and transcendent liberty which is beyond mere cultural differences and mere externals—and mere this or that. (Merton [1975], 343)

He said much the same when he spoke in Calcutta:

> I think we have now reached a stage of (long-overdue) religious maturity at which it may be possible for someone to remain perfectly faithful to a Christian and Western monastic commitment, and yet to learn in depth from, say, a Buddhist or Hindu discipline and experience. I believe that some of us need to do

this in order to improve the quality of our own monastic life and even to help in the task of monastic renewal which has been undertaken within the Western Church. (Merton [1975], 313)

Merton certainly urged his fellow monks to undertake a colossal task, and its outcome was not at all clear. But the question remains: Did he practice what he preached? We know that Merton wrote a lot about Zen, and all are agreed that his understanding of this Japanese tradition is penetrating and compelling. Does this mean that he knew Zen because he practiced it? This is not a meaningless question, nor is it posed simply to satisfy our curiosity. A personal experience of the fundamental truths of Zen—for example, impermanence, suffering, emptiness—will affect the Christian understanding of God, human beings, and the world in a way that a purely theoretical grasp of these notions could never do. Bonnie Thurston, former president of the International Thomas Merton Society, notes that Zen provided this American Trappist with a new way of understanding the essential goal of monasticism—letting go of ego—and a new way of expressing it. I believe that if this understanding does not flow from experience it is superficial and without any real impact. On the other hand, when it is founded on practice it necessitates a rethinking of the Christian contemplative experience.

Was Zen a part of Merton's monastic discipline? Our first inclination is to respond in the affirmative on the grounds that an accurate understanding of this tradition is normally the result of practice, as Zen masters themselves insist. But the actual situation is not all that clear, especially since Merton was so reticent about his own prayer life.

There are those who say he had an intuitive understanding of Zen without necessarily practicing it (MacInnes [2003]). Could this be the case because he felt that he himself was very much like the Eastern mystics? On one occasion he actually said, "I am much closer to Confucius and to Lao Tzu than to my American contemporaries . . . I am as much a Chinese Buddhist in thought and temperament as a Christian . . ." (Lipski [1983], 5). Some will find weak points in his understanding of Zen. Heinrich

Dumoulin, a professor at Sophia University in Tokyo whose understanding of Zen differed from Merton's, thought it would have been good for Merton to spend some time in Japan to get a deeper sense of the essence of Zen. At the same time the celebrated Zen master Daisetz Suzuki, with whom Merton corresponded, felt that no other Westerner had ever understood Zen as well as this monk from Gethsemani. One should be aware, however, that Suzuki's authority was never as great in Japan as it was in the West.

If it is difficult to prove that Merton actually practiced Zen, there is nothing that prevents us from believing that he did. According to Thurston "he turned to the East, and especially to Zen, in order to learn a method of prayer" (Thurston [1994], 22). By entering deeply into the practice of Zen, might he have hoped to reclaim the ancient Christian traditions of interiority? One thing is sure; he never converted to Buddhism, as he was rumored to have done. All are agreed that he always remained faithful to the Christian tradition. Where they differ is in their assessment of the degree to which Buddhism had an influence on him.

In order to come to some understanding of Merton's relation to Buddhism and especially to Zen it might be helpful to recall the beginning of his interest in the ways of the East. While he was a university student, well before he entered a Trappist monastery and without any particular religious inclinations, Merton looked for inspiration in the areas of mysticism and asceticism. In his autobiography, *The Seven Storey Mountain,* he clearly states that since he knew nothing of the Christian mystical tradition he was naturally drawn to the East. An interest in mysticism and asceticism is usually strengthened by the desire to take up the practice of meditation and thus make oneself ready for an experience that gives meaning to one's life. In fact, under the influence of Aldous Huxley, Merton was deeply moved by the thought that employing mystical techniques could bring about peace, tolerance, and charity, ideals dear to his heart. However, his study of the East at this point in his life was superficial and scattered, and ultimately without much fruit. He came to the conclusion that Eastern meditation techniques did little more than help one relax, and that as a consequence "Eastern mysticism is not true mysticism, because it lacks a supernatural dimension" (Lipski [1983], 6).

Once he entered Gethsemani it seems that Merton put aside his interest in Asia. At any rate we have no information about his relationship to Eastern religions between the time he joined the monastery and his ordination to the priesthood in 1949. In that year he mentioned in his journal that he was studying the yoga of Pantajali and that he met a worker in the monastery who had been a postulant in a Zen monastery in Hawaii. From that time on his attraction to the ascetic ways of the East grew. In his youth Merton was first attracted to Hinduism and then his studies took him to other Asian religions, including Islam. But as a monk he was interested most in Buddhism (Zen and Tibetan), alongside Taoism and Confucianism.

Merton entered the abbey of Gethsemani with the firm intention of giving himself totally to God. In the monastic traditions of Eastern religions he found a treasure he could delve into, a way of life he could investigate all the more closely because he was being formed by a monastic way of life that emphasized silence, asceticism, and contemplation. There are a number of indications—though not proofs—that Merton engaged in an experiential study of Eastern ways, at least with regard to Buddhism.

First of all he stated that he had been influenced by the teachings of the Buddha when it came to comprehending the Christian faith. David Steindl-Rast recalled that Merton had once said to Zen master Robert Aitken, "I don't think I would have understood Christian doctrine the way I do if it had not been for the light I received from Buddhism." In a letter dated November 9, 1968, Merton mentioned that he had spent eight days in retreat at Dharamsala where he was able to read, meditate, and engage in conversation. His openness to Buddhism was such that during his visit to Sri Lanka he had a sort of "illumination" at a Buddhist site in Polonnaruwa. What is especially interesting is that he described this experience using Buddhist terminology (*dharmakaya*, void, compassion):

> All problems are resolved and everything is clear, simply because what matters is clear. The rock, all matter, all life, is charged with dharmakaya . . . everything is emptiness and everything is compassion. I don't know when in my life I have ever had such a sense of beauty and spiritual validity running together in one aesthetic illumination. Surely, with Mahabalipuram and Polonnaruwa my Asian pilgrimage has come clear and purified itself. I mean, I know and have seen what I was obscurely looking for. I don't know what else remains but I have now seen and have pierced through the surface and have got beyond the shadow and the disguise. (Merton [1975], 235–36)

According to Jean Leclercq this event would have shaped the rest of Merton's life.

In spite of the difficulty of getting a clear picture of the spiritual practice of this monk, it is clear that for him there was an intertwining of Buddhist and Christian ascetic paths. His desire to establish a retreat center is an indication of this. What he wanted to do was to create an American center where Christian contemplatives and Tibetan monks would be able to live side by side as they made the legendary three-year retreat under the guidance of a lama. He envisioned his role as that of spiritual guide for the Christians and facilitator of exchanges between the two groups.

The main reason Merton continues to be an inspiration for monks involved in dialogue is that he was so convinced of the importance of absorbing Eastern religions *in situ*: "I think we must seek not merely to make superficial reports about the Asian traditions, but to live and share those traditions, as far as we can, by living them in their traditional milieu."[11] The lives of Le Saux and Griffiths gave concrete expression to this same conviction in an Indian setting.

Yoga and the Masters of Shantivanam

In this section I wish to speak about Le Saux (Abhishiktananda) and Griffiths in terms of what they had in common: their connection to mission in an Indian setting, their crucial roles in the development of the Shantivanam ashram, the place of yoga in their spiritual life, and the importance they assigned to the experience of non-duality (*advaita*) in their understanding of the divine. I do not, however, want to give the impression that the spiritual journey of Le Saux and Griffiths was similar, that they had the same approach to Hindu spirituality, or that they worked together. Le Saux was present at Shantivanam from 1950 to 1968, while Griffiths took up residence there from 1968 to 1993. Moreover, Le Saux went much farther into the Vedantic experience of non-duality and made it the basis of an internal dialogue to a much greater degree than Griffiths. Having said this, I hope the following remarks will be helpful in showing how these pioneers approached Eastern forms of meditation.

There can be no doubt that Le Saux[12] and Griffiths integrated a form of yoga into their Christian spiritual practice. Their example shows us that meditation is a privileged way to touch the Indian soul, or better, to embody the truth of the Vedanta through the experience of non-duality (*advaita*), which is the very heart of Vedanta. However, it is somewhat surprising that unlike Merton, who leaves us in doubt about his practice of Zen while at the same time displaying an obvious interest in Buddhist forms of meditation, Le Saux and Griffiths engaged in the practice of yoga but rarely spoke about it. When Merton met the Dalai Lama in India he wrote that they had a long conversation about meditation. The writings of the two Benedictines make little mention of meditation, even when they highlight the spiritual treasures of Asia.

One of the few exceptions would be Le Saux's little book entitled *Prayer*, published in 1967, which deals with meditation and yoga. But even here Le Saux does not so much address the "how" of meditating as its significance. He passes over technical and ascetic dimensions of meditation—that is, its method—to concentrate on the never completely realized goal of meditation, namely, the encounter with the divine Spirit present at the center (*guha*) of everything that is. A few pages describing the prayer of the name of God are the only ones that speak of its stages, its form, and how to go about practicing it. Le Saux here gives us some information about the way he himself prayed, but the fact that he wrote this book only toward the end of his life and in response to repeated requests from Christians in Asia indicates that he was reluctant to say much about the subject.

Why did he show such discretion when it came to speaking about meditation? It certainly cannot mean that he thought meditation was unimportant. It held a noteworthy place in the lives of both Le Saux and Griffiths,[13] the latter going so far as to say that nothing was more important than meditation (Griffiths [1992]). The only way to respond to this question is to relate their view of meditation to their missionary context. Le Saux does so eloquently when he says "O Lord, I have come to India to make you known to my Hindu brothers and sisters. And it is you who will make yourself known to me through meditation" (Coff [1994], 22). This shift is understandable in relation to the missionary ideal already referred to, which consists in knowing in order to be known, doing all that one can to grasp the profound longing of Hinduism in order to allow the riches of Christian monasticism to spring up from the soil of India. It should be noted that Le Saux distanced himself more and more from the traditional understanding of missionary work in response to the demands of a more intensive dialogue with Hinduism, a development that led to an ever-increasing conflict with Monchanin.

The Hindu ways of asceticism have a crucial role to play in the inculturation of the Christian message, particularly when it comes to elaborating a form of the monastic life that accords with the Indian spirit. In this regard the Council's Decree on the Mission Activity of the Church calls for "authentic adaptation" in relation to two types of monasticism. The first is what can be called traditional monasticism, and it retains the essential elements of the monastic establishment; the second returns to the simpler forms of ancient monasticism.

In India these forms were to be found in small communities that were like Hindu ashrams with their *sannyasa* way of life. One of the best examples of this second kind of monastic life was at Shantivanam, founded by Monchanin and Le Saux at Kulitalai in the state of Tamil Nadu on the feast of Saint Benedict,

March 21, 1950. They called it Saccidananda, a Sanskrit term that refers to the three fundamental aspects of ultimate reality: being, consciousness, and bliss.

People had already heard of this community before Vatican II, thanks to the writings of its two founders: *Ermites du Saccidananda*, published in 1956, and *A Benedictine Ashram*, which appeared in 1964. It was part of the Christian ashram movement that began at the end of the nineteenth century and became better known after Griffiths assumed responsibility for it in 1968. Shantivanam distinguished itself from earlier ashrams by making contemplation rather than apostolic ministry central to its way of life. It was there that the Christian monastic experience was brought to bear on mission and spirituality, and it is there that we can see how Le Saux and Griffiths regarded meditation. Understanding the dynamics and purpose of the ashram makes clear the place meditation had in the lives of each of these two men. In the case of Le Saux this was true for the first period of his life in India. Later he would leave the ashram in search of greater solitude.

While the Hindu ashram can be seen as the equivalent of a European monastery, there are also significant differences. In fact, they are quite dissimilar institutions. Unlike a monastery, an ashram is not permanent, or at least is not established to be permanent. It comes into being with a guru, revolves around him, and therefore dies with him if he has not designated a successor. It is an institution that supports the master/disciple relationship and makes interiority, asceticism, and meditation central to its way of life. Each member of an ashram follows his or her own rhythm of life in silence and respect for others. Making an ashram a Christian center means simplifying traditional monasticism—often identified with its large abbeys—and focusing on the experience of God and the offer of hospitality to everyone in search of truth, no matter what their religion. It should be noted that ashrams are more than a response to the need for interiority. Their value is also to be found in that they are a link to the extreme poverty found in many parts of Asia. However, there are those who claim that ashrams are too "bourgeois," out of touch with the misery and social injustice that surround them.

By means of the ashram the Benedictine missionaries showed themselves receptive to the possibility of becoming familiar with the contemplative traditions of the region and of inviting contemplatives of various traditions to journey together toward the mystery that unites them. That certainly was one of the reasons they were more interested in meditation as a springboard to the divine than in promoting a particular technique, which would not have been well received in the Hindu-Christian setting of Shantivanam, for reasons we shall see.

More than any other religion, Hinduism developed numerous and often elaborate spiritual methods, involving physiological and psychological elements, to attain inner silence. Under the heading of "yoga" these various methods—*bhakti yoga*, *karma yoga*, *jnana yoga*, *mantra yoga*, etc.—offer different ways of arriving at the same end: the cessation of all mental activity in order to allow the divine energy (*shakti*) resting beneath one's consciousness to be awakened and to lead the individual to a state of perfection.

This tells us two things: first, the importance of taking these methods seriously in order to come to a deeper knowledge of Hinduism, and second, the necessity of seeing them as a means to prepare the individual for the experience of the Ultimate. The Shantivanam ashram exemplifies this double approach. Even if Le Saux gave pride of place in his own practice to the prayer of the name of God or of any other mantra (*nâmajapa*) (see Le Saux [1967], 57), he did not propose that this be the official method at Shantivanam. No doubt meditation was an important part of the daily horarium—an hour at sunrise, another at sunset—but each individual was expected to find the way that was most personally suitable. Le Saux made it clear that yoga was not essential and should not be recommended for everyone (Le Saux [1967]). What was important was that the ashram be a place that fostered an ever-deepening consciousness that one is and that one is a part of everything that is.

The teachers of Shantivanam stressed the importance of savoring the truth of the Upanishads, of having a direct experience of the divine that went beyond words and thought. A meditation method or technique is not sufficient to accomplish this. As Le Saux insisted, it is only a preparation for the ultimate encounter with oneself, as the Vedanta expresses it, or with the Father in the unity of the Holy Spirit, according to Christian mystics (ibid.).

In the Christian understanding of this encounter, divine grace and the gifts of the Spirit are essential. A spiritual guide (guru) is also necessary; without a guide one needs to be very careful about setting out on a path that leads to union with God. Le Saux reflected on the meaning of a spiritual guide in his relationship with Ramana Maharshi, even more with Sri Gnanananda, and toward the end of his life with Marc Chaduc, his own disciple. The spiritual quest demands renunciation of anything that could stand in the way of full and absolute union with the divine. Now a meditation technique itself can get in the way of arriving at the true goal of the inner journey. At a given moment one's own particular practice will become meaningless. Le Saux was especially aware of this situation, whence his uneasiness about favoring any spiritual method to the detriment of a spontaneous religious experience. In this he was very close to the mind of the *sannyasi,* one who renounces everything, even what we might think is essential to a religious way of life. Le Saux's acceptance of this way became even more radical after the death of Monchanin, when he left Shantivanam and went to live as a hermit in the Himalayas, a setting he found conducive to long retreats and silence.

The examples of Le Saux and Griffiths make clear that yoga is a way to come into contact with the Indian soul, but that its technical and ascetic elements are of relative value. What is of ultimate importance is the experience of non-duality, where the spiritual and the material, the one and the many, the human and the divine are harmoniously reconciled.

With regard to this point it would be helpful to call attention to the way Merton differed from the teachers of Shantivanam. Certainly they all spoke of the urgent need for an encounter between the spiritual traditions of Western Christianity and Asian spiritualities. For Merton this meeting was to be found by making use of Hindu or Buddhist techniques and disciplines. For Le Saux and Griffiths it meant coming to an experience of God that was proper to these traditions. This is how Griffiths put it in 1988:

> The real encounter of the Catholic Church with the religions of Asia has hardly begun and the challenge before the monastic order today is to enter in depth into the experience of God or, as in Buddhism, of ultimate Reality, in the religions of Asia and relate that experience to the experience of God in Christ in the West.[14]

This subtle difference is not about ends, but about means, specifically the meaning and place of the Christian use of Eastern methods of meditation. The difference is due, in part, to the different contexts and priorities of each.

Merton was especially interested in Zen and Tibetan Buddhism. Both these traditions had developed specific and rigorous meditation practices. Moreover, he was a Westerner who only set foot in Asia at the end of his life and for a very short time. Therefore he had no experience of the religious/cultural context in which these methods originated. Furthermore, Westerners who are attracted to Buddhism are especially attracted to its meditation practices. In contrast, Le Saux and Griffiths had become guests of the Indian subcontinent and were looking for the essence of the monastic life. In a country where ascetic techniques and traditions of all kinds have been part of the daily life of the people for centuries, even millennia, these two Benedictine missionaries concentrated on finding India's jewel, the experience of non-duality. It was their conviction that they could reach a larger number of people if they did not limit themselves to any specific tradition.

Merton, Le Saux, and Griffith were in agreement on a matter that is decisive for understanding the motivation behind the changes that would soon have an impact on monastic interreligious dialogue. They rejected a reductionist view that regarded the adoption of a Buddhist or Hindu meditation practice as merely a way for a local church to become inculturated. For them, taking up an Eastern form of meditation had first of all to be understood in the broader context of each individual's search for truth. They believed this was the case because the adoption of such a practice leads each individual to a uniquely personal expression of the spirituality of the other.

These pioneers found themselves in dialogue after the fact. Often without their being aware of it, they were led by their thirst for the divine to seek out a non-Christian spiritual experience. For them the spiritual East was not only the field where the vine of the Good News could take root and grow; it was also the orchard where the Christian was called to harvest the fruits of his or her own conversion in order to reconnect with the depths of his or her own tradition. It is precisely in this encounter—a transformation of the classical "missionary mandate"—that the dialogue of monks little by little found its center of gravity and became a dialogue that places itself at the service of a world in urgent need of recovering its spiritual foundations if it is to survive.

Chapter 2

Dialogue for a Changing World

The second period of monastic dialogue coincides with the establishment of two subcommissions of AIM for the specific purpose of promoting monastic interreligious dialogue: the North American Board for East-West Dialogue (NABEWD),[15] now known as Monastic Interreligious Dialogue (MID), created at Petersham, Massachusetts, in June 1977, and *Dialogue Interreligieux Monastique* (DIM) in Europe, created at Loppem in Belgium in August 1977. With these structures in place, monastic interreligious dialogue soon evolved into an activity at the service of the human community and thus moved away from what had been its original link with the establishment of the church in Asia. Cornelius Tholens was among those who promoted this development. In an unpublished paper written in 1979 he proposed that the guiding conciliar document for monastic dialogue should be the Second Vatican Council's Declaration *Nostra Aetate* (On the Relation of the Church to Non-Christian Religions): "As we move away from apologetics and missionary activity as it is commonly understood, new possibilities are open to us—not those of a new way of doing mission, but those of living together with the members of other religions and sharing what we have in common!"

Even if monastic dialogue was never completely separated from the missionary setting in which it came into being, it was now becoming clear that the promise of a new age rested in large part on a spiritual exchange between East and West. In this second stage of the development of monastic dialogue monks became even more aware of the importance of the contribution they could make to a diverse and beleaguered world. When monks of different religions encounter one another they instinctively recognize their common commitment to disinterested spiritual dialogue, mutual understanding, and the experience of reconnecting with the mystery of the divine. These activities can speak to a world that seems unable to agree on what is of real value and that fears for its very survival. Thus at the end of the 1970s there emerged a new understanding of monastic dialogue. It moved away from the strictly missionary objectives of AIM, without, however, making a clean break from them, in order to evolve on its own in response to concerns that were more global and spiritual and against the background of an uncertain future for humanity.

How do we explain the changed understanding of dialogue that came about as it was being given institutional identity? What motivated the monks to look beyond Benedictine and Cistercian communities, beyond the framework of mission, to make dialogue an expression of their concern for the whole human race? What are the implications and the challenges of such a change? In order to try to respond to these questions, we need to take into consideration three points. In the first place, dialogue is akin to a new monastic Pentecost that has peace as its principal objective and that responds to concerns and deficiencies that are specifically Western. Next, this new understanding of dialogue is based on a deepened experiential as well as theoretical appreciation for Eastern forms of meditation. Its goal is a spiritual renewal at the heart of a church that has for too long disregarded contemplative silence and the interior laws of the Spirit. Finally, the ambitious proposals of monks in dialogue are grounded in an altogether novel expression of hospitality toward the religions of Asia. This new attitude caused fear and questioning within Catholic monastic orders that, while damaging to the image of dialogue in the short run, ultimately prepared the way for its future evolution.

A New Monastic Pentecost

The meetings that took place at Loppem and Petersham were different from other contemporary interreligious events in that they marked the beginning of a long-term project. In addition to standing at the origin of the institutionalized form of dialogue, these meetings solidified an intuition that would enliven the future activities of monks in dialogue. That understanding of their significance was highlighted by the Trappistine GilChrist (Denyse) Lavigne:

> Petersham was for me, not simply "another meeting" or workshop among many, not a naive attempt at dialogue, not some fad-type involvement with superficial techniques of Eastern or Western meditation. Rather, Petersham was an overture, a threshold into a new kind of monastic adventure: a journey which begins within and reaches out to all nations and peoples. I now view the Acts of the Apostles as my own journey, both within and without. I sense a profound solidarity with, and gratitude to all monks and nuns who share this journey with me, even if I never meet them. (Lavigne [1978], 5)

These words are an eloquent expression of the essence and intention of a nascent interreligious movement that understood its mission to be a common search for the truth that is the goal of contemplatives of every spiritual tradition. Together they are called to lay the spiritual foundations necessary for the survival of a rapidly evolving world. Monks in dialogue continue to believe that if East and West do not encounter one another on the level of spirituality they will collide with one another. At this second stage of development the religions of the East were once again the main object of attention. However, the concern was not simply to bring together monks of different religions, but to be open to dialogue with all religions, especially Islam, which, in the West—and particularly after 9/11—represents a growing challenge.

Out of their concern for the future of humanity, those who took part in the meetings held at Loppem and Petersham expressed their willingness to do their part for the cause of peace in the world, believing that the coming together of monastic traditions was an important part of the solution. It was especially at Petersham that this new direction for monastic dialogue was promoted. The media took notice of the breadth of vision and sense of mission that marked this gathering with headlines such as "Petersham, World Village, Setting of Monastic Colloquium on East-West Unity," and "Eastern Monks Meet the West." The makeup of the participants indicates just how much Petersham manifested the culture that was emerging from the process of globalization. Those who took part were a various and sundry lot. Alongside the sons and daughters of Saint Benedict could be found university scholars, Buddhists, Hindus, and laypeople from various Christian backgrounds, many of whom had experience with Eastern spiritual practices. Especially noteworthy was the presence of Robert Müller, who represented the United Nations. Because of his sensitivity to the massive transformations taking place throughout the world he suggested there was need for a new spirituality, and with it a kind of monasticism that would give expression to all the traditional values, but in ways adapted to an emerging global culture. By making this appeal Müller set the tone of the meeting. The discussions dealt with the question of transforming particular cultures into a world culture, with monks in dialogue addressing the place of religious experience in such a transformation and coming up with ways to speak about it. It should be noted that this was not the first time such an overarching role for monks was spoken of. Already in the report of the Bangalore congress (1973) we read: "The world today hungers for liberation, and any problem today not on a universal horizon is methodologically wrong. The monk should not be a narrow man, but the man with the planetarium consciousness" (O'Hanlon [1974], 20). A survey of the Benedictine

Order conducted by Tholens in 1975 on better ways to promote the encounter of different monastic traditions shows a similar concern when it mentions the demands that will be placed on the pioneers of dialogue: "Together they will have to face the crucial questions posed by the cultural transformation that is being experience by the whole of humanity, a transformation that challenges all religions" (Tholens [1975], 49).

It is in the light of this perspective that monks in dialogue would henceforth understand and direct their mission. It needs to be made clear, however, that this global culture to which monks want to give a spiritual foundation does not mean a unique, homogeneous, and hegemonic culture. Cultures evolve in their interaction with one another when they recognize their respective identities as well as their primordial unity. Communion among all is not to be had at the price of diversity, but rather by wholehearted acceptance of it. Monks sense that they are to give witness to their belief in a unity among all believers, a unity that is deep-seated and mysterious, already present and yet still to be fully realized. In that conviction, identified and affirmed at Petersham, lies the strength and specific contribution monks bring to dialogue. The hope of becoming one people provided those who met in 1977 a sense of meaning and purpose (Pennington [1978a]).

This sense of fraternal unity was there at the beginning—"We need to start where we are one, in the Spirit of God" (O'Hara [1977], 5)—and coincides with a new missionary spirit that emphasizes the Holy Spirit and communion. It involves waking up together, in a relation of reciprocity and mutual understanding, to the presence of the divine mystery within, in the inmost heart of all human beings, precisely at that point where communion with all beings is already a reality but still awaits its perfection here below. The words Merton spoke in Calcutta provided the key to understanding the meaning of dialogue and putting it into practice. "My dear brothers, we are already one. But we imagine that we are not. And what we have to recover is our original unity. What we have to be is what we are" (Merton [1975], 308). Faith in this eschatological unity is what drives monks to welcome with unconditional love and respect those who belong to a different religious tradition and to strive for a world in which all can live together in harmony.

The interreligious subcommissions concretized the spirit of Petersham by making peace their main objective. In so doing they made their own the monastic motto taken from the Psalms (33:15) and placed by Benedict in the Prologue to his Rule, "Seek after peace and pursue it" (RB Prol 17). By calling his monks to a life of reconciliation, the father of Western Christian monasticism shows that the monk still has a place in today's world, a point made by the Abbot Primate of the Benedictines in 1994 when he reiterated his commitment to peacemaking: "It is our task to stress the spiritual values of the various world religions in the hope that through knowledge and dialogue we who belong to monastic institutes may contribute to the creation of peace in the world. Pax is Saint Benedict's gift to us and our gift to the interreligious dialogue" (Theisen [1995], 2).

If interreligious dialogue and world peace were now to go hand in hand, it remained true that the contribution of monks to the latter would be indirect. One of the essential elements of their message was that they could only serve the cause of peace by attending to their specific objectives, the promotion and development of dialogue between religions. Otherwise they risked reducing peacemaking to the kind of negotiation diplomats engage in. Real peace is the result of a sustained encounter in which the acceptance of religious difference and openness to the divine come together. Such peace involves a sincere transformation of hearts, minds, and social structures.

We should note that this concern for world peace on the part of monks served to widen the distance between the first and second stages of their involvement in dialogue. Their concern actually revealed a decidedly Western interest in interreligious encounter that would become more and more evident as the European and American subcommissions little by little turned aside from the church in Asia and its missionary demands.

As the desire to give some structure to monastic dialogue increased, Western monks moved into action and responded to concerns that were distinctively Western. This gave rise to tensions between the interreligious subcommissions and AIM regarding the nature and purpose of dialogue between East and West. In theory at least, dialogue among Christians in Asia remained the primary objective of monks in dialogue. Rembert Weakland, the Abbot Primate of the Benedictines, made it clear at the congress in Bangalore that AIM's principal responsibility was to be of service to Christian monasteries in Asia by helping them initiate dialogue with Buddhist and Hindu monks. The head of AIM, Marie-Robert de Floris, was of the same opinion when he endorsed the necessity of creating within AIM a section devoted to interreligious dialogue.

In reality, the need to be of service to Asian monasteries was not very well understood. For this reason in 1980 Victor Dammertz, Rembert Weakland's successor as Abbot Primate, contacted American monks to insist that the first responsibility of the intermonastic subcommissions was to help the Christian monks of Asia enter into dialogue with monks of other religions. In November of the same year, the American subcommission added a new goal to its mission statement in response to the Abbot Primate's message: "encouraging and being supportive of Benedictines and Cistercians in Asia with their dialog with non-Christian monastics."[16]

However, this reminder remained a goal in theory only, disappearing behind another goal that was approved by AIM: "to make known to the monastic world of the West the vitality of monasticism in the developing countries, to stimulate understanding and fraternal sympathy, awakening generosity in helping these monasteries to resolve the numerous problems arising from the shifting context of today's world."[17]

How is one to explain this change, favoring interreligious encounter in the West to the detriment of the church in Asia, which depended so much on dialogue in order to become inculturated? Why was it so difficult to maintain both a dialogal and a missionary perspective? The reasons are fourfold: the specific role of monks in dialogue, the lack of a clear understanding of dialogue, the difficulties surrounding inculturation, and the innermost identity of the East.

The Specific Role of Monks in Dialogue

Western monks distanced themselves from their missionary activities in Asia as they became increasingly aware of the specific role they were capable of playing in the area of dialogue. The experience of the congresses of Bangkok and Bangalore showed that monks had an amazing ability to communicate at the level of spiritual practice and experience with Buddhists and Hindus, while dialogue on the doctrinal or theological level was more likely to lead to an impasse. Contact with these other spiritualities, which could involve adopting certain practices of meditation, showed that religious experience was a good basis for developing successful dialogue. Over and above their real differences of opinion and experience, monks[18] of all traditions have the same goal: the search for the Ultimate, the transcendent, that which is greater than what can be understood, felt, or imagined.

This common quest is, of itself, an invitation to be mutually enriched, to share one another's ascetic and contemplative ways, without denying one's own convictions. Even though Christian, Buddhist, and Hindu monks have their own literary sources, which are the product of different spiritual experiences, monks need no time at all to sense how close they are to one another. There are those who go so far as to claim that Eastern and Western monasticism share a common historical origin. Even if the indications that Christianity borrowed the idea of monasticism from India are "mute" and "underground" (Corless [1989]), one can still entertain the possibility that Christian monks are the descendants of ancient Indian "renunciants" (Leclercq [1986]). For the present, entertaining a possibility is perhaps all we can do, for there is no proof that currents from the East influenced the development of Christian monasticism (Åmell [1998]). This does not prevent monks engaged in dialogue from discerning a common religious archetype manifested in and through the different forms of monastic life. Monasticism as an archetype was, in fact, the theme of the first symposium sponsored by the American subcommission at Holyoke in 1980.

Monks thus discover that they have an almost natural predisposition to come together in their search for the one thing necessary that lies beyond doctrinal differences and theological disputes. Unless it is grounded in spiritual experience, dialogue with Eastern religions appears arduous and even hopeless. At the organizing meeting in Loppem the participants agreed that all Christians ought to participate in dialogue, but held that the members of the monastic order are called to take part in it in a way that is specific to them. They are, after all, in the best position to give witness to the universal character of truth and to the conviction that all human beings share the same ineffable destiny. They are also in the best position to make known the mystical treasures of Christianity to their dialogue partners.

Without isolating monks as a species unto themselves and reserving to them alone the heights of the spiritual life, it should still be recognized that while they do not play the only role in interreligious dialogue, they do have their specific role to play. At any rate, that was the opinion of Cardinal Sergio Pignedoli, the then-president of the Secretariat for Non-Christians. The institution of monastic dialogue and the new direction it took was the result of a letter he addressed to the Abbot Primate of the Benedictines on June 12, 1974. This letter, cosigned by his secretary, Pietro Rossano,[19] gave official encouragement to dialogue at the level of spiritual experience, recognizing that what had been accomplished to the present time gave promise of future success. This letter marked an important step forward in the development of monastic dialogue, not only because it exhorted monks to continue working in this area but also because it spoke of dialogue in terms of mutual understanding and enrichment rather than as a missionary activity.

Without disregarding the necessity of inculturating monasticism, the major concern of the Pontifical Secretariat was to see monasticism assume "the very important role that it alone can play in the church's encounter with religions rooted in a monastic spirituality" (Pennington [1978a], 51). The letter situated the contribution of monks in a form of dialogue that responds to the needs of a local church but attends even more to the need of affirming the spiritual depth of the universal church. It explored dialogue along the lines of mutual purification and enrichment of religious experience, and, consequently, of a greater awareness of the mystery that unites the whole body of believers. The Cardinal's letter can be summarized in three points that corroborate this point of view. First, the crucial role of monks in the encounter with other religions, especially in Asia, was emphasized. After having called to mind the success of the congress in Bangalore, the Cardinal presented the monks as the archetype of the *homo religiosus*, in virtue of which their presence at the heart of the Catholic Church is, in itself, a bridge that extends to other religions. Then he treated the challenge of dialogue that is specifically directed to Hinduism and Buddhism. He implicitly encouraged dialogue at the level of spiritual experience for the purpose of showing Asia that the Christian is also disposed to mysticism and interiority. He expressed his belief that without the monastic experience it would be difficult to present the church as a spiritual entity to Eastern spiritualities. Finally, he proposed that, moving forward, they should work for spiritual renewal in the church, recalling that during a Christian-Buddhist encounter organized by the Secretariat for Non-Christians in Bangkok in 1974 one of the major resolutions accepted by the bishops was to set up a center of prayer and meditation for lay people.

Over all, Cardinal Pignedoli encouraged the exploration and organization of paths of in-depth dialogue with the spiritualities of the East in order to bring about a contemplative renewal at the heart of the Catholic Church, which for far too long had undervalued a sense of interiority. In promoting this development he had more than the demands of mission in mind; rather, his focus turned to the need for spiritual renewal within the church itself. He was convinced that Christianity, with the monk, the embodiment of the spiritual person, at its center, is just as able to respond effectively to this situation as Buddhism or Hinduism.

Cardinal Pignedoli's viewpoint was due, in part, to the conviction of Pietro Rossano, a well-known professor at the Gregorian University, who coauthored the letter. Like Le Saux and Griffiths, he considered the "mysticism of dialogue" as the "guiding principle" of his life. It is not surprising that he was more and more attracted to monastic dialogue, the archetype of an encounter centered on religious experience. It will suffice to recall a speech he gave in 1980 to the congress of Benedictine abbots entitled "Dialogue between Christian and Non-Christian Monks: Opportunities and Difficulties," which he concluded by saying:

> Everything that can serve for edification, anything that can help one to make contact with another's inmost experiences or his starting point, so as to be able mentally to travel his road in the light of Christ, may lead to a fruitful dialogue that monks alone are suited to undertake with their brothers, non-Christian spiritual seekers. (Rossano [1981], 10)

Ultimately, the letter of 1974 expressed a tendency that would become apparent some years later in AIM's promotion of a dialogue that was not limited to the inculturation of a particular local church but was at the service of a universal objective, the spiritual marriage between East and West for the good of the whole human race. This new understanding of dialogue also flowed from a way of looking at the relationship between dialogue and mission that would soon be regarded as problematic.

The Ambiguous Situation of Dialogue

The change of direction of monastic dialogue has its roots in a tension between mission and dialogue that existed even before the creation of interreligious subcommissions. It can be seen in the original desire to separate dialogue from the specific activities of AIM. After receiving Cardinal Pignedoli's letter the Benedictine leadership considered establishing a secretariat for dialogue, but since funds were not available they gave the task to AIM. At first AIM was hesitant to expand an endeavor that was judged by some to be embarrassing, risky, and uncertain in regard to its outcome. On the one hand, AIM believed the endeavor lacked competence; on the other, it worried that dialogue might sow confusion among the faithful. They believed there was risk of compromising the identity of monasticism and the uniqueness of Christianity. Even though the congresses of

Bangkok and Bangalore recognized the central role of dialogue in monastic mission, some abbots remained opposed to the idea and did not think AIM should be financing such activities.

The future of dialogue could have been in trouble had it not been once again for the intervention of Tholens. In a letter he wrote to me on January 20, 1998, he said: "In order not to lose this battle I went to see Bishop Rossano, who was then Secretary of the Roman Secretariat for non-Christians, and requested that he ask Cardinal Pignedoli, President of the Secretariat, to write a letter to all the abbots of the Benedictine Confederation to propose that contemplative monasticism play a role in the encounter with Asian religions, given the religious character of that encounter." In May 1974, while he was in residence at the Shantivanam ashram, Tholens managed to get those responsible for AIM to accept his proposal for "interreligious closeness through monasticism," and this even before Abbot Primate Weakland received Pignedoli's letter in June of the same year.

Clearly, organized dialogue did not have an easy birth. AIM was not a completely willing midwife, and tensions would grow with the passing of time. When the Abbot Primate, in response to the letter from Pignedoli, asked AIM how to go about furthering dialogue between Christian and Asian forms of monasticism, AIM responded with three suggestions: create within AIM a special department that would be capable of providing the resources necessary to get dialogue off the ground and promote it; encourage regional encounters between Christian and non-Christian monks on specifically monastic topics such as prayer or community life; finally, take care that this department give special consideration to all the Christians of Asia.

Tholens was put in charge of organizing such a department, and he began by circulating a survey in February and March of 1975 among Benedictine and Cistercian abbots in several Western countries who were sympathetic to the cause of dialogue. By doing this he set the tone and confirmed the underlying ambiguity between dialogue and mission that has already been referred to. This ambiguity can be seen in the numerous questions that emerged: Why are Westerners being approached when the focus is really on Asia? How can one deal with a problem without knowing its context or having dealt with it or been affected by it, at least to some degree? Does there exist a certain incompatibility between the need to develop dialogue in the West and the need to get Christian monks in Asia to be more sensitive to other religions in order to support the inculturation of their church? Does this ambiguity of the relationship between dialogue and mission constitute evidence of a cultural difference between Western Christian monks and those of Asia? Once again we have an indication of the difficulty that dialogue had in finding its place in a well-defined missionary endeavor with its own weaknesses that, by the way, dialogue also revealed. We are here at the beginnings of the debate on the relationship between dialogue and mission that even today is the subject of much discussion.

So why did the focus of attention of monastic dialogue shift to Western monks? According to Leclercq the reason was the lack of enthusiasm of Christian monastic communities in Asia for this new activity, mainly because of their precarious conditions. In face of the necessities of everyday life it was difficult to free up a member of the community for dialogue who could help his confreres appreciate the spiritual riches of Hinduism and Buddhism. That may be the main reason, but it was not the only one. There were also some political issues involved that made Western monks think they alone could show Asian monks how to become involved in dialogue. In a letter Tholens wrote me on March 16, 1998, he said that the Benedictine abbots did not think it was a good idea that money sent to young monasteries in so-called mission lands should be used to promote interreligious dialogue. AIM was becoming more and more a Western enterprise charged to come to the aid of the rest of the world. Consequently, it felt that its duty was to put the expertise of Western monks at the service of their Eastern confreres. This *modus operandi* was reaffirmed by the officers of AIM in September 1977:

> The directors of AIM believe that the new perspectives that have emerged will not sidetrack AIM from its principal goal,

which is to help Christian monks in Asia undertake dialogue with non-Christian monks. Therefore our Asian brothers can not only count on the moral support of their Western brothers, but also on their competence. To insure the existence of such competence, our first task is to bring together Western monks who have already shown an interest in interreligious dialogue. (Floris [1977], 59)

In the end this approach maintained two objectives that had little in common. We have already seen the results of Tholens' survey, which showed that those who expressed interest in interreligious dialogue were not much concerned with the church in Asia. The monks who were surveyed agreed that dialogue was necessary to counter mutual ignorance and the prejudices that were still too often present among the spiritual practitioners of different religions. These monks wanted to work in a spirit of cooperation for a cause that concerned and, at the same time, surpassed them, namely, the maintenance of an authentic spiritual presence in a constantly evolving world. For these reasons Western monks believed it was imperative that they participate in the religious encounters that were being organized throughout America and Europe at this time.

In the new statutes of 1976 the AIM secretariat insisted on the necessity of supporting the dialogue of monks living in mission lands, but also of fostering dialogue with different forms of non-Christian monasticism in the West. This twofold charge can be found in objectives formulated by Tholens at the meeting in Petersham: to reflect on the importance of encounter; to understand and assimilate some of the values of Asian religions and to promote dialogue among the Christian monks in Asia; to raise the consciousness of Western Christian monks about the tremendous importance of the religions and cultures of Asia for themselves and for the contemporary world. In actual practice the second objective was only minimally honored, given the geographical and cultural distance separating the East from the West with regard to dialogue. Added to this were the difficulties of inculturating Christian monasticism in Asia.

The Difficulty of Inculturation

The growing gap between dialogue and a certain way of looking at mission can also be explained by the difficult process of inculturation. In the case of India, Western monks were faced with two difficult situations. In the first place there was the challenge of the ashram of Shantivanam, which was—it must be admitted—partially abandoned. While it was not a complete failure, it did not realize all the hopes that were placed in it. In spite of the international reputation it gained under the leadership of Griffiths it appears, in retrospect, that the initial enthusiasm gave way to a certain degree of disappointment. Even though it was reputed to be one of the bright spots of inculturation, it attracted only a few native vocations. Without going into detail it is possible to point to three reasons for this situation: a certain wariness in Christian circles about Le Saux and Monchanin's attempt in the 1950s and 60s to incorporate Hindu symbols and images into a Christian vision of the world; the difficulty for a Catholic population largely drawn from the lower castes to feel at home in renunciant spirituality (that of the *sannyasi*), which is normally reserved to the elite caste of the Brahmins; finally, as has already been noted, the desire of Indian Christians to maintain the unincultured externals of their religion—typically Western and often Portuguese—in order to counter a dominant religion with great power to assimilate other religions.

After the death of Monchanin it did not take long for Le Saux to decide to leave the ashram and become a hermit in the Himalayas in order to satisfy his intense desire to penetrate more deeply into the mysteries of non-duality (*advaita*). In spite of its limitations, Shantivanam under the direction of Griffiths enjoyed considerable success in the areas of interreligious dialogue and interiority. If it did not live up to the hopes of its founders by becoming a model of inculturation, it still responded to the needs of numerous young people from Europe, North America, and Australia who were looking for a more intense experience of the divine. In this way Shantivanam remains a potent symbol of the urgent need for a mystical approach to the Gospel. Griffiths played a key role in responding to this need when he took over the direction of the community in 1968 in response to the request of Le Saux, becoming, in effect, a "Christian guru" for a host of people from the most diverse backgrounds. Thanks to him the ashram acquired a dynamism it had never had before. In it many who desired a deeper spiritual life found a way to become reconciled to a church that had not satisfied their need and from which they had become estranged.

The reconciliation mediated by Shantivanam reinforces the theory that an encounter with Eastern religions provides Christians an opportunity to go more deeply into their own often unknown spiritual traditions. This is the point Le Saux made when he wrote in a 1967 letter to Odette Baumer-Despeigne: "I believe that it is necessary to go to the Hindu sources in order to be able to draw more deeply on our own Christian sources" (Baumer-Despeigne [1990], 535).

It was also difficult for the monks of Europe and America to understand that the planting of Christian monasticism in Asia was a challenge that could only be met by Asians. Western monks may have been experts in the area of dialogue but Asian monks had serious reasons for not being very receptive to collaborating with them, if for no other reason than that in India religious pluralism and the peaceful coexistence of religions was a tradition going back over a thousand years. Asian Christian monks were not very happy about being told how to enter into dialogue with the local religions they themselves had come from, especially since it was Westerners who some centuries earlier had insisted that their relationship to Christ had to be stripped of every trace of another religion. In response to the criticism that it was being too paternalistic, the AIM secretariat changed its name from *Aide à l'implantation monastique* (Assistance for the Implantation of Monasticism) to *Aide inter-monastères* (Assistance between Monasteries).[20] The acronym AIM remained the same, but out of a concern to eliminate any trace of colonialism that might be communicated by the word "implantation" the meaning was changed to emphasize fraternity and the mutual enrichment of Christian monasteries in the East and the West (Gordan [1979]).

At the same time, monks and nuns involved in dialogue preferred a contextual approach and were not very comfortable with the centralized *modus operandi* of AIM. Whether in Europe or in Asia, the responsibility for developing a local or regional dialogue that addressed the situations and challenges that were theirs fell to those who lived there. This approach was already evident in the results of the 1975 survey, but now that the subcommissions for dialogue had to be financially self-sufficient it was even more pronounced. At the pan-Asiatic conference held in Kandy in 1980 the Abbot Primate made it clear to the monks of Asia, who were living in such close proximity to Eastern traditions, that they had the primary responsibility for engaging in interreligious dialogue in their regions. The role of their American and European counterparts would remain secondary:

> It is up to you, monks and sisters of Asia, to engage in dialogue and to determine what Benedictine life in the monasteries of Asia today should be like. The monasteries of other continents cannot assume this responsibility because, even with the best of intentions, they are not fully aware of the problems you face. In order to continue the necessary acculturation of Benedictine monasticism in Asia, you have to live in an Asian milieu day in and day out. Even more, you have to be Asian.[21]

Since then, Christians in the East have no longer depended on their Western brothers and sisters to guide them in dialogue. In fact, on the last day of the congress Asian-born monks expressed the desire to meet among themselves, without the presence of even such outstanding pioneers as Bede Griffiths, Francis Mahieu (Acharya), or Mayeul de Dreuille.

The Innermost Identity of the East

There is a final point that explains why monks in dialogue little by little separated themselves from missionary work in Asia: the concept of "the East" itself. In fact, "the East" refers not so much to a geographical location as to an interior reality. This point of view was expressed at the Bangkok congress when the Abbot Primate noted that when taking a cultural or anthropological point of view people can discover within themselves characteristics that are both "Eastern" and "Western" (O'Hara [1977], 4). The point was made again at a symposium held in Holyoke when Raimon Panikkar suggested that East and West were anthropological rather than geographical places (Panikkar [1982]). Even if this idea was colored by a certain orientalism, Panikkar's intention was not to minimize the historical development of the religions of the East, thereby reducing them to some "fictitious East." What was being rejected was the still widespread tendency to categorize biblical religions as Western and non-biblical religions as Eastern. If, in fact, the religions still in existence are Eastern in origin, it remains true that they have been subject to both Western and Eastern influences. The terms "Eastern religions" and "Western religions" should be used with caution. Europeans and Americans still think of the East as a cultural monolith that stands over against another monolith, that of the West (Batchelor [1994]).

By emphasizing the anthropological aspect of these categories, monks call attention to the twofold dimension of their approach to dialogue. First of all they show that Asian religions are not an alternative to the perceived weaknesses of Christianity; nothing is gained by opposing an "ignorant and murky" West to an idealized East that possesses "the truth" (Blée [1998]). Monks also favor the internal and psychological dimension of their dialogue by making connections between their religious traditions and the spiritual depths of human nature.

The East puts us in touch with the feminine side, where intuition, symbol, and immanence are in the forefront, in contrast to the West, where the masculine characteristics of reason, doctrine, and transcendence are accentuated. Dialogue with Buddhism and Hinduism offers Christians the opportunity to pay attention to the neglected dimensions of their personality. Griffiths insisted on this point when he set out to promote the marriage of East and West (Griffiths [1982]). Pierre de Béthune did the same when, in an article that appeared in 1981, he referred to the definition Karl Jung gave of the East:

> What is this "Orient" where the Christian life has equally to take root? C. G. Jung once said: "It seems certainly true that the East is at the origin of the spiritual changes through which we are passing today. Nevertheless, this East is not a Tibetan monastery or some meeting of Mahatmas, *it is in us*." We feel that it is time to awaken this "Orient within us, " namely all the aspects of our personality which have become atrophied in our Western civilization; the place given to intuition, symbols, bodily expression, acceptance of what is tangible—in short, the feminine pole of our personality. Yet this polarity must not be over-emphasized. (Béthune [1981], 10)

Monks attribute to the East an even deeper meaning, one that goes beyond psychological categories. They also discover a metaphysical dimension, seeing it as a symbol of the divine, of the ultimate reality beyond all dualities. This metaphysical dimension is—at one and the same time—at the heart of and beyond all particularities. The Sri Lankan Jesuit Aloysius Pieris, an advocate of monastic dialogue, speaks of the "Orient within" as the "Kingdom of God in us and among us" (Pieris [1988], 84). But it is Merton who especially catches our attention: "Asia in its purity . . . is clear, pure, complete. It says everything, it needs nothing. And because it needs nothing it can afford to be silent, unnoticed, undiscovered. It does not need to be discovered. It is we, Asians included, who need to discover it" (Merton [1995], 84). Whether it be with respect to its psychological or metaphysical dimension, the "East" cannot be reduced to a designation of the religions that originated in India or the rest of Asia. In addition to being a dialogue partner with its own unique characteristics that have to be recognized as such, the East is also a mirror that enables Western contemplatives to discover aspects of their relationship to the divine that have been forgotten; it shows them their weaknesses and the importance of remedying them for the good of all. It is also the place where Benedictine monks discover their role in the creation of a more just society. In other words, the intimacy of an internal dialogue with Buddhist and Hindu spiritualities allows monks to reach into the depths of their own being whence they can draw on the energy needed to break with routine and contribute to world peace.

The Mirror of Ascetic Paths

The examination of Eastern forms of meditation is at the heart of the mission of monks who are engaged in dialogue, contributing to its implementation and defining its character. With the creation of subcommissions for interreligious dialogue, this examination became a priority. An intense interest in methods of meditation from other religious traditions is not an expression of curiosity, a passing fancy, or even less a lack of appreciation for one's own contemplative tradition. Not content to limit themselves to responding to the needs of mission in Asia, monks became the artisans of a new apostolate in response to the cry for an authentic spirituality anchored in the experience of daily life.

A Pastoral Necessity

For monks, the interest in Eastern meditation coincided with the discovery of a ministry to the confused youth of the 70s who were hungry for a deeper spiritual life. The foundations of Western society were being shaken by countercultural movements and protests against the alienation brought about by Puritanism, conformism, materialism, and consumerism. The religious scene was marked by a massive exodus of young people from religious institutions and a passionate search for a spirituality not bound by moral and dogmatic constraints. Their search was often without direction and in many cases led them to look to Asian spiritualities in their quest for liberation here and now. Among those Westerners who turned to Hinduism or Buddhism—or groups inspired by these traditions—to practice yoga or any other form of meditation, an increasing number felt the need to reconnect with their Christian roots, or at least to find a spiritual guide in a setting that was familiar to them. The first place many turned to in their search for guidance was the monastery.

At the congress in Bangalore there were already a good number of young European and American hippies who were making their way through India in search of "authenticity." But it was especially at the meetings in Petersham and Loppem that monks were made aware of this phenomenon. The discussions at these meetings and the spirit that animated them revolved around two fundamental poles. The first, as we have already seen, was related to the desire to look at everything in the context of a worldwide culture of peace. The second was connected to the concern to rediscover the spiritual roots of human intelligence and to affirm the place of contemplation in human activity—a concern that goes hand in hand with an interest in Eastern meditation. Both Petersham and Loppem shared a common concern, but the meeting in the United States gave greater emphasis to the first pole while the meeting in Europe emphasized the second.

On both sides of the Atlantic monks were sensitive to young peoples' sincere interest in spirituality and took them seriously. They did not regard the desire of the young as a passing phenomenon or the plight of some marginal individuals, but as the sign of deep need that demanded a response, and even more as an indication of a malaise at the very heart of the church that could no longer be ignored. The unpublished report of the meeting at Loppem indicates that the participants' starting point was the conviction that "structures fulfill their function when they flow out of experience. When they become rigid, they provoke a reaction from monks and nuns in all cultures, because one can then find religious who are no longer engaged in a spiritual quest." Jean Leclercq also emphasized the importance within the monastic dialogue movement of the question of Eastern forms of meditation and the problems this caused for those in charge of AIM.

> [Within the European commission the double task] of providing information and making contacts does not always meet with the same interest, understanding, or trust in our own monasteries.

> Nonetheless, the influence of Eastern religions appears to be growing and demands our attention. In order to obtain a better idea of this influence and to determine how we ought to respond, in 1984 DIM sent a questionnaire to its members to gather information on the presence of Hindu or Buddhist centers in the West, the reason so many young people and adults were now being drawn to the East and its religions, the role of monks in the encounter with non-Christian but still monastic religions, etc. The responses were illuminating and showed that at the present time, whether in Italy, the United States, France, Holland, or Germany . . . these religions are growing rapidly, especially among the young. Why are they looking to another religion and other methods for a spiritual experience? How should Christian monasticism respond to this new era of religious pluralism? (Leclercq [1986], 204)

One of the reasons monks took this phenomenon seriously was that they desired to offer some guidance in an area where people could easily be led astray. Monks knew they could serve as a protection against the dangers represented by pseudo-mystics and their promises of intimate contact with the divine. They also faced new questions.

The fundamental question for Christianity is whether or not it can offer people a way to interiority similar to that offered by Eastern spiritualities. In order to respond to this question we have to rediscover the mystical roots of the Christian tradition and also learn about Eastern spiritualities, not just through study but experientially. The second question, closely linked to the first, is what spirituality is best for today's pluralistic world, a world where the erosion of traditional markers intensifies a longing for truth and sharpens the fundamental existential question: What is our reason for existing? The willingness to deal with these questions establishes the terrain from which monks can offer a spiritual foundation for the global culture that is emerging, a foundation where East and West, by means of their interaction and complementarity, would become the unexpected leaven for a durable peace that is both interior and exterior. But to be up to this task requires preparation.

Guides Who Need to Learn

Among the young people who approach monks there are those who have known altered states of consciousness and mystical experiences that are disorienting psychologically and even physiologically. In order to understand these states it is necessary to have had some experience of them. A priori answers or readymade formulas that can be applied to every case will not do. Monks will need to become explorers, getting to know Buddhist and Hindu methods of meditation by actually beginning to adopt them. It is possible to talk about them from the standpoint of one's own Christian practice, but only up to a certain point. It is only personal experience that will prepare one for the task of speaking about them with authority and relating to them with confidence. At Loppem some monks were encouraged to specialize in non-Christian religions and Eastern methods of meditation. A recommendation was made that monks be trained as spiritual directors who would be knowledgeable about Eastern practices and able to guide those interested in them. They were invited to integrate some of these practices into their own spiritual life and to take part in study sessions to help them come to a fuller understanding of these practices and teach them to others.

Benedictine monks realized that it was not possible to interact with Asian spiritualities without an experiential knowledge of them. Le Saux showed the way: "And, before comparing and relating the two approaches to the divine mystery, the Christian must first try to understand, to plumb the depth of the Eastern religious experience" (Le Saux [1981], 216). At Petersham the participants were also conscious of the need for such preparation: "[O]ne must experience the depths of another tradition before he can formulate valid concepts in its regard. Looking from the outside in, we deal with appearances and projections of our own limited values, whereas finding a tradition from within we come to know by experiencing with our whole being" (O'Hara [1977], 33). In order to understand a religious tradition that is not one's own it is necessary—to the degree this is possible—to enter into it and to approach it through and beyond concepts and interpretations that inevitably present it in a limited and partial way. The documents of the subcommissions returned to this point several times. For example, the American *Bulletin* took note of the congress of the South-East Asian Major Superiors (1983), which encouraged Christian religious to study and practice Asian methods of prayer. Mention was also made of the sixth congress on Christian-Buddhist meditation at the Naropa Institute in Colorado (1986), where the participants agreed that only someone who practiced an Eastern form of meditation could truly enter into a dialogue between East and West. Setting out on such an adventure is no simple matter. It involves making one's way toward the unknown and being willing to call everything into question. But it also involves rediscovering oneself as a God-seeker and it offers the possibility of opening new horizons and moving beyond illusory certitudes and well-established routines.

What led monks to become involved in this new apostolate was less a sense of duty than a conviction of the importance of encountering Eastern spiritualities in order to recapture the essentials of their own tradition. After the fact they found themselves engaged in an internal dialogue with Buddhism and Hinduism—hence the distinction between a summons that is *heard* and a summons that is *felt*. As we have seen, the fathers of the council and the fathers of dialogue stressed the importance of acquiring an experiential and discerning knowledge of the ascetic ways of the East: a summons that was *heard*. One can respond to it or not. A summons that is *felt*, on the other hand, does not come from the outside. It is a deeply interior longing to taste the divine through contact with another tradition. In this case, entering into relationship with the other springs from love or an existential necessity, and not from a sense of duty or obligation. Griffiths described his attraction for the East as a thunderbolt (Griffiths [1982]). Le Saux undertook his interreligious "saga" after having sat in the presence of the silent and radiant Ramana Maharshi, one of the great Hindu mystics of the twentieth century. After this encounter he could think of nothing but becoming a "Christian Ramana." The gift of the East, and of India in particular, is to challenge the spirituality of Western Christians, several of whom have written about their disconcerting and yet revelatory experiences: the experience of enlightenment (Merton [1995]), of plenitude and non-duality (Tholen [1979]), or of interiority.[22] It should be clear that the Christian who, when it is right to do so, adopts an Eastern practice of meditation does not do so for some ulterior motive.

Adopting an Eastern form of meditation is the expression of an intense desire to encounter the divine, a desire that needs to be shared with those who are ready for a similar spiritual quest, no matter what their religious affiliation. If there is no *felt* summons, it will be hard to respond to a *heard* summons; on the other hand, a *felt* summons can only be fully expressed if it is supported by a *heard* summons. Furthermore, a *heard* summons influences the way monks receive Western young people who come to them for guidance. The monks do not put themselves on a higher level, but rather recognize that they too face the same difficulties and risks. Monks who are responsive to this new pastoral situation are themselves drawn to the East in search of a more integrated spirituality. Their challenge is to be both teacher and disciple. They can no longer skirt around embarrassing questions by appealing to their authority or repeating doctrinal formulas. Monks become fellow seekers. Often the young people who come to see them are firmly grounded in the practice of Zen or yoga; some may even have had experience of advanced mystical states, in which case they are in a position to enrich the vision and spiritual experience of monks and contribute to the development of their dialogue.

While there exists a reciprocal relationship between lay people and monks, rather than a relationship between an all-knowing master and a naïve disciple, it remains true that monks have the advantage of being anchored—in the best of cases—in an experience of contemplation and discernment that reveals the richness of their age-old tradition. If that is the case, their search for the divine through contact with Eastern spiritualities is all the more meaningful. Their path to the core of another religion becomes the archetype of a broader spiritual search, one that is often less informed but no less sincere and revelatory. Monks become spiritual guides but are also fellow pilgrims. As they make their way to the inner sanctuary they travel along new paths on which they meet a growing number of lay people who are also searching for ways to integrate the treasures of Asia into their Christian spirituality.

The Urgency of Integration

This new apostolate demands more than a simple preparation for a specific and immediate problem. Monks in dialogue recommend a careful consideration of Eastern forms of meditation that call into question some particularly Christian ways of looking at things. At Petersham the participants identified some areas to be explored. Tholens and the young lay people spoke enthusiastically about the values they discovered in the East, values they believed could enrich Christianity. One of the questions was precisely what the West would gain by being open to Eastern values. In relation to the ascetic practices of Buddhists and Hindus several points were made: the importance of physical posture, the symbolic value of the *asana* (postures), the relationship between *apatheia* as found in the church fathers and the equanimity taught by the Buddha, and the necessity of a spiritual teacher.

It was especially at the meeting in Loppem that involvement with Eastern forms of meditation became a central concern. The participants at Loppem did not come from as wide a background as those at Petersham, but the forty who gathered there were highly qualified and well informed about the matters they were addressing. Most of them were religious and clergy, but there were also monks from other religions and individuals who were experts on the subject of dialogue, among them Marcello Zago, who would become the secretary of the Pontifical Council for Interreligious Dialogue. They dealt with questions that were quite specialized and therefore not readily accessible to the public at large. In his study of AIM, perhaps because he was not present at Loppem, Leclercq hardly mentions the European meeting, but he does describe in detail the one that took place at Petersham.

Be that as it may, Loppem was extremely important, and the discussions that took place there were every bit as forward looking as those at Petersham. We have still not fully appreciated or understood the breadth and depth of its vision.

Responding positively to the conclusions of Petersham, the participants at the meeting in Loppem began by calling to mind the current world situation. We live in a world that is being transformed and where all peoples share a common destiny. We cannot ignore contemporary sociopolitical realities, the great religions, or their spiritual paths. This is a time of transition that calls for new syntheses to bring together common values and to comprehend the identity of each, in the East and in the West.

After having spoken of this unprecedented social development as a sign of the times, an invitation from God to take action, the participants addressed the conditions needed for a contemplative and theological renewal. In particular they explored the possibility of a renewal that emerges from dialogue with Eastern religions undertaken in response to the request made by Western youth to bring the riches discovered in Buddhist and Hindu traditions into their Christian way of life. In the face of this situation the participants were clear about their responsibilities. The unpublished minutes of the Loppem meeting contain the following: "In a world where experiences are nourished by different cultures, Christian monks sense that they have a special responsibility to foster this integration. Their life has to be a sign that all can understand, no matter what their religious affiliation." The study of Eastern forms of meditation follows from the necessity of making known new vistas of Christian spirituality. There was agreement with Merton, who believed that openness to Buddhism, Hinduism, and the other great traditions of Asia was a unique opportunity to discover the potential that was being lost in his own tradition (Merton [1975]). Here we have one of the big concerns of this second period of monastic interreligious dialogue. It can be seen, for example, in the annual meeting of the European subcommission that took place in June 1984 and at which Zago was present. The participants agreed on the necessity of creating a new spirituality that would remain totally Christian while at the same time incorporating Eastern values. This point of view was shared by Bede Griffiths, who wrote, "We were given the challenge of rethinking our religion no longer only in the light of Western thought patterns, but of Eastern as well. In this way we would be able to discover another dimension of Christianity. . . . This moment in history can be as decisive for contemporary Christianity as was the transition from its original Jewish setting to the Greco-roman world for the primitive church."[23]

This was not the first time the West sought out the treasures of Eastern spirituality. During the Romantic period of the nineteenth century there was an oriental renaissance led by such notable figures as Friedrich Schlegel, Novalis, and Eugene Burnouf. And of course there was the influential Theosophical Society and its leader Madame Blavatsky. This second Western renaissance was seen as the fulfillment of the first in that it situated antiquity much farther back than Rome or Greece. India was regarded as the true cradle of humanity, the location of the original and universal religion that was capable of bringing about the unity of the human race and saving it from its superficial materialism—an idea already put forward by Voltaire (Batchelor [1994]). Monks in dialogue distanced themselves from this romantic approach. For them it was not a question of a reactionary or anticlerical opposition to Christianity in favor of something that was authentically spiritual or of making the Christian religion a pale copy of the pure religion hidden in Asia. Their intention was not to mold the specificity of the Christian tradition in the cauldron of the East. Rather, they hoped that bringing East and West together would lead to a mutual enrichment and a harmonious relationship between openness to the other and rootedness in one's own tradition (Dinges [1978]). Moreover, monks were attentive to the fact that the interaction of these two spiritual currents represented a challenge to the present generation that had to be taken seriously. "Throughout its history the Church has encountered strong currents that at first were foreign to it; little by little these confluences brought about great advances in faith and sanctity. Is it not fitting that monks should be, in the way that is proper to them, the artisans of this historic encounter?" (Leclercq [1986], 205).

Toward a Theological Reformation

The integration of Eastern methods, as proposed at Loppem, coincided with a desire for a major renewal of theology. The foundations were laid for a long-term project of theological reflection on experience. The monks were aware of the need to provide a theological framework for their proposal of integrating certain Eastern ascetic elements into their specifically Christian way of life. They also realized that they needed to provide this service for the entire church and not just for the monastic orders within it. They knew it would be impossible to bring about a change in Christian thinking if this new way was not supported theologically. What was at stake was not just a dialogue involving monks, but a way of helping all Christians see the importance of other religious experiences in order to come to a better understanding of the divine reality. They proposed putting brochures in monastic guest houses to provide young people with a better understanding of non-Christian religions, reviewing a psychotherapeutic evaluation of methods of meditation, and compiling an anthology of non-Christian spiritual texts that could be used in community prayer. In the last analysis the challenge for the participants was to find ways of affirming the universality of the church. They believed it was important for theology—which was addressed to all the baptized—to take account of the spiritual experience of Christians of all cultures as well as of adherents of other religions. Theology needed the nourishment of religious experience, more precisely the different religious experiences of people everywhere. On this point the monks present at Loppem believed they were competent to speak.

> It may well be that monasticism is a privileged setting for this kind of reflection, for the monastic tradition has always looked at the various expressions of inner experience. It will be so all the more today if it is open to all the ways in which we approach God, the Absolute, the Father, the Ineffable, and to the multiple manifestations of the Spirit of Christ who draws all things to him. (Unpublished report)

Fortified by this conviction, the European monks elaborated a program of theological reform grounded in bold theological research and invited theologians to collaborate with them. They proposed organizing symposia that would bring together experts in the area of interreligious dialogue. They also recommended that monks specialize in the study of other religions: "The time has come for monks to engage in a serious comparative study, both historical and doctrinal, of Christian and non-Christian monasticism for their own good and for the good of all" (Unpublished report). Ultimately what they were proposing was a whole body of systematic work that would require a solid and wise theoretical formation and involve an experiential knowledge of Eastern spiritualities. On the basis of such a program they gave themselves the mandate to reexamine theology under at least three headings: spiritual, sacramental, and methodological.

The minutes of the meeting at Loppem first report on the need to take a new look at spiritual theology in the light of all that had been gained from responsible experimentation with the spiritualities of Asia and the way they were actually lived out in that primeval monastic tradition. Eight points were listed: (1) indicate the principal goal of the spiritual life and its intermediate goals; (2) emphasize the critical role of meditation for authentic personal fulfillment and right action; (3) reflect on the necessity for including the body in one's spiritual practice; (4) evaluate the importance and appropriateness for spiritual progress of methods taken or adapted from the East; (5) compare the contribution of these methods with those of what is called charismatic prayer and more traditional forms of Christian prayer; (6) study the underlying psychology and anthropology of the religions of Asia and their methods of meditation; (7) undertake a comparative study of Western Christian monasticism and Asian forms of monasticism (taking account of Eastern Christian monasticism); and (8) look more closely at the nature, role, and practice of celibacy in the different monastic traditions. These points express three important desires: to recapture the essence and richness of religious experience, to recover the path that leads to that experience, and to accomplish both in a pluralistic setting.

Those who gathered at Loppem then turned their attention to sacramental theology. They began by recognizing that the religions of Asia developed a rich repertory of visual symbols and symbolic gestures that manifest a successful integration of the body in spiritual practice. They recommended a comparative study of the symbolic universe of Buddhism and Hinduism in particular, and also that of Christianity, in order to restore the meaning of symbol in Christian liturgy and sacraments.

Finally they raised the issue of theological methodology. By favoring language that is rooted in the experience of the object studied, Eastern spirituality calls into question a Christian theology that is too deductive. The monks believed that the tight bond between truth and experience in Asian religions is a value Christian theology can incorporate in order to become more authentic. Against the background of this need to link truth to experience they put forward three questions: How can the interior experience of the Holy Spirit become the place where the word of God is received in the church of Jesus Christ and in that way become the foundation of theological discourse? How can this experience spur theology to emphasize the mysterious, ineffable character of God and God's presence to human beings? Finally, are there more adequate ways of thinking about the relation between transcendence and immanence, unity and participation? These questions showed that Eastern forms of meditation act like a mirror in which Christians, particularly contemplatives, take a new look at their spiritual and mystical heritage. Even more, these questions revealed the kind of reception they give to strangers, to those who pray and think differently. Adopting other ascetic paths was for them an occasion to embrace a new and fuller understanding of the meaning of hospitality.

Hospitality as the Foundation

The relationship of monks to Eastern forms of meditation is, in fact, a fresh expression of hospitality as the primordial gesture of Christian conduct, and calls for a redefinition of the missionary spirit. Saint Benedict made hospitality a typically monastic calling, whence the advice given by the American Trappist, Kevin Hunt, to monks interested in dialogue: Begin with hospitality. "That's something we are good at; it is second nature for those who live according to the Benedictine Rule."[24] While monks have always been eager to practice hospitality, they have usually not been so willing to accept the faith and beliefs of the other.

It is precisely here that something new has come into the picture: the only way we can receive strangers is by receiving them with their most cherished spiritual longings. To love our neighbor means that we also love what constitutes their relationship to transcendence. There is also something new about the way hospitality is expressed. While it used to be thought that hospitality only meant receiving someone into your home, it is now to be expressed by willingness to be received by someone else. How, in fact, can you properly receive someone else if you have not previously been received? (Béthune [1998]) This idea was vigorously defended within the monastic movement for dialogue and put into practice by its pioneers. Merton invited his fellow monks to become familiar with Eastern religions by immersing themselves in the traditional settings of these religions in order to go beyond a superficial relationship (Merton [1975], 313). Monks very quickly realized how important it was to become familiar with other believers on their home turf. At the close of the congress in Bangkok two Christian monks went to spend a day in a neighboring pagoda (Leclercq [1986]). The importance of such an experience was subsequently mentioned on several occasions, especially by David Steindl-Rast at the meeting in Bangalore. Later, just before the formation of the interreligious subcommissions, monks who received Tholens' survey in 1975 agreed on the necessity of situating dialogue at the level of lived experience rather than of a merely intellectual exchange, noting that such an experience comes out of a shared life. "It may be that monks from one civilization will spend some time in a monastery of another, or perhaps small groups of monks from different cultures will work together without any particular end in mind other than to live together as equals and in mutual respect" (Tholens [1975], 50). This same concern was expressed at Petersham. There the suggestion was made to "work out an exchange program between monks and nuns from the East and the West," a proposal that was quickly implemented. Only a few years later both subcommissions set up such a program with Buddhist monks. At first it was the European monasteries that, beginning in 1979, made it possible for a group of monks to spend several weeks in Zen monasteries in Japan. And then in 1982 the Americans welcomed Tibetan monks in their monasteries (Blée [1999c]).

These exchange programs have been one of the principal activities of the subcommission, and certainly the most publicized. Christian monks were introduced to a traditional Buddhist world by being allowed to take part in its ascetic way of life. More generally, it raised the consciousness of the whole monastic order to the importance of spiritual dialogue with Asia. There was, it should be noted, a difference in approach between the Europeans and the Americans. To a greater degree than their confreres from North America, the European monks, in their desire to live the life of a Zen monk as completely as possible, opted for a radical hospitality that made it possible for them to follow the rules and extreme rigor of Zen monastic life—and also to partake of its joyfulness. This meant that staying in a Japanese monastery was only open to Christians who already had some experience of Zen practice. In the United States the approach was a little different. Christian monks who stayed in Tibetan monasteries in India or Tibet were not expected to follow the daily horarium of their hosts or to submit themselves to any particular ascetic discipline. The idea was not so much to have an experience of the monastic life of the Tibetans as to visit them in a spirit of attentiveness and friendship. Whatever the arrangement, the exchange programs made possible a greater familiarity with what had been foreign and also provided the participants with a greater degree of self-understanding.

If reciprocal religious hospitality finds its most radical expression when Christians adopt another ascetic path, and even more when they do so to help effect a renewal of theology, the actual implementation of this kind of hospitality gives expression to more modest expectations. Not all monks in dialogue feel called to go so far in their acceptance of the experience of someone else. Often they have very little or no experience in this area, and so have to prepare themselves to meet the challenges of this new activity. Hospitality allows them to take the first step toward a deeper encounter. The first step is that of friendship, and it is taken with all the greater confidence when it is done under the auspices of Buddhist and Catholic authorities.

Pope John Paul II gave his support to the program of monastic hospitality by granting an audience to the Tibetan and Japanese groups after their stays in Christian monasteries. The Dalai Lama himself selected the Tibetan monks who would participate in the exchanges and received a report from each group. Furthermore, he invited the Christian monks to meet him during their trip to India. These exchanges responded to two of the major objectives of the subcommissions: to develop a dialogue between East and West in the monasteries of Europe and America and to make the religions of Asia more aware of the spiritual riches of Christianity. Even more basically, they represented the archetype of a new community, the model of a humanity where different peoples live in peace, recognizing their original oneness and relishing the joy of being together, without compromising their respective differences. Nonetheless, in spite of this encouraging development of monastic dialogue the ambitious program put forth by Loppem and Petersham is still far from being realized. Without doubt this is due in part to the resistance and misunderstandings that have arisen within the Benedictine and Cistercian orders.

Resistance and Suspicions

In the course of the second phase of intermonastic dialogue the emphasis was on the discovery of the other. Creativity was promoted in the search for ways to bring about a spiritual renewal in the church and major changes that would, so it was hoped, benefit everyone. Individuals strove to redefine their relationship to religious difference on the basis of heart-to-heart relationships. These efforts necessarily called into question more conventional ways of acting that had become the norm. Confident that they were fundamentally in accord regarding the goal of interreligious dialogue, some contemplatives of different traditions tended to express their love for others in ways that could lead them to disregard church rules and not take into account the more cautious approach of other believers. It is not surprising that their activities provoked resistance within the monastic orders. These conflicts are revealing, for they allow us to understand the way dialogue will evolve. It will be worth our while to look at them more closely.

Avant-garde Experimentation?

The root cause of the problem was not the lack of understanding or the incompetence of monks with regard to dialogue. Even less did it involve getting mired in activities that are in opposition to the Christian faith. Rather, the problem arose because of some incidents that were regarded as avant-garde experimentation. The task of the subcommissions was, above all, to raise the awareness of monks who did not know of or had no interest in interreligious dialogue. Armand Veilleux, the first president of the American subcommission, had already made that point in a February 26, 1980 letter to Marie-Robert de Floris, prior to the meeting that took place at Holyoke in November: "I am convinced of the importance of this East-West Dialogue. I am also aware of the difficulties connected with it and know how delicate the issue is in certain quarters. I sincerely believe that our working-group should continue its task of raising consciousness without needlessly raising fears or reactions."[25] This idea would become the cornerstone of the monastic movement for years to come. To change the mind of people who have no interest in dialogue, who are even suspicious of it, requires diligence and patience. On the other hand, to call their attention to the occurrence of avant-garde experiments in dialogue, as important and relevant as they might be, would only get in the

Dialogue for a Changing World 85

way of their conversion. It should be noted that this criticism concerned the American subcommission most of all. It was there that the tensions were especially pronounced, going so far as to lead the entire interreligious movement to adopt a new *modus operandi* that will be treated in the next chapter.

After the meetings in Petersham and Loppem the AIM secretariat at its meeting in December 1977 moved to have two subcommissions for dialogue set up, one in Europe and the other in the United States. The European subcommission was established at the conclusion of the meeting at Loppem and confirmed at its first meeting, which took place on February 21, 1978 at Vanves. The establishment of the American subcommission took place six months after the meeting in Petersham. Marie-Robert de Floris, who was in charge of AIM, asked that this be done officially on the occasion of the meeting of the "American permanent working group" that had been called by Armand Veilleux to be held at the Rickenbach Center of the monastery of the Sisters of Perpetual Adoration of Clyde, Missouri, January 6-8, 1978.

This time there were fewer in attendance and the group was more homogeneous than at Petersham. This closed meeting of monks and nuns responded to the wishes of the Abbot Primate, who asked that after Petersham and Loppem there be formed "a small group of monks willing to work on behalf of greater openness between Christian and non-Christian monastic orders" (Leclercq [1986], 136).

The Controversy around Intercommunion

The report describing the official creation of the American subcommission shows how unpalatable the resolutions adopted at Petersham were. The delay might be explained by the unexpected election of a new Abbot Primate, but I believe there was another reason, one that was more important and also more sensitive, and that was not mentioned in the minutes of the subcommission. Leclercq reported somewhat timidly that "during the meetings which took place, especially in the United States, there were incidents that raised questions, and they occurred in a setting where false steps are simply not acceptable" (Leclercq [1986], 139). These somewhat enigmatic remarks refer to intercommunion, that is, communion offered to persons other than Catholics during the celebration of the Eucharist. In the Catholic Church only baptized Catholics are allowed to take communion; apart from some specifically determined exceptional situations, other Christians are not offered the Eucharist, even though the Catholic Church recognizes the baptism of Protestant and Orthodox Christians. Given this state of affairs, intercommunion is extremely controversial. The practice raises all sorts of questions and creates a fear that it could destroy the sacramental system at the heart of the Catholic Church. The following situation, described in a letter Pascaline Coff wrote me on March 9, 1998, shows how sensitive the matter can be:

> AIM in France received a complaint from a Japanese abbot who saw a photo of Brother David Steindl-Rast holding a piece of bread during a para-liturgy. He mistakenly thought the picture was taken during the celebration of the Eucharist. This was the first time we sent the Bulletin [of the American subcommission] to our monasteries in Japan, doing so at the request of someone in the Secretariat in Rome.

The incident of intercommunion that took place at Petersham happened by accident. Contrary to what some claimed, it was neither encouraged nor planned. Tholens was at the center of the controversy. During the distribution of communion a "non-Christian" came forward with the faithful. Tholens, the celebrant, was unwilling to refuse him communion. Pennington, the organizer of the conference, reacted by referring to the church's position on this matter. Tholens offered me his point of view on what happened in a letter dated December 18, 1997:

> I never knew what had taken place behind my back, but it seems that I came close to being condemned by Rome! I never responded. My opinion about intercommunion is that we may not, as a matter of course, go against what the law lays down. But we are not robots, and when someone comes forward to receive communion in special circumstances—someone who

feels "in communion" with me—I will not refuse to give communion to such a person.

That was not the first time that such an incident took place. During a symposium on world religions that was held at the Benedictine monastery of Mount Savior (New York) in 1972, Raimon Panikkar celebrated a Eucharist at which some Hindus came forward to receive communion. The abbot of the monastery reminded people of the restrictions regarding intercommunion, to which Fr. Robert Vachon,[26] one of the participants, responded that imposing such restrictions was not Christian. It should be noted that Vachon regularly allowed intercommunion at the Centre Monchanin in Montreal, a practice that provoked much debate in the late 60s and early 70s between the cofounder of the Centre, Jacques Langlais, a Holy Cross priest, and the French theologian Henri de Lubac.[27]

All this goes to show that the encounter between religions can even call into question the way to carry out one of the most basic symbolic acts of the Christian faith. It also shows how demanding, even frustrating, interreligious dialogue can be. "The discovery of radical incomprehensibility is even more painful because it happens at a time when a deep bond can be formed. It is a reality which is part and parcel of the dialogue" (Béthune [2002], 39).

The minutes of the meeting at Petersham make no mention of the fact that intercommunion took place there. According to Mayeul de Dreuille, who was present when it happened, the reason is that no one said anything about it during the meeting. It was only later that a religious who was not present at the Mass heard what had happened and reported it to his superior, giving him to understand that intercommunion had been planned for, when in reality it happened by accident. The superior in question informed his superior general in Rome. An explanation was called for and given, and that was the end of the matter—except that people continued to talk about it and distorted what had taken place. Even if the controversy was unintended, it still damaged the credibility of the subcommission in the eyes of AIM. For this reason it seemed wise to delay its official establishment until the next meeting. That did not prevent the same subcommission from becoming the object of lively criticism some years later when it held its first program, a symposium on the monk as universal archetype, at Holyoke in 1980.

Panikkar was the principal speaker at that symposium, and he stirred up controversy by defending the idea that the monastic life could be lived in all walks of life, that one could be, as he put it, a "hidden monk" or a monk in the sense of a universal archetype. Some monks saw this as a jab at institutional monasticism, which, according to them, was being devalued.[28] Confusion was also caused by Panikkar's celebration of a silent Mass. Sometime later, one of the abbots on the American subcommission—who, as it happens, was not present at the meeting—resigned and no longer participated in monastic interreligious dialogue. The reason he gave was the lack of respect for the rubrics of the eucharistic celebration.

It should be noted that the fact that these incidents were reported by only a small number of people indicates that they were not all that significant. They were, however, enough to create a sense of uneasiness. Even if, in the case of Holyoke, Panikkar asked pardon of those he had offended, the activities that were denounced had some major consequences. Following the symposium in 1980, AIM, which had financed the event, began to distance itself from the American subcommission and was reluctant to approve its activities.

Outside the Monastic Institution

At the founding meetings, as we have seen, the participants adopted resolutions that in many ways went beyond what the monks themselves could accomplish. At least that point would soon be made, along with repeated comments about how to prevent such problematic incidents from happening again. Tholens' survey was quite clear about the nature and limits of a specifically monastic dialogue and the importance of distinguishing it from theological and missionary interests. However, things turned out quite differently.

In Europe what was proposed was a long-term theological study beginning with an examination of the spiritual techniques of Buddhism and Hinduism. It was at Petersham—which had a vision that was described as vast, impressive, and vitally important for the future of the church and humanity—that the proposals went beyond the monastic institution. The participants moved that the new organization be attached to the United Nations and proposed that a monk be officially named to it. On the recommendation of Robert Müller, the American permanent working group hoped to acquire the status of a nongovernmental organization. At their meeting in December 1977 the directors of AIM responded negatively to this proposal:

> Abbot Tholens brought forward the proposal made by Dr. Müller at Petersham that the monastic order have an observer at the United Nations to keep monastic communities informed about major spiritual movements on the international scene. Some directors objected that it was impossible to accept such an invitation because it is not the role of the monk to get involved in major world problems. This role rather belongs to the laity who are prepared for such work or to official organs of the Holy See who are delegated to collaborate in specific areas. (Leclercq [1986, 129)

Moreover, the participants at Petersham encouraged lay participation within the new organization. There was also a plan to create a university committee that would study the spiritual heritages of both East and West. Another proposal was to establish loosely organized centers of Christian meditation (on the model of an ashram) to respond to the need to offer Christians, Buddhists, and Hindus the possibility of coming together for the study of meditation. These centers would be open to receiving lay people who would like to live there for a time. In order to accomplish this the proposal was made that monasteries be asked to provide financial help and trained personnel. Their enthusiasm only served to heighten the anxiety of the leadership of AIM, which immediately replied that monks should remove themselves from the dialogue of experts and from theological discussions, which are not their field of activity, and confine themselves to dialogue that specifically deals with monastic observances. In the case of the American subcommission, the anxiety was all the greater because at that time neither the name of the organization—North American Board for East-West Dialogue (NABEWD)—nor the title of its *Bulletin* made any reference to the "monastic" dimension of dialogue (Gordan [1979]).

The Role of Centering Prayer

There is one final problematic point to mention : the promotion of Centering Prayer as an activity of the American subcommission. According to Pierre de Béthune, "Some members of NABEWD give the impression that they are using the structures of the Board to promote programs such as Centering Prayer, which are not, properly speaking, within the domain of intermonastic dialogue. They are excellent programs, but they cause some confusion in the minds of outside observers who wonder 'What exactly is the goal of this Board?'"[29]

Centering Prayer was initiated by Willing Meninger, Basil Pennington, and Thomas Keating on the basis of an anonymous fourteenth-century work, *The Cloud of Unknowing*. It was Keating who did most to propagate this form of prayer. In June 1987, in his role as president of the American subcommission, he sponsored a conference on this specific form of contemplative prayer and its practice. Moreover, the *Bulletin* promoted it repeatedly: there were announcements of retreats and articles about it. In the annual report, Centering Prayer was frequently mentioned as the only interreligious activity of some monks. This project of the Colorado Trappist was certainly commendable in that it allowed monks, clergy, and lay Christians who were attracted by Eastern religions to have an experience of the spiritual life in their own tradition. In *Intimacy with God*, Keating proposed a vision of the church that his organization, Contemplative Outreach, was charged with propagating. He envisioned the creation of a network of communities of faith engaged in the process and dissemination of Christian transformation.

All this led a number of abbots to ask some questions. Has Centering Prayer now become one of the objectives of NABEWD? How does promoting it contribute to an understanding of Eastern traditions? While it offers a new spiritual synthesis, it does not encourage interreligious dialogue. It really does not make people aware of the importance of interaction with the East, nor does it confront the practitioner with the reality of religious difference, a *sine qua non* for true dialogue. It should be added that the endorsement of Centering Prayer did not always benefit the American subcommission. Mother Angelica, a media-savvy, militant Catholic in the United States publicly identified it as a New Age practice, a charge Keating rebutted in the *Bulletin* of NABEWD (Keating [1993]).

Although some may have given that impression, the principal activity of NABEWD was not the promotion of Centering Prayer. On June 4, 1991, Keating wrote to Patrick Regan, president of the American AIM,[30] deploring certain rumors that were making the rounds.

> I am surprised to learn that the primary goal of NABEWD would be helping North American participants recover the contemplative dimension of the monastic life. Even though that would be an excellent idea, it is nowhere to be found in our literature. If the members of your Board have that impression, I would appreciate it if you would correct this misunderstanding.

It is true that the practice of Centering Prayer was an activity encouraged by the American subcommission. In fact, it was a way of responding to one of the objectives established by the subcommission during its meeting at Petersham: to encourage Christians to go deeper into their own contemplative tradition and thus make it possible for them to engage more fully in a spiritual dialogue with the traditions of Asia. By his promotion of Centering Prayer, Keating aligned himself with the wish formulated by Mayeul de Dreuille in 1978: to inform Western youth of the existence of a Christian monasticism that is as capable of responding to their longings as are the Eastern traditions.[31] But there were still some abbots who were uneasy about the fact that the American subcommission was being used to promote a particular method of prayer.

For all the above reasons some monasteries, especially in the United States, threatened to discontinue their contributions, which would have resulted in serious financial hardship for AIM. Mission and dialogue—especially dialogue—found themselves in difficult straits, and a solution had to be found quickly.

Henri Le Saux (Abhishiktananda) celebrating the Eucharist with Raimon Panikkar (left) and Giorgio Bonazzoli (right) in Yesu Ashram, Varanasi, 1965.

Pan-Asiatic Congress, Bangkok, 1968. Rembert Weakland, Abbot Primate of the Benedictine Confederation (left); Somdet Phra Ariavong Sankarat, Supreme Patriarch of the Thai Buddhists (right).

Pan-Asiatic Congress, Bangkok, 1968. Cornelius Tholens (center). To his right, Thomas Merton and Jean Leclercq.

Pan-Asiatic Congress, Bangkok, 1968. Francis Mahieu (Acharya) and Thomas Merton.

Pan-Asiatic Congress, Bangalore, 1973. Left to right: Jean Leclercq, Yves Raguin, Patrick D'Souza, and Francis Mahieu (Acharya)

Pan-Asiatic Congress, Bangalore, 1973. Left to right: Hugo M. Enomiya-Lassalle, Odo Haas, Mayeul de Dreuille, and Marie-Robert de Floris.

Pan-Asiatic Congress, Bangalore, 1973. Bede Griffiths and Sarananda.

Petersham (Massachusetts, USA), 1977. Left to right, first row: Donald Corcoran, Sarvagatananda, Joseph Chu-Cong, George Seidel, Denyse Lavigne, Satchidananda, Mayeul de Dreuille, Jean Leclercq, Cornelius Tholens. Second row. Unidentified, Katherine Howard, Mary O'Hara, Edward Bednar, Helen Wang, Virginia Lee, Armand Veilleux, Susan Beaman (?), Wayne Teasdale, Bernard Peters, Joseph Farrell. Third row: Ewert Cousins, Edward Hulme, Paul Marechal, David Toussain, Basil Pennington, Theophane Boyd, Roy Mauer.

Loppem (Belgium), 1977.

Spiritual Exchange II; European DIM (Japan, 1983). On the left, Notker Wolf, Archabbot of St. Ottilien.

Samu (manual work) during a Spiritual Exchange program in Japan.

Spiritual Exchange II; European DIM (Japan, 1983). Left to right: Notker Wolf, Simone Tonini, Jeroen Witkan, and Pierre de Béthune.

Spiritual Exchange IV; European DIM (Japan, 1990). Center: Yamada Etai Roshi. To his right, Michael Fitzgerald, Secretary of the Pontifical Council for Interreligious Dialogue. To his left, Pierre de Béthune.

Hospitality Program II; North American MID (India/Tibet, 1995). Left to right: Mary Margaret Funk, James Wiseman, Aaron Raverty, Pascaline Coff.

Gethsemani Encounter I, opening ceremony; North American MID, 1996. H.H. the Dalai Lama. To his left, Abbot Timothy Kelly.

Gethsemani Encounter I. Maha Ghosananda and Gilchrist (Denyse) Lavigne.

Gethsemani Encounter I. Plenary session with Maha Ghosananda.

Chapter 3

Autonomy and Assessment

The third period of monastic interreligious dialogue was dominated by the attempts of monks involved in dialogue to find their place within the Benedictine family. If the preceding periods had been marked by enthusiasm, the discovery of other forms of monasticism, creativity, and new experiences, it was now time to take stock. Extending from the mid-eighties to the mid-nineties, this period was marked by stepping back in order to reinvigorate dialogue, to correct misunderstanding, and to go deeper in the exploration of religious otherness. In response to the criticism and tensions provoked by their ventures into the area of interreligious dialogue the monks involved did what they could to gain the trust of their monastic brothers and sisters. Their task was all the more demanding because this third stage of development coincided with the rise of a conservative movement within the Catholic Church. One of the objectives of this movement was to close the door on initiatives of dialogue that had arisen in response to the spirit of Vatican II.

The attempt of monks involved in dialogue to gain the trust of their fellow monks resulted in two major changes. Structurally, the interreligious subcommissions became independent of AIM.

With regard to their vision of monastic interreligious dialogue, they articulated the specific nature of their mission for the first time. These significant changes revealed that dialogue was in crisis and had to find a way to reach maturity by defining itself and taking a position. This time for seeking greater freedom and growing in self-confidence was divided into three stages. First, monks involved in dialogue established their position within the monastic order by separating from AIM and looking for ways to bring the European and American subcommissions for dialogue closer together. After the organizational restructuring had taken place, the monks then articulated the characteristics and challenges of intermonastic dialogue, feeling a special urgency to do so because of the publication by the Congregation for the Doctrine of the Faith of the *Letter to the Bishops of the Catholic Church on some Aspects of Christian Meditation*[32] in 1989. Because of their experience and expertise, monks involved in dialogue felt obliged to respond. Finally, the debate about the place of Eastern ascetic paths in the Christian life became the occasion for international cooperation that brought about a deeper understanding and clearer statement of the specific nature of monastic interreligious dialogue.

Finding Their Place in the Order

Today the dialogue of monks is regarded as a credible activity, but it was not always so. Monastic authorities always supported its development, but some abbots had their doubts. When subcommissions for dialogue were created in 1978 the AIM secretariat expressed its concern that it was not qualified to engage in dialogue. The Abbot Primate of the Benedictines encouraged monks in dialogue to move forward, asking them to consider the suggestions of Simone Tonini, a theologian with special expertise in interreligious affairs and abbot president of the Sylvestrine Congregation, whom the Vatican had indicated for membership on the central committee of AIM. Because of his knowledge of the religions of Asia he was invited to participate in intermonastic meetings. His presence was all the more important and reassuring in that he was known to be somewhat conservative. While Tonini was able to quiet the fears of certain abbots who had questions about some of the activities of monks in dialogue, there were still others who continued to make their disapproval known. It should be added that Tonini, whom the Vatican had appointed to insure orthodoxy, got so involved in dialogue that he became a convert to the cause.

The Isolation of the American Subcommission

It was especially after the symposium at Holyoke that widespread suspicion cast a cloud over the future of the interreligious movement and also over the future of AIM. Because of its involvement in what some thought were avant-garde activities, the American subcommission, at that time known as the North American Board for East West Dialogue (NABEWD), very quickly found itself in conflict with several abbots. But the problem went farther than that. Its isolation within the order harmed the cause of dialogue in general. In an August 26, 1991 letter addressed to Thomas Keating, president of the American subcommission, Patrick Regan expressed his concerns:

> . . . the relationship between NABEWD and DIM needs some clarification. According to the Internal Regulations both are "subcommissions" of the general secretariat of AIM in Vanves. But their relationship to each other is not specified. This, we think, leaves NABEWD somewhat isolated. It is not really a part of DIM in Europe. It is connected to the general secretariat of AIM at Vanves. But that connection to us seems somewhat remote. At least it does not seem as close as the relationship between DIM and the general secretariat of AIM. Consequently to some NABEWD seems insufficiently linked to the larger Benedictine and Cistercian complex.

The isolation of the American subcommission was made all the more complete by the decision of AIM not to finance it any longer. AIM underwrote NABEWD during the first three years of its existence. Its decision to cut off financial aid coincided, paradoxically, with the subcommission's desire for greater independence. In fact, when it began, NABEWD asked AIM in France to cover the costs of its initial activities, but indicated that it wished to be financially independent as soon as possible. The irony is that it was AIM that distanced itself from the American body. It continued to support the European subcommission (DIM) until 1988 when, thanks to a major gift, DIM was able to cover the costs of operations with its own funds.

AIM distanced itself from NABEWD because its own financial resources were at risk. The policy of AIM, the mother institution, had been to finance the two subcommissions (NABEWD and DIM) with money given to it by Benedictine and Cistercian monasteries. However, several American monasteries had simply stopped paying their assessment because they refused to finance activities connected with interreligious dialogue. While their suspicions of interreligious activity were partly caused by the American subcommission's failure to state its mission clearly, they were also the result of a lack of awareness of the importance of dialogue at all levels of the monastic orders. Whatever the case, since the wellbeing of NABEWD, as well as that of AIM, depended in large part on the generosity of the American monasteries it was important that neither of them lose time in responding.

A New Bond Between Mission and Dialogue

Left to itself with regard to finances, the American subcommission no longer needed to heed the directives of AIM. Faced with the possibility that it would lose all credibility, monastic authorities consulted the Pontifical Council for Interreligious Dialogue. The council asked the Abbot Primate and the congress of abbots that it be charged with overseeing NABEWD and that it serve as a liaison for the entire monastic interreligious movement. What resulted was the nomination of a general coordinator to be a liaison with the European and American subcommissions and report on their activities to the person in charge of AIM as well as to the Abbot Primate. In June 1985 the Abbot Primate, Victor Dammertz, asked the Belgian Benedictine Pierre de Béthune to accept this responsibility. He was appointed to chair a central committee made up of monks from different regions and language areas of Europe and the United States and was given the responsibility of coordinating the activities of dialogue at the international level and doing what was necessary to resolve the sources of tension within the American subcommission.

The process of improving relations between the partners on both sides of the Atlantic was twofold: a gradual and inevitable separation of the organization for monastic interreligious dialogue from the authority of the secretariat for mission (AIM) on the one hand, and a closer relationship between the European and American subcommissions on the other. These two activities went hand in hand and reinforced one another.

For the sake of its own survival AIM was forced to withdraw its financial support from the American subcommission. However, this did not mean that NABEWD could then seek the financial support of American monasteries, since AIM had the sole right to do that. Without AIM's approval of its proposal to raise funds from American monasteries NABEWD ran the risk of becoming even more marginalized. AIM gave NABEWD that permission on condition that it remove from its documents all references to a legal connection with AIM. On January 30, 1992, the president of AIM, Marie-Bernard de Soos, wrote to Katherine Howard, executive director of the American subcommission, to confirm the decision that had been made a month earlier by the Alliance for International Monasticism: "We all ardently desire to see NABEWD emerge from its isolation and take its place in the monastic orders, and I am happy that you want that as much as we do. We have to restore our bonds and combine forces in order to make interreligious dialogue, in which we are involved, a vibrant reality in the monasteries of our confederation."

The administrative break between the secretariat for mission (AIM) and the interreligious subcommissions (NABEWD and DIM) was now inevitable. The desire of NABEWD for administrative independence was also shared by the members of the

European subcommission (DIM). This led Pierre de Béthune to emphasize in an unpublished article he wrote in 1991 how important it was for monks in dialogue to maintain a link with the secretariat for mission, if for no other reason than to maintain its legitimacy: "It is important that our (European) commission be officially mandated by the monastic order, of which AIM is a significant body, in order to accomplish in the best way possible its task of consciousness-raising in our monasteries. For this reason it is the Secretary General of AIM who confirms the nomination of the members of DIM and assures the connection between the DIM subcommission and the governing body of AIM."

It should be pointed out that the reason the interreligious subcommission felt constrained by being a part of AIM was because dialogue was more and more being seen by the Christian community as a separate and legitimate activity. On the one hand, the monastic movement for dialogue had gained no little interreligious experience. On the other, the famous World Day of Prayer for Peace held at Assisi in 1986 represented a highly symbolic starting point for the involvement of all the baptized in dialogue.

The Restructuring of the Interreligious Commissions

In December 1992 the members of the American subcommission envisaged a new structure for dialogue that would be simpler and better adapted to their mission. In order to reflect the decentralized character of monasticism and the dialogic character of the interreligious subcommission they opted for a structure that would be favorable to mutual respect and cooperation among all the groups and individuals concerned. Moreover, they wanted a structure that would be supportive of initiative and creativity at the international, national, regional, and local levels.

In June 1993 it was the turn of European monks involved in dialogue to consider the restructuring of the movement for interreligious dialogue. They did this at a meeting in Göttweig in Austria that would be decisive for the future of the subcommissions. The presence of the Abbot Primate, Jerome Theisen, who was eager to see dialogue become better known within the Benedictine confederation, made it possible to bring up the question of the structural organization of interreligious dialogue and its place within the monastic order. Together the Abbot Primate, the head of AIM, and the general coordinator of the interreligious subcommissions decided that the time had come to grant monastic dialogue its autonomy. All that remained was to find the appropriate structure. That was worked out after consultation with the synod of abbot presidents of the Benedictine confederation and the Cistercian Abbots General. The definitive structure was approved by the Abbot Primate. In a November 1994 letter to the Benedictine confederation he announced the creation of a general secretariat to supervise all activities in the area of interreligious dialogue.[33]

The new structure has two principal characteristics: first, a general secretariat was established, to be both independent of and complementary to AIM and to represent the interreligious commissions as a whole. Since they were no longer subject to AIM, the American MID (Monastic Interreligious Dialogue) and the European DIM (*Dialogue Interreligieux Monastique*) were no longer subcommissions, but became extensions of the new general secretariat for dialogue and would henceforth be called "commissions." The secretary general was now the key person in the new structure. He would function as an intermediary between the interreligious commissions and Benedictine leadership, submitting reports on monastic interreligious activities to the Abbot Primate of the Benedictines and the Abbots General of the two branches of the Cistercian Order, as well as to the Pontifical Council for Interreligious Dialogue, which, however, does not play a role in the administrative affairs of the general secretariat. Nonetheless, the synod of presidents of the Benedictine Confederation can ask it to provide assistance and to give advice on particular questions.

The second characteristic was that the general secretariat could eventually include other continental commissions, thereby ensuring the global character of the monastic movement for dialogue and the freedom of each commission to choose activities that respond to conditions present in the continent it represents. By acting as a liaison between the different commissions, the secretariat can prevent the duplication of projects in different regions.

At the present time, in addition to the European and American commissions, there are commissions for India/Sri Lanka and Australia. The Indian/Sri Lankan commission, known as Benedictine Interfaith Dialogue (BID), was officially approved in 1995, but its beginnings go back to 1993, following an intermonastic exchange initiated by Tai Situ Rinpoche, a Tibetan religious leader who invited a group of Christian monks from Europe to his monastery, Sherab Ling. It was there that Bede Griffiths gave his last public conference.

The Australian commission was established in 1991 and in May 1994 identified itself as the Australian Monastic Encounter (AME). Its uniqueness is to be found in the fact that it has included not only Benedictine and Cistercian monks, but Buddhists and Hindus as well. After having experienced some difficulties, it regrouped in 1995 as the East-West Meditation Foundation. Work has begun to create commissions in Southeast Asia, Africa, and South America.

With the amicable negotiation of an administrative separation between the secretariat for mission and that for dialogue the interreligious monastic movement turned a new page. The link between mission and dialogue, however, was not broken, as can be seen by a recommendation made at the European meeting in Göttweig: "A representative of AIM should be part of the council of DIM, and one from DIM on the council of AIM, so that the concerns of mission and dialogue be always present within each Secretariat."[34] Collaboration is advantageous to both bodies because of the complementarity of their objectives, which the Abbot Primate defined in an April 13, 1993 letter to the American commission (MID) as follows: "I see AIM as helping new and struggling monasteries, especially in the third world, in matters of formation and finance. I see MID in terms of understanding and dialogue between religious groups. Of course, the point

Autonomy and Assessment 109

of departure is the monastic life pursued in various religious traditions."

The Dynamism of Transatlantic Cooperation

The movement for dialogue was now freer, but it was also more fragile because it had to be credible in and of itself. In addition, the members of the American commission had to repair their image within the larger monastic community, especially for abbots who were skeptical about the cause of dialogue and therefore wanted to keep their distance. As a result, at least seven activities were undertaken, activities that ultimately helped to restore the credibility of MID:

1. Bringing onto the board of directors persons who were well known, respected, and inspired confidence;

2. Giving evidence of a clear understanding of what it means to be a monk—obviously a reaction to the notion of a "clandestine monk" developed by Tholens and Panikkar—and placing only professed monks on the board of directors;

3. Doing away with all imported cultural trappings—for example, wearing the yellow saffron robe characteristic of Indian renunciants, but that in a Western setting would look odd and give rise to suspicion and misunderstanding;

4. Partnering with people respected by the media. The best example would be Abbot Timothy Kelly's invitation to the Dalai Lama to participate in a Buddhist/Christian monastic dialogue at the Abbey of Gethsemani—a dialogue the Dalai Lama himself had proposed to the American commission at the Parliament of the World's Religions in Chicago in 1993;

5. Using the term "monastic" in the name of the organization and its *Bulletin* in order to clarify the kind of dialogue in question, to respond to the criticism of those who complained about its absence, and to parallel the European commission;

6. Incorporating the American MID as an official Catholic organization. The change of the name of the *Bulletin* and the organization became official when incorporation took place. On January 25, 1993, NABEWD was officially incorporated in the state of Minnesota under the name Monastic Interreligious Dialogue, with its seat at Saint Benedict's Monastery in Saint Joseph, Minnesota, the monastery of Sr. Katherine Howard, who was then executive director. Incorporation made it possible for MID to be listed in the Official Catholic Directory of the United States.
7. Promoting cooperation with the European commission—perhaps the most significant action of all.

Attempts had been made very early to increase contacts and cooperation with the European commission. In a report of activities dated May 12, 1980, Armand Veilleux, the first president of the American subcommission, wrote: "NABEWD believes that collaboration with the European DIM would be most desirable and wants to look into the possibility of more frequent contacts." In 1982 there was a proposal that monks from Europe and America take part in a pilgrimage to India financed by DIM. In general, however, the two organizations had little to do with one another until 1985, the year in which the Belgian Benedictine Pierre de Béthune was made coordinator at the head of the central commission. Before that the lack of contact between the two commissions can be explained by the distance that separated them and by the fact that they had different interests because of where they were located.

When Béthune took office there began a period of communication and cooperation between the European and American subcommissions. It was also a time of greater freedom and an occasion for growth in maturity and wisdom. Their previous relationship had sometimes been rocky. However, as paradoxical as it might seem, mutual ignorance and misunderstandings can actually strengthen the vocation of monks for dialogue when there is the will to overcome these obstacles. The monastic interreligious movement showed its authenticity when monks succeeded in establishing dialogue between their organizations in spite of difficulties, thus demonstrating their ability to engage in dialogue within their respective communities and between them. The cooperation between the interreligious subcommissions was a kind of apprenticeship for dialogue. While their relationship was always cordial, it was clear that they had some distance to go in respecting each other's sensitivities. On the European side Béthune complained that he was not invited to attend the annual meeting of NABEWD in 1986. Regan admitted that he sometimes felt like an outsider at some meetings in France and Italy.

What happened in 1986? Charged with keeping an eye on what was happening in the North American subcommission, Béthune traveled to the United States to visit the principal centers of NABEWD and take part in the annual meeting that was going to be held at Saint Anselm's Abbey in Washington in December of that year. During the meeting he made some suggestions about how to improve the American subcommission's credibility. Strangely, the minutes of the meeting, which were published in the February 1987 issue of the *Bulletin*, made no mention of the presence of Béthune. The omission was not soon forgotten, and five years later was still the topic of heated discussions. On April 28, 1992, Béthune wrote to Keating, president of the American subcommission, to defuse a misunderstanding:

> In 1985 at the time of the meeting of DIM at Mariastein, Father Abbot Primate . . . wanted me to supervise NABEWD. . . . This viewpoint was accepted officially by NABEWD as it appeared in the bulletin. . . . But this has never really come about. I was able to recognize this at the time of my trip to the USA in 1986. . . . But especially at the meeting of the Board in Washington, I noticed there wasn't any expectation in my regard. My opinions were received with sympathy along with the others, but a little lost in the whole.

Two months later, on June 8, 1992, Keating reassured Béthune, letting him know that the arrangements made at Mariastein had been perfectly agreeable to NABEWD, but adding that "this was not as clear to the commission as it should have been."

With the passage of time it is possible to see this tension in a positive light. While it caused frustration, it was also part of the dynamism of dialogue and definitely moved it toward greater maturity and freedom. In spite of their different sensibilities, the American and European monks recognized the need to go beyond their respective cultural limitations. Dialogue with monks of other religions is meaningless if it is not founded on a dialogue *ad intra*. Pascaline Coff was explicit about this when she wrote to Patrick Regan on January 16, 1992. In the name of the subcommission she apologized for the misunderstanding that took place in 1986: "Intermonastic dialogue, in which we are all engaged, is a sacred work that demands compassion, understanding hearts, and even reconciliation and pardon when necessary." Regan said much the same when he replied a few days later, "Now that dialogue is taking place at an international level, we are all called to transcend the limits of our own culture, even to accept trials for the good of our encounter with the other." There can be no doubt that transatlantic cooperation rested on a solid base and that the sharp tensions between the American organization and its European counterpart were, as Mayeul de Dreuille put it in a letter written February 4, 1996, "not between Europe and America, but between conservative and progressive tendencies in the two continents."

Transatlantic cooperation began modestly with the presence of an American representative at the annual meetings of the European subcommission and vice versa. Once the restructuring took place, an international bulletin was created in 1995. However, the first major act of cooperation dates from 1991 and became an especially important occasion for affirming the specific character of monastic dialogue. What brought the two commissions together was the publication of the famous *Letter on Christian Meditation* that elicited a strong reaction from monks involved in dialogue.

Christian Meditation in Question

The restructuring of the interreligious commissions went hand in hand with a clear statement of the specific character of monastic dialogue. The latter is what gave strength and cohesion to the former. The affirmation of the monastic identity of dialogue was the result of a collective effort brought about when the Congregation for the Doctrine of the Faith published the *Letter on Christian Meditation* on December 14, 1989. It had been signed on October 15 of the same year by Cardinal Ratzinger. Once again the concern was with the adoption by Christians of Eastern forms of meditation.

The monastic reaction that followed the publication of the *Letter* had a decisive impact on the development of the subcommissions, contributing to their closer relationship and thus giving them the confidence they needed to move forward to greater independence. It also gave monks the chance to act in concert by agreeing on the scriptural, spiritual, and theological bases of their experience of dialogue. Since the episode was so important for the development and energizing of monastic dialogue, it will be good to look at it more closely.

Cardinal Ratzinger's Admonition (1989)

We can begin by looking at the content of Cardinal Ratzinger's *Letter*. The document is addressed to bishops for the purpose of defining Christian prayer, while at the same time cautioning Catholics who are tempted to make use of the spiritual practices of Asian religions. It is necessary to articulate the foundations of Christian prayer, it says, because of the number of Christians who are being attracted to Eastern forms of meditation. The main question the author addresses is whether or not the Christian heritage can be enriched by developing a form of prayer that incorporates foreign elements.

First of all he recalls that Christian prayer should follow the counsel of the church and defines the nature of Christian prayer as essentially a personal, intimate, and profound dialogue between the human being and God. Then he identifies some erroneous ways of praying to be found in the contemporary religious world. He compares them to Gnostic and messianic heresies prevalent in the primitive church, and by so doing he adopts the tone of the early Christian apologists.

He denounces the belief that matter is evil and insists that grace is not a good the soul possesses by right. He also asserts that, for the Christian, knowledge of the divine is inseparable from love. According to the *Letter,* the danger of Eastern methods of meditation lies in forgetting the earthly—whatever can be grasped by the senses—in order to submerge oneself in the divine sphere. Placing an imageless Absolute on the same plane as the God revealed in Christ is tantamount to giving in to a negative theology that defends the idea of submersion in the indeterminate abyss of the divinity. However, union with God has to take into account the human being as a creature. Christian prayer is not in any way about the absorption of the human self in the divine self. Instead, the *Letter* insists on the necessity of speaking of the otherness of God and thus of the reality of the Trinity, in which the yearning present in the prayer of other religions finds its fulfillment.

At the same time the author does not reject anything that is true in these religions and says it is legitimate to take certain useful elements and assimilate them into the meaning and practice of Christian prayer. With regard to the concept of "emptiness," so central to the practice of meditation without object, the author explains that this does not mean emptying the mind of all images and concepts, but rather of renouncing egoism. He warns against the temptation to think of the divine as purely immanent and insists on the necessity of going beyond the ego. This ego must never be identified with God, who, though in us and with us, is a mystery that completely transcends us. Being lifted up to God is a gift and not the result of our efforts or of a technique that owes nothing to revelation. In prayer we are not led by our likes and dislikes but by the Holy Spirit who, in Christ, leads us to the Father. While the author accepts the idea that authentic practices of meditation coming from Eastern Christianity and from other religions can help those who pray to place themselves in the presence of God in a spirit of inner recollection, he immediately affirms that all forms of Christian prayer go through Jesus, who is the way to the Father, as he himself said.

The *Letter* also offers important cautions to those who adopt other ways of praying without sufficient preparation and then sometimes experience problems they cannot resolve.

So why did monks engaged in dialogue feel the need to react so strongly to this document? The reason is that the *Letter* did not just recommend prudence; it touched on what is at the heart of dialogue in two different ways, both of which called for interpretation. First, it cast doubt on the validity of apophatic contemplation, which had been honored in the church since the time of Dennis the Areopagite and was practiced and promoted through the ages by such spiritual masters as Eckhart, John of the Cross, and Henri Le Saux. Second, the *Letter* tended to lump together the great Asian traditions with recent derivations such as Transcendental Meditation.

If that was its intention, the *Letter* indirectly cast doubt on monks engaged in dialogue because what had brought them together was an experience of the divine born out of silent contemplation, prayer that goes beyond words and is at the same time deeply rooted in the body. Monks felt they were a target of the *Letter* for two reasons: first because of their apophatic approach to Christian prayer, which can appear to minimize the separation between God and humans, and second because they had put such effort into gaining a deep familiarity with Eastern spiritualities, an effort that was not always regarded positively within Catholic circles (Béthune [2003]).

However, the advice to exercise prudence was not addressed to Benedictine and Cistercian monks, whom the Cardinal held in high esteem, but to Christians who wanted to quench their thirst for interiority by indiscriminately engaging in Eastern practices, or practices influenced by the East, and thus ran the risk of syncretism. But appearances can be deceiving.

Monks Charged with Treason

The questions and concerns raised by the *Letter* about monks who practice Buddhist or Hindu forms of meditation predate the creation of subcommissions for monastic interreligious dialogue.

Among the documents that influenced the contents of the *Letter* was an article by the celebrated Swiss theologian Hans Urs von Balthasar entitled *"Meditation als Verrat,"* which appeared in the periodical *Geist und Leben* in 1977 and referred explicitly to Benedictine monks. The French translation of this article was published in 1983 in *Des bords du Gange aux rives du Jourdain*, and it appears that Cardinal Ratzinger's *Letter* of 1989 drew from this source. For example, the two documents limit their view of the spirituality of the East to Zen, Yoga, and Transcendental Meditation. Eastern religions are identified with the longing to escape the prison of the world found in Greek philosophy. The two documents go on to suggest that Eastern meditation is characterized by egoism, and they emphasize the importance of looking to the fathers of the church for inspiration when it comes to assimilating these non-Christian practices.

Des bords du Gange aux rives du Jourdain is a collection of writings by authors who deplore the influence of Eastern practices on Christians, especially monks. They point out that in some monasteries Buddhist monks have come to introduce Zen to the whole community. "One such abbey in Holland has an area set aside for a zendo that is larger than the church, and the monks are free to absent themselves from the Divine Office to go there for meditation. One cannot count the religious houses where people are no longer upset by such practices, including one in Segovia that has the body of Saint John of the Cross" (Balthasar [1983], 7). These comments refer, no doubt, to the East-West spiritual exchange program that has been taking place since 1979 between members of the European subcommission and Zen Buddhists from Japan.

Balthasar vigorously and sweepingly denounced the use of Eastern practices by some Benedictines:

> And then there is the absolutely ridiculous dilettantism that brings counterfeited Asiatic methods to Europe . . . a charlatan mélange of pseudo-Zen with various expressions of mock poverty and psychoanalytic group dynamics . . . that would do little more than make you laugh if, in fact, you did not have to cover your face in shame at the church's loss of fundamental

values and this act of treason that is taking place at the very heart of this same church . . . even Merton and the Benedictines at Bangkok and Bangalore did their best to find some kind of equilibrium on this bobbing see-saw. (Balthasar [1983], 161)

This Swiss theologian, who authored a working document for the congress in Bangalore (1973), believed that Christian monks had compromised themselves by adopting practices implicitly identified with the serpent and the Antichrist. They were guilty of treason (*Verrat*) and adultery (*Ehebruch*) by their betrayal of the incarnate and crucified love of God (Balthasar [1977]). Perhaps the author's indignation was a sign of his high regard for Catholic monasticism. At least that is the impression given when he asks himself: Could anything worse happen? The contemplative orders are, after all, the spiritual heart of the church. He then continues in these terms:

> No more intimate or lethal wound could be inflicted on the church than the abandonment by religious orders of that form of meditation they are called to practice as representatives of the church and of the entire world in order to take refuge in a non-Christian form of meditation for their own personal enjoyment. (Balthasar [1983], 160)

It should be noted that Balthasar's article, which certainly made waves on the international level, was published in 1977. That was a decisive year for monastic interreligious dialogue with the meetings that took place in Petersham and Loppem. It is altogether possible that it heightened the anxiety of some abbots at the very time subcommissions for dialogue were being created.

Monks involved in dialogue did not remain passive in the face of such accusations. AIM asked Pierre Massein, a Benedictine who taught at the Institut Catholique in Paris, to express his opinion on the matter. He did so in a 1979 article entitled "*Le point de vue bouddhiste et le point de vue chrétien sur les techniques de méditation.*"[35] Massein dealt with the prejudices that were entrenched in Christian circles and got in the way of an accurate understanding of Eastern religions.

Massein's article did not prevent the publication, ten years later, of the *Letter* signed by Cardinal Ratzinger. There is no evidence that he was familiar with the response of this French Benedictine. Of course, the *Letter* was not addressed to Benedictines, and it hardly could have been, given the fact that intermonastic dialogue had always had the support of the Pontifical Council for Interreligious Dialogue and on several occasions had received the support of Popes Paul VI and John Paul II. While the subcommissions may have aroused suspicion and incomprehension among those who were more conservative, they always enjoyed the backing of Catholic authorities concerning their involvement in an in-depth and existential dialogue with other spiritual and ascetic paths.

Numerous and Varied Reactions

Whether they were the intended recipients or not, monks felt an obligation to respond to the *Letter*, not only because it all but denied the possibility of a profound encounter with the spirituality of the East while remaining true to the fundamental values of Christianity, but also because it ignored the decades-long experience of dialogue they had accumulated in their interreligious subcommissions. The *Letter* became the subject of interpretation and provoked varied reactions. We can point to five (Blée [1996b]).

The Letter *encourages the very thing it denounces.* The first reaction interprets the *Letter* as an encouragement of apophatic prayer, the study of Eastern religions, and engagement in interreligious dialogue. Those who held this opinion regretted the negative interpretations of those who reduced the letter to a warning against the use of non-Christian forms of meditation in order to seek union with God. They believed that it offered an invitation to engage in practices elaborated in other traditions as long as they were looked at from a Christian perspective. For these monks the purpose of the *Letter* was to remind bishops of the meaning of Christian prayer; it did not intend to reject Eastern practices. If the meaning of Christian prayer was understood and these other methods were found to be helpful, so much the better. This reaction was typical of the official members of the subcommissions. It consisted of justifying their own actions by saying that the *Letter* supported them.

Consternation and severe criticism. In spite of the efforts of Catholic authorities to receive the *Letter* as a supportive and encouraging document for those who led a contemplative life, there were those who felt that it mainly conveyed suspicion. Those who put forth this second type of reaction focused on the *Letter's* omissions. They denounced its superficial view of Eastern forms of meditation and also its inadequate understanding of Christian prayer, which glossed over what was most meaningful in the Gospel and in Christian tradition.

Good intentions and inadequacies. The third type of reaction combined the two previous ones. Here we find a concern to bring out the good intention of the *Letter*, but also a need to point to what it fails to say. In his article "May a Christian Practice Zen or Yoga?" published in the *Bulletin* of the American subcommission, the Indian Jesuit Ama Samy states that the *Letter* contains good advice and solid doctrine, both of which are up to date and can be a great help for spiritual directors or anyone else. At the same time he notes the inadequate and incoherent ways in which these otherwise valuable teachings are presented.

The comments of Pascaline Coff to the *National Catholic Reporter* (May 11, 1990) are in line with this type of reaction: "The document is a good start, but it's far from being a complete treatise on Eastern and Western prayer." She regretted the absence of reference to Christian mystics and Eastern religions in the *Letter*'s definition of authentic prayer. While the *Letter* did not reject out of hand Eastern forms of prayer, she explained, neither did it present them as worthy of attention from a spiritual point of view.

Defending Centering Prayer. A fourth reaction sought to defend the validity of a form of contemplative prayer that was widely practiced in some circles of monks involved in dialogue. Centering Prayer was presented as a response to the appeal of Cardinal Ratzinger that Christians go more deeply into their own tradition and renew the practice of Christian contemplation. The *Letter* became an occasion to defend the essence of this kind of contemplative prayer that, as we have seen, had already aroused suspicion within American Catholicism. Emphasis was placed on its profoundly Christian character in an effort to show how it was different from Eastern methods. The problem with this approach was that it did not do justice to Eastern forms of prayer and their undeniable influence on the renewal of Christian contemplation that had taken place at the heart of the dialogue of religious experience. The influence of Zen, yoga, and Transcendental Meditation was passed over in silence, while Centering Prayer, which was already well known, was described in detail. For example, Thomas Clark wrote:

> One of the exercises of interiority which has come into favor in the past few years in the United States has been termed Centering Prayer. Like other recent approaches to prayer, most of which have been influenced by Zen Buddhism, Transcendental Meditation, or other currents of Eastern spirituality, it directs the focus of mind and spirit inward, toward the self, the center, the still-point. (Keating [1978], 49)

Bede Griffiths, however, was clear on the influence of Eastern methods on Centering Prayer:

> The art of the mantra consists in the repetition of a sacred word or a verse from the Bible, which has the effect of "centering" the person, unifying all the faculties and focusing them on the indwelling presence of God. The discovery was made in Spencer Abbey under the influence of the Maharishi's Transcendental Meditation and led to the concept of "centering prayer." (Griffiths [1992], 39)

This fourth reaction to the *Letter* of Cardinal Ratzinger refused to recognize any connection between Centering Prayer and Eastern forms of meditation, or at least ignored them. It held to the idea that the long Christian contemplative tradition that goes all the way back to the fathers of the desert in Egypt, Palestine, and Syria was never broken and now has come to blossom in the form of Centering Prayer. Since it had already been taught by the first Christian monks, it has nothing to do with Eastern practices. On this particular point I believe it would be good to be a little more nuanced. While it is true that Centering Prayer in itself is not something new in Christian mysticism, it is also true to say that the discovery of the ascetic paths of Buddhism and Hinduism has been, and continues to be, a catalyst for the reaffirmation—and not just in monastic circles—of a contemplative life that for a couple of centuries had been all but ignored in the Catholic Church. This debate showed once again that among monks involved in dialogue there are different ways of thinking about a relationship to Eastern forms of meditation.

The fifth kind of reaction is of particular importance, so it will be treated in more detail.

Continuing the Debate

This reaction proved to be decisive in the course of events and came from Pierre de Béthune, who adopted a courageous and constructive stance. In March 1990, during his term as consultor to the Pontifical Council for Interreligious Dialogue, he submitted an unpublished report to the council. After having shown that the *Letter* did not pass judgment on other religious traditions or even on their spiritual methods, he made clear that it was not directed to practitioners or teachers of meditation methods, but to Christians engaged in an experiential encounter with other religions. On the basis of this assessment he made his principal point: the *Letter's* tenor is pastoral and doctrinal, but it is not dialogic. He went on to say, "When someone wants to avoid entering into dialogue but takes up matters that are intrinsically connected to dialogue, it is very difficult to avoid falling into attitudes that are opposed to dialogue." Even though he acted in good faith, the author of the *Letter on Meditation* strayed into the domain of dialogue without intending to. To speak about Christians who practice Zen is inevitably to present Zen in a certain way and to provoke a reaction among Buddhists. "By not taking into consideration the dialogic dimension, which is now a constitutive element of Church life, the authors of the *Letter* considerably weakened the case they wanted to make to Christians." Béthune reproached the author of the Vatican document for not having listened to those within the church who had already studied the problems raised by the meeting of spiritualities and the adoption of Eastern methods. Cardinal Ratzinger had not even consulted with the Pontifical Council for Interreligious Dialogue before issuing the *Letter*; he simply asked the council to promulgate it.

In order to make up for this omission, Béthune proposed entering into dialogue with the Congregation for the Doctrine of the Faith to continue the work of discernment by listening to the many Catholics who had adopted "a form of Christian meditation deeply influenced by other types of meditation and who testify that it has been a help to their Christian practice." He concluded his report by saying that, with the help of the subcommissions and experts, he intended to conduct a survey on the actual practice surrounding the dialogue of religious experience. Cardinal Francis Arinze, who was then president of the Pontifical Council for Interreligious Dialogue, gave his support to Béthune's proposal.

On July 7, 1991, Arinze published a letter on monastic interreligious dialogue in response to Ratzinger's *Letter*. He began by recalling the major stages of monastic dialogue—Bangkok, Bangalore, the letter of Cardinal Pignedoli—noting that at each step there had been encouragement from the highest levels of the Catholic Church. He then recalled the support his council had always given to the spiritual exchanges between East and West. Finally, he called attention to the rich experience that had been accumulated by the monastic interreligious subcommissions, to which should be added the personal experience of numerous monks who integrated Eastern practices into their monastic life, as well as the teaching of Eastern methods of meditation given in Christian monasteries by Asian monks who live in or are visitors to the West.

The letter, signed by Cardinal Arinze, was a rebuttal of the criticisms made by Balthasar, who denounced the behavior of monks at the pan-Asiatic congresses sponsored by AIM and the infiltration of non-Christian practices in Western monasteries. It was also intended to counterbalance and complete the 1989 *Letter* by encouraging the monastic subcommissions to evaluate their long experience of dialogue for the good of the Benedictine family and of all the church.

> The time would seem to be ripe to make an evaluation of this experience, to see the benefits which have come from contacts with other forms of monasticism and spirituality, but also to examine some of the problems arising in this domain. . . . The Letter of the CDF has given sound guidance in setting forth the nature of Christian prayer and meditation. There are nevertheless questions which require further study, particularly with regard to the integration of different forms of spirituality. (Arinze [1992], 16)

In short, the *Letter on Christian Meditation* was the occasion for the interreligious subcommissions of Europe and America to collaborate for the first time by clarifying the nature of their dialogue.

Interreligious Dialogue for Everyone

The turmoil created by the *Letter* of the Congregation for the Doctrine of the Faith ultimately gave strength and cohesion to the process of restructuring the subcommissions. It also led monks involved in dialogue to recommit themselves to a path the *Letter* treated with doubt and suspicion. In order to demonstrate this we need to look at the response given by monks involved in dialogue in an article entitled *"Contemplation et dialogue interreligieux. Références et perspectives tirées de l'expériences des moines,"*[36] published in 1993 in the journal of the Pontifical Council for Interreligious Dialogue.

It is not enough to make experiences happen; they have to be reflected on, and what has been experienced has to be put into words. That is exactly what was recommended by this document, a veritable leap forward in the history of monastic dialogue. In response to Cardinal Arinze's encouragement the monks of America and Europe shared with others their experience of dialogue with Buddhism and Hinduism especially, but also in some cases with Islam and Judaism. For the first time these monks made an appraisal of their experience of dialogue over a period of fifteen years.

Contemplation and Interreligious Dialogue (1993)

Their document was worked on in two phases. First a questionnaire was sent to European and American monks. About fifty responses from seven countries were sent to a committee composed of five French-speaking Europeans who met in April 1993 to record the responses. The second phase consisted in producing a synthesis of the responses received. A three-person working group was charged with producing an outline based on the themes that had emerged. A first draft, prepared by Béthune, was discussed at the annual meeting of the European subcommission at Göttweig in June 1993 and sent to several experts, one of whom was Panikkar. At this same meeting, as we have already noted, the decision was made to set up an independent structure for monastic interreligious dialogue. In retrospect it can be said that becoming clear on the specific nature of its mission is what gave DIM the assurance it needed to be structurally independent of AIM.

In July 1993 Béthune asked those in charge of the American subcommission to have their members review the document; they did so at their annual meeting in August of the same year. The final text was made public in November, and each subcommission appended its own bibliography. The American subcommission published the document some months later in its *Bulletin* (January 1994). The final version of the document was the result of a long consultation in which the American subcommission (MID) played an important role in the first stage (responding to the questionnaire) and the European subcommission in the second (analysis and redaction). Still, the text was above all the work of Béthune, who initiated the project and was the final redactor. In fact, he published it under his name with the title *Par la foi et l'hospitalité* (Béthune [1997; English 2002]).

The document focuses on the question of the adoption by Christians of a contemplative practice taken from another religion. The concern was not a new one; it was already present in the first period of monastic interreligious dialogue. The document situates the experience of monks at the crossroads of the dialogic movement and the contemplative renewal, two extremely significant developments, first of all in the context of inculturation (the first period), and then in response to the increasing search for interiority in the West and the necessity of putting in place the spiritual underpinnings of the emerging global culture (the second period). But the document treats the question from a new angle. It clearly places the adoption of Eastern forms of meditation at the heart of the monastic journey of dialogue and furthermore describes this practice as something that concerns the whole church.

The 1993 document positions monks in an explicit relationship with the meditative practices of the East. It shows that adopting these methods is an important means for making dialogue with other religions fruitful, and it lays out the conditions for arriving at this goal. At the outset the author identifies three ways for Christians to engage in Zen or yoga: adopting a practice without allowing oneself to be influenced by the milieu in which it originated; practicing a way of prayer influenced by Eastern spirituality and then reworked according to a Western mentality—one thinks here of the Christian meditation of John Main, the Centering Prayer of Keating, or the Zen of Dürckheim. Without judging or rejecting these two approaches, the author does not expand on them, since they do not lead to the desired dialogic attitude. In fact, they do not take religious difference into account, that is, they do not attend to what it is in the borrowed practice that reveals the specific character of the religion that shaped it. Therefore Béthune favors the third approach that, following Panikkar, he terms "intrareligious." He limits himself here to the practice of contemplation in the context of dialogue and aims at clarifying what is meant by the "dialogue of religious experience." The substantive issue is certainly not to talk about contemplation, but to engage in a non-Christian practice of contemplative silence. What this involves is the acceptance into one's own self of another kind of religious experience, another way of thinking and feeling, and to do so by the adoption of a form of meditation from another religious tradition.

It is significant that the author does not refer to the ascetic paths of the East in terms of "meditation," but as "contemplative paths fashioned in other religions." His choice of terminology is significant. It points to the fact that monastic dialogue is the product of the highest aspiration of the spiritual quest. Monks of different backgrounds recognize that their encounter is rooted in the silence of divine union that is beyond all words (Le Saux [1981]). To speak of Buddhist and Hindu contemplative paths rather than forms of meditation is a way of identifying their most noble aim, namely, the achievement of awakening (*satori, nirvana, moksha*), and also its purest form, a form of meditation without object, just conscious presence to reality as it is—which is also the best way of describing Christian contemplation. But it is important to know what Christian tradition of contemplation is being referred to, and to do this the author makes use of the *Scala Claustralium* of Guigo the Carthusian (twelfth century), who speaks of *lectio, meditatio, oratio*, and finally *contemplatio*, the highest degree of the spiritual life. Against this background he is able to cast more light on the specific character of monastic dialogue. Within the church there are, in fact, a number of different ways to understand and practice contemplation. Béthune opts for the apophatic tradition.

The originality of this document is also to be found in its presentation of internal dialogue with the ascetic paths of Asia as the means to a new religious consciousness within the church. In fact, this kind of dialogue is presented as the most meaningful kind of interreligious exchange. An intimate relationship to other religious practices is no longer restricted to a few pioneers as it was in the first days of AIM. Greater openness and ever-increasing cultural exchange mean that the vocation of the fathers of dialogue has now become much more common, affecting a growing number of monks whose experience is making an indelible mark on contemporary monasticism.

The document makes the reader aware of the need to make intrareligious dialogue a common monastic concern. The adoption of Eastern forms of meditation is not just the business of a few monks but concerns the entire Benedictine world. For this reason Béthune offers some guidelines to prevent the marginalization of monks involved in dialogue: they should be in touch with their superior, have the trust of their community, not upset those who are less informed, and be personally rooted in their own monastic tradition. On this last point the author refers to Merton, for whom contemplative dialogue "should be reserved for those who have been formed by years of silence and a long habit of meditation [and] . . . for those who have entered very seriously into their own monastic tradition and are in authentic contact with the past of their own religious community" (Béthune [2002], 60). Not becoming marginalized is important for the practitioner, for his community, and also for the entire movement of dialogue. The 1993 document responds to the need for monks to find their place within their own communities by insisting that monastic dialogue is legitimate, since it is the fourth kind of dialogue referred to by the Pontifical Council for Interreligious Dialogue, namely the dialogue of religious experience. The document actually begins with the definition of this kind of dialogue as it was given in the pontifical document *The Attitude of the Church toward Followers of Other Religions: Reflections and Orientations on Dialogue and Mission*, a definition that affirms that contemplation in dialogue contributes to the development of interreligious dialogue, which has become an essential element of Christian identity in today's world. One thing is certain: the document brings an element of boldness that was lacking in the 1989 letter. It encourages the adoption of other contemplative paths and presents the conditions for doing so with all humility, simplicity, and discernment. An Eastern tradition is to be chosen with care, the authority of the teachers should be verified, and one should be informed about the cultural, historical, and theological background of the practice adopted. This 1993 text does not replace the *Letter* of Cardinal Ratzinger: it is not a doctrinal exposé but an expression of monastic wisdom. But what its author hoped to accomplish is just as great: transforming religious consciousness and making this internal dialogue an ecclesial reality.

Raimon Panikkar and Monastic Dialogue

The efforts to explain the significance of the new ventures of the fathers of dialogue helped to create a shift in thinking—from that of seeing the adoption of Eastern meditation practices as something that only concerned a few pioneers to seeing it as a responsibility incumbent on a whole community. The ability to understand and articulate the process and demands of interreligious dialogue made it possible for more people to be ready for this new adventure and to set out on it with greater understanding. More than any other theologian it was Panikkar who played a decisive role in the development of monastic dialogue. Because of his close relationship with Le Saux he was a bridge between the time of the pioneers and an institutionalized form of dialogue. In addition, by creating and articulating the concept of intrareligious dialogue he became a dominant figure for understanding the nature and the specific role of monastic dialogue and the tensions it can bring about.

Panikkar accompanied his close friend Le Saux in his pilgrimage to the sources of the Ganges and in his reflections on dialogue with Hinduism. The monk and the theologian influenced each other. Panikkar had privileged access to the rich experience of Le Saux, and in return he helped Le Saux put this experience into words and free himself from his tendency to think of everything in doctrinal terms. The internal dialogue of this Benedictine *sannyasi* from Brittany strongly moved Panikkar and inspired him to understand his own relationship with religious otherness and to develop his concept of intrareligious dialogue.

Le Saux spoke of dialogue that was "religious at its deepest point" to designate the same kind of encounter (Le Saux [1981]). In this way he wanted to take account of his own Christian experience at the heart of Hinduism; his message was his journey. He did not intend to work out a theology of dialogue *a priori*, even though he was aware that his writings would have theological repercussions for future generations. He assumed the burden of his dialogic experience in the name of the church, the Christian community, and more broadly, humanity. All the same, it remains true that not everyone was convinced of the theological importance of the writings of Le Saux. It was precisely here that Panikkar played a decisive role. He brought his erudition and academic experience to bear on the experience of his friend—which in many ways he found similar to his own—thereby bringing him to the attention of the world outside monastic circles.

Panikkar is not a monk, but monks are deeply indebted to him. He proposed a theoretical framework that made it possible to grasp the ins and outs of internal or intrareligious dialogue. Even though this concept was developed outside a specifically monastic context, it continues to inspire many within the monastic interreligious commissions.

Panikkar also influenced the development of monastic dialogue by his presence and his avant-garde vision. For example, at the pan-Asiatic congress in Bangkok he proposed the establishment of a center of monastic studies for Buddhists, Christians, Hindus, Muslims, and others. In this center the monks would together foster common monastic values: mastery of self, silence, detachment, simplicity, harmony with the rhythms of nature, etc. The idea for the creation of such a center came from his conviction that monks throughout the world speak the same language. In such a center they would be able to become experientially aware of this fact and express it to one another. By their example they would also be able to contribute to harmony among all people (Åmell [1998], 61).

Several of the people most active in monastic dialogue were inspired by Panikkar. One of them was Armand Veilleux, the first president of the American subcommission. At the meeting in Petersham he made reference to the idea that interreligious dialogue presupposed intrareligious dialogue. It is no exaggeration to say that Panikkar was a fellow traveler with monks on the journey of dialogue. That was the opinion of the American Benedictine Steve Gruber, who wrote, "In a shrinking world where diverse cultural expressions begin to share and compete for the same neighborhood, we are offered a guidebook for dialogue at the core of human activity, religious faith and practice." And he added, "As monastic communities remain in the vanguard of the Catholic Apostolate of East-West dialogue, Raimon Panikkar's vision offers accessible groundwork for rich interfaith exchange."[37] Ten years later Béthune would say much the same thing.

Conscious of Panikkar's influence on him, Béthune told me in 1993 that he took it upon himself to visit him in order to tell him how much he owed him and to hear what he had to say. He was, he said, extremely important in helping monks involved in dialogue clarify their ideas and giving them spiritual strength. He went on to add that this dependence was relative in that it did not imply an uncritical acceptance of all of Panikkar's ideas. Béthune gave full acceptance, however, to Panikkar's intuition that dialogue is a rich resource, a spiritual path in itself. Following this intuition, Béthune spearheaded a new stage in the evolution of monastic dialogue, which now placed itself at the service of a new way of thinking.

Only for an Elite?

The question can be asked: Is intrareligious dialogue for everyone? Or is it only for a few? Without restricting it to an elite, one has to admit that it is not necessarily for everyone. It is not exclusive, but it is selective, and this for three reasons. First, intrareligious dialogue presumes a particular vocation, one that is still not common and cannot be forced, a vocation founded on a deep desire to enter into relationship with adherents of other religions. Second, it requires that one have an experience of contemplative silence. It is in the intimacy of one's relationship to the divine—where, in Christian terms, the Holy Spirit opens us to the mystery of the Father—that the acceptance of the other is most authentic, and it is easier to experience the joyful fellowship of recognizing each other's deepest longings. That is why contemplative practice is one of the requirements for becoming a member of the American commission. As surprising as it may seem, this practice is not something that can be presumed.[38] Finally, the intrareligious experience is demanding and can even be dangerous. To engage in it one needs to be well grounded in the Christian faith and have the benefit of an appropriate intellectual and spiritual preparation. Le Saux himself never recommended straddling two religions and humorously advised people not to imitate him: "One clown in India is enough!" (Coff [1994], 24). His, however, was an extreme case, and he was in an environment that was not very supportive.

In spite of these observations, it must be said that the number of monks who follow an intrareligious path is increasing. This path has been thought of as reserved for people of strong character, but there are considerations that indicate it should not be regarded so restrictively. If it is true that all authentic interreligious dialogue is founded on an intrareligious experience (Panikkar [1985]; Le Saux [1981]), and that dialogue is the vocation of every Christian, it can be deduced that the intrareligious dimension has a place in the life of all the baptized. Bethune was clear about this when he told me in 1997 "It should be for everyone." He expressed the same opinion in the preface to the proceedings of the famous intermonastic encounter that took place at Gethsemani in 1996: ". . . monastics are not alone in endeavoring to pursue this 'dialogue of spiritual experience,' as the Pontifical Council for Interreligious Dialogue designated it since 1984. All Christians are called to reach this level in their meetings with believers of other religions" (Mitchell and Wiseman [2010], xiv). Odette Baumer-Despeigne took a similar position when she said about the spiritual adventure of Le Saux, "This confrontation between an oriental spirituality and a Christian spirituality is, in a certain manner, the problem all Christians have to face today, each one according to his or her personal character" (Coff [1994], 23).

This may seem like a contradiction to what was said earlier, but in fact it signals an evolution of the status quo and of understanding. Furthermore, there is an increase in the number of persons who are better prepared to undertake this new journey. Finally, it indicates a recognition that a broadening of intrareligious dialogue is something that has to happen if we are to see a better world. The document of 1993 provides a stage for the prophetic words of Le Saux to ring out with greater clarity than ever before:

> The solution for the crisis of the world must be found in common by all people of good-will, by all men devoted to truth, in whatever way the truth may have manifested itself in the depth of their hearts. Their dialogue will be a searchlight which will probe the present societies of men, but will first scan the heart of those taking part in it. It will be the test of their allegiance to truth alone in their respective religious or humanist commitments. (Le Saux [1981], 210)

Dialogue, not Assimilation

For the whole of the monastic interreligious movement the adoption of a form of contemplative prayer that comes from another religion is the essence of a fruitful encounter. There is, however, a way of doing this that must be avoided. The document of Pierre de Béthune (1993) warns against a temptation that has always beset the church, that of assimilating the religious paths it has encountered. Assimilation does not satisfy the demands of genuine dialogue. In fact, dialogue and assimilation are mutually exclusive.

To assimilate elements from another tradition into one's own relationship to the sacred means incorporating them in such a way that they lose their quality of otherness. To detach them from the surroundings that have shaped and formed them is, in effect, to take them hostage, to use them to make up for what is lacking in one's own tradition, or to dominate the other. In every case the elements that have been taken over are not presented as borrowed but as one's own. What is problematic about the process of assimilations is not the fact that we borrow certain things—a common enough occurrence in the history of religions—but that we pass over in silence the mutual exchange that benefits us. In fact, it is precisely because such an exchange allows us to grow existentially that it should be given credit. That is essentially the message of the 1993 document.

Assimilating the other means refusing to recognize that he or she is different. As a result there is no vis-à-vis, and thus no dialogue. The same thing happens when only the similarities are attended to in an interreligious encounter. In this case all one is doing is looking for oneself in the other, or making the other into oneself. It is futile and even against the very nature of dialogue to want to find agreement simply because elements from different traditions strike us as identical, when in reality they support different religious bodies and belief systems. But it still remains true that every instance of authentic dialogue involves being enriched by contact with the other and then integrating into one's vision of the world and one's practice the values and conduct that have been discovered. Unlike assimilation, such integration is the fruit of mutual comprehension and of an exchange founded on respect for the religiously other, and not the consequence of an illusory self-sufficiency. Integration is part of the dialogic process; assimilation sets up an obstacle to it.

The 1993 document thus affirms its preference for a certain way of entering into dialogue. We can see two major tendencies in the monastic experience of dialogue. The first is the intrareligious movement described in the 1993 document: dialogue is what follows hospitality; it is in the acceptance of another contemplative path, whose otherness is respected and maintained, that the encounter takes place. The second, which is implicitly rejected, follows another logic. Here dialogue necessarily involves a certain power struggle. Christian monks are required to perfect their contemplative practice as a way of developing confidence in their own methods and thus being able to resist becoming disciples of their Buddhist and Hindu partners who offer to share their advice and experiences.

Hiding behind this attitude is the refusal to admit that everything has not yet been said in the Christian tradition and that it might be enriched by non-Christian ascetic paths that in many ways are much more refined. Ignored is the testimony of all those monks who complain of something lacking in their own tradition when they want to develop a more intense and integrated spiritual life (Béthune, [2002]). Even more, they are suspected of not knowing their own tradition. What finally happens is that they are simply advised to do without the other. The irony of this situation is that the logic at the heart of such counsel is the same that is used to justify the process of assimilation! Contrary to the statement that we "should not hesitate to take the fruit of the age-old wisdom of the East and 'capture' it for Christ" (Pennington [1978b], 5), I believe it is necessary to "hesitate" for as long as it takes to allow our gesture of openness to be motivated by gratitude toward the other and accompanied by a desire to understand the other in all his or her specificity, originality, and difference.

The 1993 document rejects the temptation to assimilate and with it the refusal to allow oneself to be transformed by religious otherness. But it also is against the idea that one can have a foot in each tradition, that one can be everywhere and nowhere. Béthune writes: "Dialogue can only take place between partners sure of their own identity and concerned to ensure the reciprocal nature of the exchanges" (Béthune [2002], 69). In every case what is to be avoided is relativism. Dialogue is the way par excellence: it is in dialogue that one's own identity is fully assumed. And dialogue demands that one accept the other precisely as the other is most strikingly and undeniably different. The only way one discovers oneself is through the shock of encounter and the testing that comes through adversity. "Thus, by receiving into our hearts the stranger with all the questioning that he provokes, we know that he is in some way a messenger of our God. That is why we can with justice hope to receive much when our interfaith involvement is animated by an attitude of faith" (Béthune[2002], 66).

Encounter with the other as other is an opportunity, not a danger. The great challenge of our time is to make such encounters part of our spiritual practice. There is no doubt that the influence of Buddhism, Hinduism, and Islam is immense, not unlike the influence of Greek philosophies and numerous religious currents in the course of history. Our challenge today is not just to find ways for Christianity to survive these outside influences, but also and above all to seize the opportunity to bring the church onto a larger playing field, that of the whole human race, so that everyone, Christians and others, can together work for peace in the world. To do so is not to compromise the teachings of the Gospel. On the contrary, it is a way to respond to the invitation given by the Gospel, and repeated by the conciliar declaration on religions, "to work sincerely for mutual understanding and to preserve as well as to promote together for the benefit of all mankind social justice and moral welfare, as well as peace and freedom" (*Nostra Aetate* 3).

Basically, what the 1993 document proposes is a way of understanding the specific nature of monastic dialogue. It argues that a typically Christian spiritual sensibility is what leads monks to seek an encounter with Eastern spiritualities rather than a desire to assimilate these spiritualities. It invites monks to explore a spirituality of dialogue and lays the primary foundations for such a spirituality. Béthune's document is not a synthesis of intermonastic experience but the fruit of his reflection on the first stage of a long-term project. He provides an official and practical foundation for an exploration that will be taken up by present and future generations, an exploration that envisions a relationship with religious otherness as the privileged way to union with God.

Chapter 4

Developing a Spirituality of Dialogue

If someone were to ask what monks involved in dialogue actually accomplished over the past thirty years, I would say first of all that change happens slowly. Sometimes the energy invested produces less than optimal results. This does not cause a feeling of discouragement or resignation among those involved as much as patient endurance coupled with a sense of isolation. In addition to lack of means, extremely busy schedules, uncertainty about who would succeed them, and sometimes a lack of response from their dialogue partners, monks dedicated to the cause of dialogue had to accept the demands inherent in the task of raising awareness and also be willing to put off certain undertakings, either because they did not receive the necessary approval or simply because the monastic community was not ready to accept them. But that was the price that had to be paid if dialogue was to be generally accepted.

I would quickly add, however, that when monastic dialogue is seen within a historical perspective it gives a much more fruitful and promising impression. Monastic dialogue only really began with Vatican II and it has made impressive strides in this very short period of time. It took but one generation for the followers of Saint Benedict to become key players on the interreligious stage, drawing on their particular charism to show that dialogue must be a heart-to-heart exchange that gives concrete expression to the hope that it is possible to be open to the other while remaining faithful to your own tradition. While the scarcity of means may have limited the development of dialogue, it also was a source of strength in that it preserved the movement from the constraints that inevitably accompany institutionalization. Nourished by their conviction, their faith, and the dynamism of their members, the monastic commissions have been energetic and creative, showing that they could set their course with a great deal of freedom.

Years of involvement in dialogue led monks to a point at which they could begin something new and thus open another period of their history, one marked above all by an investigation of the spirituality of dialogue. The document already referred to entitled *"Contemplation et dialogue interreligieux. Repères et perspectives puisés dans l'expérience des moines"* provided new ways of going about this activity. Even though it made relating to religious difference the basis of a new form of spiritual activity, it only provided a general orientation and left it to others to work out the implications by asking such questions as "How does our relation to the Buddhist, to the Hindu, or to some other religious experience make it possible for us to draw closer to Christ or to God?" In fact, the dialogue of spiritual experience is more an opportunity for our faith than a threat to it.

The interest of monks in a spirituality of dialogue was shown with the publication in February 2003 of a special issue of the *International Bulletin* of the secretariat for Monastic Interreligious Dialogue to mark the twenty-fifth anniversary of the creation of the American and European commissions. Titled "Expériences monastiques de dialogue interreligieux" (EMDI), it brought together the statements of monks and nuns who recounted how dialogue had influenced their relationship to the divine.

Unlike the text of 1993, this one made no attempt to synthesize the experiences recounted, for two reasons. It was judged premature to make such a synthesis, and the statements had been gathered in response to an invitation of the Pontifical Council for Interreligious Dialogue (PCID) to examine the essential link between dialogue and spirituality, a link that was regarded as both promising and disquieting. In March 1999 Cardinal Arinze published a letter inviting the bishops to send him their reflections on the spirituality of dialogue for the purpose of preparing a detailed report on the subject.[39] The study was initiated to address a concern that was not, therefore, limited to monastic circles. It involved the whole church. The work of formulating a position would take into account the advice and experiences that were received, not only from monks but from others as well.

The Cardinal's letter followed a plenary meeting of the PCID in October 1998 to address this topic and more generally the question whether or not it was possible, from a theological point of view, to pray together, a question that had become more important as a consequence of the interreligious encounter in Assisi in 1986 whose organizers rejected the possibility out of hand. In addition, there was the phenomenon of a growing number of Christians who began to speak of their "double belonging"—Christian-Buddhist, Christian-Hindu, or Christian-Taoist (Blée [2000])—a theme that was addressed for the first time at a congress in Brussels organized by *Voies de l'Orient* that brought together Christians from different denominations and backgrounds (Gira and Scheuer [2000]). The question was obviously a delicate one, and in some settings it could create confusion and threaten good judgment and the identity of an unwavering Christian faith.

Once again, monks who had now been involved in dialogue for thirty years and had become skilled at entering into communion with adherents of other religions were able to provide their expertise, and to do so with a maturity based on experience. There had been earlier instances of such communion, but from this point on it became more characteristic of the activity of monks and a sign that the movement had entered into a new phase of its development. The famous 1996 encounter at Gethsemani in the United States was a decisive moment in the history of the movement.

In this last chapter, which will be more analytic than descriptive—and thus somewhat longer—my intention is not to sketch the portrait of a fourth stage of monastic dialogue, still less to make a synthesis of all the experiences that have been mentioned up to this point. Such a historical perspective would not give the full picture. I would instead like to look more closely at the spiritual dimension of monastic dialogue, which I will present as a return to the desert, the desert of otherness. I do not intend to speak for the monks themselves or to exhaust the richness of their experience. Rather, I will limit myself to indicating some lines of thought that are deserving of further study in order to get a better sense of the nature, the challenges, and the conditions for connecting dialogue and spirituality.

In order to accomplish this objective I will consider four different aspects of the question. First I will show what makes dialogue spiritual by identifying various elements that allow communication to become communion. Then I will come back to the adoption of Eastern methods of meditation by Christian monks to show that this is an activity that fosters the emergence of a spirituality of dialogue and also provides an opportunity to identify a tension within the church vis-à-vis the contemplative life. Next I will show that the spirituality of dialogue implies moving away from familiar landmarks and returning to the desert, a place of silence and solitude that does not separate monks from other human beings but that, on the contrary, creates the necessary condition for entering into a relationship with another believer. Finally, I will conclude the chapter by recalling that intermonastic dialogue and the spirituality it engenders are fragile developments. If they are to endure and bear fruit they must be handled with care.

From Communication to Communion

The spiritual nature of dialogue becomes evident when it is grounded in the essential unity of the dialogue partners. This basic unity is expressed by interreligious prayer, which consists of coming together in one place to pray together, either by using a common ritual or meditating in silence. This approach to spiritual dialogue is different both from the approach adopted at the celebrated gatherings at Assisi and from the approach taken by ecumenical groups who envision a coming together of Christians of different confessions. At the prayers for peace that took place in Assisi in 1986 and 2002 the adherents of different religions were not able to come together for a common expression of their respective spiritualities.

As for ecumenical groups, what they envision above all is finding a way to reconcile the issues that divide them in order to bring about unity between the two sides. Here, as was the case in Assisi, unity is seen as the result to be achieved by dialogue. In a monastic approach to dialogue, however, the unity of the adherents of different religions is seen as the point of departure. For monks, encounter is made possible by their conviction that in God everyone is already mysteriously one, and that this indescribable unity is revealed in the contemplative life. What is involved here—as can be seen in the lives of Merton, Le Saux, or Griffiths—is faith and not some vague feeling of commonality. The more one descends into the depths of one's being, the more one draws near to the source from which all drink. To live in the presence of the divine reinforces one's awareness of unity with the other and with the entire universe.

Monks strive to actualize this unity-in-Christ (Gal 3:28-29) that is hidden in the Spirit of God who is present in the hearts of all by allowing every form of communication to become communion, without in any way denying what is specific to each person or tradition. Dialogue is spiritual when it invites the partners in dialogue to grow together in the Spirit and to anticipate the "kingdom of God," an expression the Christian tradition uses to designate the universal presence of the living God at work in humankind. In Christ this presence transforms and frees human beings from within and invites them to come together in love and reconciliation to form a communion that will only come to fulfillment at the end of time.

In this section I would like to go deeper into the meaning of the challenges and characteristics of dialogue understood as growing together in the Spirit. I shall do this in four stages. First of all I will briefly refer to the historic encounter that took place at Gethsemani and indicate what made it an unprecedented occasion of communion between the Buddhist and Christian participants. Then I will look at the fact that dialogue is spiritual because it is anchored in the search for the kingdom of God—even more, because it allows access to God's kingdom. After that I will highlight the external aspect of this quest: dialogue favors the expression of an eschatological community that brings together unity and diversity. Finally, I will consider the interior aspect of this same quest. I refer here to a dialogue of mystical experience in which the Christian comes to an experiential discovery of the process of spiritual transformation that is proper to another religious tradition.

The Gethsemani Encounter

We were asked to arrive at the Louisville, Kentucky, airport on July 22, 1996. It was not difficult to identify our group: shaved heads, black and white habits, yellow, saffron, or red robes (Blée [1996b]). We came from the four corners of America, from Europe, Australia, and Asia. Our destination was the Trappist Abbey of Gethsemani. We were all prepared to take part in an unprecedented event in the history of dialogue. Over the course of five days, twenty-five Christian monks and an equal number of Buddhist monks came together around the topic "Meditation and Contemplation." The Dalai Lama was the key participant, and it was not the first time he had come to the oldest Cistercian monastery in the United States. In April of 1994 he had made a quick visit to the grave of his "good spiritual friend," Thomas Merton. In fact, it was because of the great affection these two men had for one another that Gethsemani was chosen as the location for this encounter. The event was sponsored by the American commission (MID) and took two years to prepare. At the Parliament of the World's Religions in Chicago in August 1993 the members of this commission organized a meeting with the Dalai Lama, and at its conclusion he proposed that a new step be taken in the coming together of different monastic traditions. He felt that both Christian and Buddhist monks were ready for a more profound expression of dialogue. The Gethsemani Encounter was the result.

Even though about one hundred observers were invited, only the monks were allowed to speak during the formal sessions of dialogue. The reason for this was not to give the impression that monks belonged to an exclusive club, but to allow for a certain degree of intimacy among the participants. It was precisely this quality of intimacy that quickly made this event historic, the happy outcome of long and careful preparation. At Gethsemani Béthune saw the fruit "of a process of interior evolution, a profound change in thinking, thanks to which the monastic orders, Buddhist and Christian, are now able to recognize themselves as forerunners of a spiritual unity that is prophetic for all humankind" (Mitchell and Wiseman [2010], xii). He then compared it to the congress that was held in Bangkok: "What only a few rare people could understand in 1968 was openly revealed at Gethsemani to all the participants, Buddhists as well as Christians. All were profoundly touched by Merton's description of the experience that we had lived during our days together: '[T]he deepest level of communication is not communication, but communion. It is worldless'" (Mitchell and Wiseman [1997], xv). Gethsemani was, in fact, characterized by a realization of Merton's hope for a shift from communication to communion and the benefits that would flow from that evolution. There were at least four features that indicated that such a shift had taken place.

1. In the opening ceremony the Dalai Lama and the abbot of Gethsemani, Timothy Kelly, together planted a pine tree at the entrance to the monastery. This symbolic gesture suggested that Buddhists and Christians were together opening a new era, giving birth to a unique way of being in the world that must be protected generation after generation. It hardly need be mentioned that the tree is a universal symbol for the central pillar of the world and of the human body; it also symbolizes the road that leads upward from the visible to the invisible. During the ceremony the Dalai

Lama spoke of the tree of interior spirituality that must be nourished every day. The roots of the tree symbolize that we all drink from a common source but produce many different kinds of fruit. From this multilayered symbolism the Dalai Lama pointed to the need for understanding, communication, and prayer in common, at least in the form of silent meditation. He added that a variety of religions is preferable to one alone, because the spirit has need of different kinds of nourishment, as does the body.

It should be pointed out that it was the Dalai Lama, an adherent of another religion, who called Christians to deeper dialogue and to interreligious prayer. By so doing he rejected the idea that other believers would be upset if Christians pushed for a more intense form of spiritual encounter—a point of view that was often repeated by the organizers of the 1986 Assisi meeting. Moreover, the Dalai Lama made it very clear that, while favoring a spirit of communion among the partners in dialogue is extremely important, this does not imply ignoring differences—a point that is fundamental in all forms of dialogue.

2. A spirit of communion among the partners in dialogue arose when ways were found to pray together. Some of the most powerful moments during the gathering occurred during the period of silent meditation that began each day and during specially prepared evening rituals in which everyone could actively participate.

3. On several occasions throughout the conference the participants were encouraged to speak on their own behalf and not as official representatives of a church or as the defenders of a particular doctrine. Participants spoke from the heart of their own personal spiritual experience. As a result, the discussions and the meeting as a whole were marked by a depth of honesty that is only possible when all agree to honor openness and commitment.

4. Finally I would mention the fact that most of the sessions took place in the monastery's chapter room, a location that

is normally off limits to anyone but a member of the monastic community (Gerry [1997]). The fact that permission was granted to use this space shows that the close bonds between Christians and Buddhists were stronger than particular regulations. Furthermore, the sharing of material space became an apt symbol of the expanding interior space that characterized the members of these two communities.

In the last analysis the Gethsemani Encounter was a sign that monastic dialogue had come of age. The dialogue partners had developed close friendships and a solid knowledge of one another's religious traditions. They were therefore able to enter into a deeper level of dialogue, as can also be seen from the events that followed the meeting at Gethsemani. For example, the Christian participants were so open to a Buddhist understanding of the Christian monastic life that they asked four of the Buddhist participants at Gethsemani to provide a commentary on the Rule of Benedict.[40] A second Gethsemani Encounter (2002) offered the participants a chance to share their vulnerability by speaking about their experience of the transformative dimension of suffering,[41] and a third (2008) brought Buddhist and Catholic monks together to investigate the ways in which the wisdom of their respective monastic traditions might help a world becoming ever more conscious of a looming environmental calamity.[42] These events became the basis for a broader discussion on the meaning of a spirituality of dialogue that was needed if the dialogue partners were to establish an even deeper communion.

Seek the Kingdom of God!

The spiritual character of dialogue depends on what motivates it and the maturity of the person who engages in it. To arrive at this level of dialogue one must be guided by truth and love (Le Saux [1981], 211). Dialogue has no strategic goals, not even peace. As paradoxical as it may seem, the real end of dialogue is not peaceful coexistence or reciprocity, for the only way to bring these about would be through some kind of negotiation. Peace cannot be imposed! This is not to say that negotiation has no place in interreligious encounters, especially at a time when increasing numbers of political conflicts on the local and international scene are often at least partially religious in nature. However, the dialogue of monks, and more generally, the different ways in which internal dialogue is experienced, show that the interreligious encounter cannot and should not be reduced to diplomatic activity.

Where, then, is the challenge located? It is to be found precisely in the willingness of monks to enter into a relationship of openness and trust with the other and to take the first step in the way of love. In other words, the only thing monks ask of dialogue is the openness dialogue asks of them. Even then, this kind of openness to the other cannot be achieved on their own. It is only by faith and through the action of the Spirit that it is possible to go beyond their natural tendencies and the fear that prevents genuine encounter. Their capacity for openness to the other coincides with their willingness to be led by divine grace. The only true dialogue lies beyond dialogue—that is to say, in the silence of the Spirit where prayer begins and hearts are united. In silence of this kind monks find the strength to welcome difference with love, patience, and discernment (Le Saux [1981], 220).

What this means is that dialogue is not the primary end of the contemplative life, but rather a crucial manifestation of a life of prayer that is attentive to the active presence of God and that knows the search for God is ongoing. That is why the interreligious commissions insist that their members practice contemplative prayer. This requirement is in accord with the document of 1993, *Contemplation and Dialogue*, which puts contemplation first, unlike the pontifical documents *Dialogue and Mission* (1984) and *Dialogue and Proclamation* (1991), whose titles reflect their emphasis. Contemplation opens the way to dialogue. "Seek first the kingdom and the justice of God, and dialogue (or the ability to dialogue well) will be given to you in abundance" (Béthune [2002], 65).

The "kingdom of God" is at the heart of the Christian experience. It is described as a salvation event that begins with conversion of heart and is experienced as a gift rather than a human achievement. The kingdom is not only a future reality we wait for; we experience it here and now, though not yet in its fullness. This is the Good News proclaimed by Jesus in his invitation to be open to this liberating presence that transcends time, space, and every kind of division.

For monks this kingdom is the very heart of dialogue. This does not mean that they avail themselves of dialogue in order to make it happen, as if it were something far off and not a part of the world we inhabit. For them dialogue is rather the very manifestation of God's kingdom, understood as the Spirit-induced transformation of this world on the way to its fulfillment. By referring to the concept of God's kingdom, monks situate dialogue in the Judeo-Christian tradition that begins with the history of the Jewish people and the promise of a Messiah and then continues with Jesus, who immediately after his baptism makes the kingdom of God the core of his preaching. Today dialogue is spiritual by the very fact that it reaffirms the primacy of God's kingdom in Christian practice. Furthermore, monks recall that if the church centers its preaching on Christ as the way, the truth, and the life, Christ's preaching focused on the kingdom of God that was already present and not on himself. Highlighting this point, however, does not mean minimizing the figure of Christ, placing him in parentheses, as it were, in order to be more theocentric and to find common ground with other believers at any price. The fear that this might happen has been the reason contemplatives are often criticized for watering down Christology by stressing the unutterable mystery of divine oneness. Making fewer references to Christ is not a sign that he is being forgotten. Actually, the very opposite is true. The Christian who is most circumspect about asserting Christ's divinity is often the one who bears him powerful witness without feeling the need to wave a flag. It is true, though, that contemplatives do have a tendency to distance themselves from a God-man Jesus who has nothing in common with ordinary human beings. Rather, they give Jesus a privileged place as master, a Jesus whose life we can share, not only the suffering that has been so emphasized by Western

Christianity but also his transfiguring light and glory. Monks in dialogue, following Le Saux, Griffiths, and Laurence Freeman, the Benedictine who currently directs the World Community for Christian Meditation, invite each person to recognize him- or herself as a companion of Jesus here below, with the possibility of already having a share in his resurrection (Matus [1984], 133). What it takes to do that is submission to the Spirit that has been sent to us, letting the Spirit lead us to follow the master and witness to him by our acceptance of the outsider, the stranger, and even those who may be regarded as enemies because they do not believe as we do.

It remains for theology and exegesis to show us just how Jesus invites us to opt for entering into dialogue with those who have traditionally been considered enemies because their beliefs are not the same as ours. Dialogue is not something we have to do because present circumstances ("the world" in Gospel language) demand compromise. Rather, it is a vibrant expression of a Christian way of acting to which "the world" summons us. To be a disciple of Jesus means setting out on ways that lead to an ever more demanding participation in the kingdom of God, whose richness and diversity are much greater than can be captured by theology and dogma and whose evolution cannot be predicted. In our days interreligious dialogue is one of those ways, and it is this that makes it a place of spirituality. Dialogue is also such a place because it allows for spiritual growth.

Dialogue prompted by the Holy Spirit leads one to a deeper encounter with and more generous response to this same Spirit, in short, to a fuller awareness of the work of the Holy Spirit in oneself and in all of creation. Faith gives birth to dialogue, and dialogue, in turn, nourishes faith (Arinze [1997], 375). In other words, dialogue is both the fruit of seeking the kingdom of God and also the door to enter it. Dialogue makes it possible to deepen one's relation to the divine. According to the Australian John Dupuche, "The heavens opened more widely at the meeting of the traditions; the Divine Mystery appeared all the more wonderful" (EMDI, 32[42]). Dialogue is spiritual because it is an integral part of Christian development; it is an occasion to grow in humility, devotion, faith, wisdom, and love (Arinze [1997], 376). Monks agree that the qualities that make for a healthy spiritual life are also the ones needed for dialogue, and that dialogue enables them to purge their faith of many tensions and to discover new dimensions of the divine mystery. The Spanish Benedictine Ramon Alvarez Velasco puts it this way: "To search for God in dialogue with other religious traditions helps us to understand the spiritual gifts spread out by God in the other religions" (EMDI, 4[26]). If the Spirit leads monks along new paths, namely those of internal dialogue, that same Spirit also makes it possible to undo old habits and to become free of anything that would stand in the way of being in accord with the will of God. The Spirit grants what is needed to pass from simple verbal exchange to communion and to contribute here below to the fulfillment of the kingdom.

The Communion of Saints

Looking at how the kingdom of God comes to fulfillment will help us understand the rich and complex spiritual dimensions of dialogue and identify the ways it can be developed. The kingdom comes to fulfillment both externally and internally, corresponding to the idea that "history and interiority are two equally valuable channels for an authentic experience of the Divine" (Dupuis [2001], 35).

By the exterior fulfillment of the kingdom of God we mean the historical and communal development of the active and universal presence of God among human beings. Dialogue brings together adherents of different religions in a spirit of communion, and by doing so—to speak in Christian terms—anticipates the kingdom of God. Dialogue does not create the kingdom or construct it according to a predetermined plan; rather, it makes it visible and explicit, revealing the unity that already exists and underlies diversity. Dialogue gives the kingdom a particular hue, for it is different from the exclusivist perspective that was dominant in the church for centuries, and also from the inclusivist perspective that became widespread after Vatican II. The kingdom cannot be identified with the visible church. It goes beyond the boundaries of the church to include every believer who is saved by divine grace in ways the Christian cannot even imagine (see Dupuis [2001], 390). Did not Jesus say, "Many will come from east and west and will eat with Abraham, Isaac, and Jacob in the kingdom of heaven" (Matt 8:11)? The anticipation of the coming of the kingdom by the interreligious community does not affect the reality of the church or make it of secondary importance. On the contrary, it is the church that is responsible for the existence of the interreligious community by virtue of its fidelity to the Spirit of Christ, whose love for everyone directs us toward a communion that is not only rooted in religious belonging but transcends it. Monks in dialogue make us aware of this perspective and do so by their three ways of representing the interreligious community.

First of all, monks—Buddhists, Hindus, and Christians—remind us that the world is fleeting. Our condition is one of exile; every individual will depart this life, and we all need to keep death daily before our eyes. Monks remind us that the kingdom is not only earthly but also heavenly, and that it is only in the heavenly realm that it will reach its fulfillment. This does not mean that this world is without value. On the contrary, only what is bound to the Spirit will find its fulfillment after death. As Simeon the New Theologian puts it, "The one who does not live eternal life here below will not enjoy it later on" (Panikkar [2006], 25). This is the hope that nourishes the patience of monks when difficulties prevent dialogue from producing any immediate results. They see dialogue as a path to the kingdom that "will certainly bear fruit, even if the times and seasons are known only to the Father (cf. Acts 1:7)" (RM 57).

Second, the interreligious community is founded on faith in a God of relationship, not a God of solitary and indifferent transcendence. The trinitarian God, one in nature, manifests the divine internal relationship by the multiplicity inherent in creation. This characteristic of the divine, manifested in reciprocal exchange, rests on two theological considerations. On the one hand, in God, who is the source and the destiny of all things, we are all one; on the other, God's self-revelation is never total, for what reveals God also hides God. In each theophany God communicates in a particular way the power of the divine saving act, and yet God is not fully revealed in any particular manifestation. God is manifested in power, but always in a relative way. Who would dare to suggest that they had marked out and exhausted all the possible ways in which God allows us to draw near? Faith impels Christians to go beyond the boundaries of the church in order to uncover another facet of the divine and to enter into ever more expansive surroundings where God is at work.

In the third place, it is clear that the interreligious community, looked at as a foreshadowing of the kingdom, does not have any territorial, religious, or political boundaries. Accordingly, it is not limited to Christians, nor it is identified with the visible church. It does not spring from heredity or belonging, but from an experience of conversion that is available to everyone and shatters the divisions of the established order. No one is excluded, but no one can claim a monopoly. The interreligious community brings together people who are not distinguished by their creed or their common identity, but by their "good will." They are not interested in doing something in order to achieve an end product; they do not look at the other in terms of what the other has to offer. Their will is to let the will of God have free rein and to be led by the power of the Spirit, that devouring fire that makes saints of all it touches.[43]

Dialogue is spiritual because it brings to light the "communion of saints" at the crossroads of traditions. Paul described this communion as a relationship of equality among those who have stripped off the old self and put on the new (Eph 4:22-24). In this communion there is no longer Greek and Jew, circumcised and uncircumcised, slave and free, but only free men and women who are united in the Spirit with sentiments of compassion, kindness, humility, meekness, and patience (Col 3:9-12). To repeat, the members of this community recognize each other not because of some common title, but because of the experience of transcendence that is proper to them. The mission of the church is not thereby lessened. It is still the sacrament of the kingdom. By the very fact that it bears witness to Christ it gives rise to an

Developing a Spirituality of Dialogue 151

interreligious community that gathers believers from various backgrounds around the divine mystery, a mystery that has been grasped through and beyond the cultural and religious particularities of each individual.

Two questions now arise. How does communication become communion? How does interreligious dialogue fashion the "communion of saints"? To answer these questions we can turn to Merton, who made communion the characteristic of all authentic dialogue. For him communion contributes to the solution of the present crisis in that it reveals a profound unity that goes beyond words and formulas. He says it is necessary to arrive at this state of communion on both the preverbal and postverbal levels (Merton [1975], 315). The first level refers to a predisposition of mind and heart to accept the stranger. This means freeing oneself of all those routines, programs, and habitual ways of acting that keep us from being open to what is new and unexpected. We have to accept the fact that the road is not laid out in advance but is created step by step. Monks are summoned to rediscover what it means to be a traveler, a pilgrim, or even an exile, for this is the condition that will allow them to be receptive to dialogue and confrontation and also to accept the "grace of renewal, precisely through encounter" (Béthune [2002], 212). It is at this stage, when dialogue is just beginning, that hospitality is most important. When the partners in dialogue do not know one another, or when their knowledge of one another's religion is based on nothing but preconceptions, a "preverbal" welcoming makes it possible to live in communion with religious difference even before any serious discussion takes place. The "postverbal" level refers to an encounter that goes beyond words and understanding and takes place in the silence of an experience of the Ultimate that cannot be produced by a verbal exchange. Without these two levels dialogue would be reduced to a simple discussion—not that that is an obstacle in itself. Discussion is very important, and the spirit of communion that is established between the partners in dialogue only improves it.

Spiritual dialogue—in this case, that of monks—sets up this close connection between communication and communion, between interreligious discussion properly speaking and the intrareligious sense that we are bound to one another at a level that transcends our respective positions, between the communal dimension of the exchange and the internal dialogue that gives it its dynamism and authenticity. In their ongoing task of developing a spirituality of dialogue monks are called to attend to both dimensions, holding them in tension and causing them to interact.

The Inner Laws of the Spirit

The process of developing a spirituality of dialogue invites the Christian to attend as well to the interior dimension of the active and universal presence of the living God in humanity. It is not easy to deal with this all-important point of the dialogue of religious experience. It has not received much attention from theologians and so it immediately raises suspicions. All I will do is lay out the question and propose some avenues of reflection.

The kingdom of God that Jesus speaks of in the gospels is usually interpreted as a communal and ecclesial reality. It takes place in history but, like a treasure hidden in a field (Matt 13:44), it is to be found first and foremost in the depth of the human heart. When the Pharisees questioned Jesus about when it was coming, he replied: "nor will they say, 'Look, here it is!' or 'There it is!' For, in fact, the kingdom of God is among you" (Luke 17:21). The Greek word *entos* (in the midst of) is most often understood by exegetes to mean "among" rather than "within," thus emphasizing the communal dimension of the kingdom. However, the other meaning of the word—"within" or "inside"—should not be easily dismissed (see Panikkar [2002], 207; Freeman [2000], 152). Theologians and exegetes tend to be skeptical about this second translation. The reason for shying away from translating *entos* as "within" or "inside" is the fear that it would lead to a Gnostic interpretation that makes knowledge of the kingdom accessible only to a few initiates rather than a historical and communal reality accessible to all. But even if such a fear is justified, it should not be overemphasized lest it undermine contemporary efforts to stress the contemplative dimension of Christian spirituality.

The experience of monks involved in dialogue shows the importance of this interior dimension of the kingdom, expressed in the New Testament teaching that the human being is the temple of God (John 14:17, 1 Cor 3:16; Rom 8:9-11). In the words of Timothy Radcliffe, "Perhaps herein lies the ultimate vocation of the monk—to reveal the beauty of this emptiness [the void at the center of my being, where God can pitch his tent] . . . to be individually and in community temples in which the divine glory can dwell" (cited by Christine Daine in EMDI, 29[40]). Access to the kingdom is not to be found in some exterior place; it is present within each person and its only boundaries are those of the physical body (1 Cor 6:19). Self-knowledge is absolutely indispensable (Le Saux [1981], 205) because it allows us to make ourselves receptive and attentive to the divine presence so that we can say with Paul, "It is no longer I who live, but it is Christ who lives in me" (Gal 2:20).

Interreligious dialogue aids awareness and acceptance of this interior dimension of the kingdom. In making another religious experience their own, Christians have to deal with spiritual energies that are part of a different anthropological and theological universe. For example, describing his practice of zazen, Benoît Billot writes, "I learned to breathe and to put my life into my breathing. Abdominal breathing especially released the energy carried by the pelvis. I learned to hold myself straight without becoming stiff, and I could sometimes feel the energy circulate from the top to the bottom of my body" (EMDI, 7[27]). This description takes us to the very core of interreligious dialogue, which is treated in an especially clear way in the works of Henri Le Saux. By taking on Hindu spiritual practices Le Saux became aware of the role of *shakti*, the individual and cosmic force that leads the yogi to complete liberation. Le Saux related this force to the Holy Spirit, without, however, making them identical realities (Le Saux, [1967], 45).

Christian monks most often take up the way of dialogue by adopting a contemplative form of prayer that has been elaborated in another religion. The dossiers of 1993 and 2003 (*Contemplation et dialogue interreligieux. Repères et perspectives puisés dans l'expérience des moines* and *Monastic Experience of Interreligious Dialogue*) provide a precious documentation of these monastic experiences of dialogue and show that Zen meditation or yoga helped monks to live out a more embodied spirituality. This kind of spirituality involves a rediscovery of the body, sexuality, and subtle psychophysiological energies—in other words, the rediscovery of unknown or neglected aspects of the work of salvation (*oikonomia*) as it has generally been understood in Christianity. One becomes aware of a whole anthropology and the role it can play in the way that leads to divine union. Béthune goes so far as to say that Christians can find here an anthropology worthy of an incarnational theology (Béthune [2002], 71).

The above citations indicate the positive role Eastern methods have played in bringing about a rediscovery of a sense of interiority and, in a special way, the relationship of Christian spirituality to the Holy Spirit, which is neither an idea nor a vague sentiment nor an entity foreign to this world. Monks involved in dialogue recognize the Holy Spirit as the power, or better yet, the divine will that is present at the heart of creation For Le Saux the "Spirit is Wind, Space, Fire. He is also the Dove that sports in space. And Spirit is water too. And Spirit is matter which sanctifies" (Stuart [2000], 318). Thus it is not surprising that coming into contact with certain Hindu or Buddhist traditions makes it possible to discover the body as something positive insofar as it participates in the salvation willed by God. According to Benoît Billot, Western culture places little value on our corporeality in its approach to spirituality. Rather, it has a tendency to nourish a mistrust of passions and feelings, which it identifies with pleasure, enjoyment, and productivity. Billot expresses a certain degree of surprise when he writes: "But in zazen meditation and all that pertains to it I discovered a teaching at one and the same time simple and complex, oriented to help the meditator live fully in the body" (EMDI, 7[27]). In fact, the body comes to be seen not only as the dwelling of the Holy Spirit but also as its most vibrant expression. This, I believe, is what Marc Chaduc meant when he wrote about his teacher, Le Saux: "They were days when Swamiji discovered ever deeper abysses of his soul. . . . The inbreaking of the (Holy) Spirit snatched him away from himself and shone through every inch of his being (*shariram*) an inner apocalypse which at times blazed forth outwardly in a glorious transfiguration (December 1974)" (Baumer-Despeigne [1983], 327).

Most often it is the practice of zazen or yoga that leads Christian monks to new ways of experiencing the spiritual life. However, sometimes this new experience happens apart from the practice of non-Christian forms of meditation. The experience of Philip St-Romain is a case in point. Even though he himself was not a monk, St-Romain caught the attention of monks involved in dialogue. His story suggests that certain spiritual advances can go beyond an individual's religious allegiance.

St-Romain was devoted to contemplative prayer, and at a crucial moment in his spiritual journey he had a powerful experience of an explosion of spiritual energy accompanied by psychological and physiological phenomena that were new to him and sometimes quite painful. In order to understand what was happening, and even more, to regain his equilibrium, he turned to Hindu anthropology, that of *hatha yoga* among others, and found in its central concepts of *kundalini* (*shakti*) and *chakras* the categories that described his own experience (St. Romain [1991]).

These categories are often wrongly associated with New Age. In fact, they are part of a specific religious context to be found at the heart of the ancient culture of India and serve to identify the stirring within humans of a power that is both personal and cosmic and that ordinarily remains dormant at the base of the spinal column. Once it is awakened, however, this power can rise to the top of one's head and bring about an interior transformation that leads to an intuitive and blissful knowledge of reality and frees one from limitation and suffering. It was this experience that drew St-Romain to become involved in the dialogue of mystical experience[44] (Johnston [1995], 105). This dialogue was driven by the urgency of his search and allowed him to interpret his experience, to deepen it, and to be receptive to new spiritual horizons. We have here, I would suggest, what Merton meant when he spoke of communion lived on the postverbal level.

Once again it was a monk who insisted on the importance of this unfamiliar feature of spiritual dialogue. In his preface to St-Romain's book, Thomas Keating, ex-president of the American subcommission, invites the reader to appreciate the meaning of these interior happenings for the renewal of contemplation. What they point to is the presence of an energy at work in the lives of many people who are dedicated to contemplative prayer (St-Romain [1991], 5). He was not alone in saying this; other monks have referred to this energy as a phenomenon we need to know more about and that has implications for Christian spirituality (Griffiths [1992], 42; Le Saux [1967], 61; Freeman [2000], 117–18, 155; Matus [1984], 155).

Monks have become interested in this internal dialogue because of pastoral concerns. We are in the presence of little-understood spiritual energies that, as we well know, can be seen—more often than one might think—in all sorts of settings and more often than not in a chaotic way.

These energies produce a great deal of anxiety and can be the cause of intense psychic trauma. The situation can be aggravated if the trauma is diagnosed as a purely psychological disorder and is treated with the wrong therapy or, in those cases in which the situation is correctly diagnosed, if the person has recourse to an uninformed spiritual director. Monks therefore need to become familiar with these manifestations of spiritual energy in order to guide those who have experienced them. As Keating notes: "as Christian contemplation becomes better known, a number of persons who have experienced the awakening of *kundalini* through Eastern techniques may wish to return to their Christian roots, where their spiritual condition needs to be understood" (St-Romain [1991], 9). The corresponding position had been supported at the initial meeting in Loppem, where monks were encouraged to study the psychological and anthropological underpinnings of Asian religions as well as their methods of meditation.

Developing a Spirituality of Dialogue 157

There is also a theological reason for paying attention to these manifestations of the interior life. Such concrete experiences make us aware of hitherto unknown dimensions of the divine mystery, of divine gifts showered on every culture and religion. Christian theology to some degree depends on the responses given to questions that are raised by these spiritual experiences: Is the awakening of *kundalini* an experience that is common to all religions? Is the rising up of this energy the result of ascetic practice or of grace? Is it possible to identify *kundalini* with the Holy Spirit, as some have done? If, as St-Romain proposes, they are two different realities, Christians cannot but recognize that there are some elements in common (Le Saux [1967], 47). Keating, for example, thinks *kundalini* might be active in the stages of the spiritual life described by Theresa of Avila in *The Interior Castle* or by John of the Cross in *Dark Night of the Soul* (St-Romain [1991], 8). As the document *Contemplation and Dialogue* (1993) rightly noted, theology will again have to address the questions that generated theological reflection in the first centuries of Christianity—for example, the relationship between nature and grace, the importance of the apophatic dimension (that is to say, the right relationship between word and silence), or the question of the right interpretation of the Scriptures (finding a middle way between historicism and esoterism) (Béthune [2002], 72).

It is not possible to deal with all these questions here, but the questions themselves form the basis of a promising internal dialogue. It should be noted that becoming involved with these kinds of spiritual energies can be a risky undertaking for those who do not know what they are dealing with. Le Saux advises the greatest caution, but he also says that some individuals are called to take up this path of internal dialogue. He believes that in so doing he discovered his own call: "It is probably better for most people to pass the Shakti by, than to be a carrier of it without realizing it. But some are capable of it. It is for them that I should like to have a place beside the Ganges to receive them" (Stuart [2000], 318).

We should mention one other point that makes interreligious dialogue a sensitive undertaking: the seal of secrecy. If believers have an obligation to explore the mystical and psychophysiological underpinnings of their experience of God for the benefit of spiritual dialogue, what becomes of the confidential nature of one's relationship with the divine? Just how much can one share about the graces and trials that accompany one's own spiritual development without the risk of compromising it? Whether one keeps silence out of humility or because one is afraid of betraying an intimacy or of being misunderstood, the question of how much one should share of one's spiritual experience lies at the very heart of dialogue.

Ultimately, an experiential relationship to religious otherness entails far more than one might expect. Speaking of the practice of Zen that transforms one's prayer life by taking one's consciousness down to the heart and the stomach (*hara*), Béthune writes: "As we borrow these methods, many elements of our spiritual life are overturned. A re-evaluation takes place. Certain convictions that seemed central lose their attraction while other gospel values make a new impact" (Béthune [2002], 34).

Looking at these spiritual facets of interior transformation does not mean isolating oneself in an esoteric, occult, or paranormal universe. There is a power that is properly divine and that, at the deepest levels of awareness and faith, heals, makes whole, and gives life. This divine power must be distinguished from all the peripheral phenomena that can be side effects, such as ecstasy, visions, and other unusual occurrences. These phenomena are not an essential part of true mysticism, unlike the loving encounter with a personal God who is revealed in and through our very physical existence. It is true that the dialogue of spiritual experience is not very common, and it is not for everyone. It should also be said that those who feel they are called to engage in it are not necessarily more spiritually advanced than those who do not. But it is deserving of special attention. To minimize its importance—simply to relegate it to psychology, New Age, or even neurology—would be to fail to take advantage of this new opportunity to reintegrate the interiority that goes with it into Christian spirituality and theology.

Beyond Spiritual Techniques

The trends of intermonastic dialogue identified in the previous chapters show that Eastern methods of meditation played a central role in both the challenges and the development of dialogue at the level of spiritual experience. Some may think this role has been somewhat exaggerated. That would certainly be the case if Eastern methods of meditation were reduced to simple exercises in order to make Christian prayer more expansive. In that case they would simply be instruments responding to a passing need. However, monks engaged in dialogue look at them differently. The document *Contemplation and Dialogue* (1993) refrained from looking only at the technical aspect of these methods, thus reducing them to nothing but an exercise to prepare for Christian prayer. It was concerned, rather, to preserve their uniqueness, their otherness and specificity, and to show that they constitute not just a method but a distinctly different way. It is thanks to this approach that monks engaged in dialogue were able to contribute to a double development in the history of interreligious dialogue: that of understanding their Buddhist and Hindu partners in dialogue and holding them in the esteem they deserve, and that of promoting a contemplative renewal within their own tradition.

Even if not all monks engaged in dialogue make use of an Eastern form of meditation, the practice of yoga, Zen, or Vipassana is a hinge point in the monastic interreligious edifice. This involvement points to a weakness at the heart of Western Christianity's mystical approach to the divine. What we are faced with is a problematic situation that cannot be addressed by simply borrowing one or the other method of meditation or figuring out whether or not it is all right to integrate foreign ascetic elements into Christian prayer. The fundamental question is a very delicate one, and much more complex and critical than it might appear. In asking it we need to remember that it will teach us as much about the Christian vision of the world as it does about the vision of our partners in dialogue.

This question can be briefly looked at under four headings: (1) the success that Eastern forms of meditation have had in the

West; (2) some misunderstandings that give the impression they are identical with New Age and thus create an obstacle to the working out of a spirituality of dialogue; (3) the fear of Gnosticism that lurks in the background of the ongoing debate within Christianity; (4) a growing awareness of the fact that Eastern ways of meditation are not simply techniques or methods, but a spiritual way that is rooted in a cultural milieu with its own inner coherence. A consideration of these points will help in the development of a spirituality of dialogue by making clear the challenges of a monastic pastoral ministry offered to Christians engaged in a spiritual quest that draws them to look to Asia.

An Influence that Cannot be Denied

The interest of Westerners in Zen, yoga, and other forms of Buddhist or Hindu meditation is undeniable. It is impossible to keep track of all the retreat centers that have sprung up, and the waiting lists of those who want to participate in the programs they offer get longer and longer. Some would consider this interest to be little more than a fashionable pastime or the latest feel-good religious fad. However, there is something more profound and permanent here. On the one hand the interest witnesses to an interreligious encounter in search of new spiritual categories; on the other it is a sign of the degree to which the religions of Asia, especially Buddhism, have become a real presence in the West. What we are seeing is the emergence of the third generation of European and American Buddhists. The influence of these spiritualities is here to stay. In fact, it will even become stronger, if one can believe the predictions that Asia will become a dominant player on tomorrow's geopolitical stage. Increased cooperation with the emerging continent in the areas of economy, culture, and politics will certainly mean increased cooperation in the area of religion as well. Irresponsible words and actions would be the only thing that could bring about a lessening of this phenomenon, or even worse, make it appear to be an obstacle to the Christian faith.

The success of Zen or yoga in the West can be explained by the fact that these practices respond to a need for a spirituality that does not shy away from the deep existential questions that are too often neglected in Christian circles. Those who have taken up Eastern ways of meditation do not want to be converted to any particular creed. Many who practice a Buddhist or Hindu form of meditation think that if you are searching for the truth, words are of no use. Just sit and observe who you are! This kind of meditation appeals to Westerners who have been fashioned by modernity and science and who have little time for a church that is moralistic and resistant to change. Obviously the church is more than this stereotyped image, just as Buddhism is more than the practice of meditation. Nonetheless, Western practitioners hold on to those elements of Buddhism that correspond to their way of thinking. We can point to three dominant features:

A scientific way of looking at things. Science is founded on reason, good judgment, experimentation, and analysis. Buddhism supports such an approach in that it recommends that a teaching be accepted because it produces tangible results and not just because someone in authority—even one's own master—proposes it. Of course, this is an ideal to be striven for and it is not always realized in practice. Still, the central teaching of the Buddha is to be grasped through an experiential approach that involves determining the cause of the suffering that is part and parcel of the human condition and finding the remedy for overcoming the alienation that is the cause of this suffering. This approach makes no reference to an external power or to the concept of God (a concept that is often wrongly understood), or to the biblical narrative, which is often difficult to understand because it seems so far removed from the here-and-now life of the faithful and so ultimately becomes just one more story among so many others.

The priority of experience. In our day it is clear that there is an increased sensibility to the importance of personal experience in defining our relationship to others, to the world, and to truth. Truth is now defined not in reference to dominant ideologies but in terms of what one can experience—thus the importance accorded to experience in the grasp of reality. What has been lived or experienced becomes the criterion of truth. Something is no longer true in itself; it is true for oneself. Given this modern awareness, Eastern spiritualities arouse interest because they accentuate the idea that only an interior transformation will be able to bring about a positive and lasting change in society. When I wake up, says the Zen monk, the whole world wakes up.

Asceticism. There is a surprising social phenomenon in our time that needs to be looked at more closely. Young people are deliberately subjecting themselves to suffering, often at the risk of death. Evidence of this phenomenon can be seen in tattooing, body piercing, extreme sports, delinquency, or suicide. To different degrees these practices are an implicit, if unconscious, expression of the importance of suffering; that is to say, they point to the recognition that all renewal, all new life, implies a loss, a death to oneself. In Christian terms this message is vividly expressed by the parable of the seed that must die if it is to bear fruit. Young people seem to be remembering or rediscovering this truth, but are unsure how to put it into practice because they lack supportive surroundings and intelligent mentors. The "rites of passage" have been all but eliminated in the life of the church, and little value is placed on asceticism. In the hope of not scaring away potential vocations to the priesthood or religious life, ascetical practices are now presented as old-fashioned and irrelevant. However, the increased participation in Tibetan, Zen, or Vipassana retreats indicates something else. These retreats are very demanding. Contrary to the superficial understanding we sometimes hear expressed, meditation is not a method for relaxation, but a demanding practice that requires rest between long and difficult periods of sitting. Eastern ascetical practices, beginning with silence, attract interest in our societies to the degree that they promote freedom and equilibrium rather than feelings of guilt and other negative emotions.

It is certainly helpful to reflect on the needs that are met by Eastern spiritualities, but it is even more important to determine the ways in which they respond to those needs. That question is one that a spirituality of dialogue can respond to. While some Westerners who have been baptized and brought up as Christians decide to leave their religion of origin and become members of a Buddhist or Hindu center, there are others who choose to experience another religious tradition while remaining faithful to their own. Such people choose to live with the tension that results from being rooted in their own religion and while at the same time being associated with another. This tension is what gives rise to the intrareligious experience (Blée [2003b]). Some are disturbed by this new but ever more common situation, seeing it as a source of confusion in a world that has already lost many of its landmarks. Others see a sign of hope in the fact that bridges can be built between cultures and religions, bridges that will lead to a Christianity that is truly universal and a world that is at peace. I believe these forward-looking Christians have a major role to play in a time of religious pluralism, provided they have received sufficient training and supervision. First of all, they are acutely sensitive to the deficiencies in their own church in the area of spirituality. Second, they are able to understand other religious approaches and appreciate their greatness and their limitations. Finally, they are capable of assessing the risks and promises of dialogue and committing themselves to it with both courage and caution. Their expertise is all the more valuable in that the kinds of meditation that have emerged from Buddhism and Hinduism or been inspired by these religions are numerous and very different from one another. Furthermore, they are taught at different levels of proficiency and with various objectives in mind, depending on the tradition, the place, or the teacher. The world of meditation is complex, and therefore amalgamation is inevitable. It is tempting to put everything on the same level, giving rise to misunderstandings that in the end work against the development of a spirituality of dialogue.

Misunderstandings and New Age

Monks involved in dialogue have achieved a level of expertise with regard to Eastern forms of meditation, but their intentions are still not well understood and their activities can sometimes create suspicion, as can be seen in the official document on New Age, *Jesus Christ, the Bearer of the Water of Life* (JBWL). It was published in 2003 by the Pontifical Council for Interreligious Dialogue and the Pontifical Council for Culture, and counsels caution vis-à-vis the errors of New Age, which the author contrasts with the true picture offered by the Christian faith. The document offers guidance to Christians whose search leads them to follow ways that can be risky and at odds with those of their own religious community. Nonetheless, the text is problematic in that it includes Eastern religions among the questionable beliefs.

The document presents New Age as a compilation of various elements, many of which are closely or distantly related to Buddhism and Hinduism. This is true to a certain extent, but the problem is that no distinction is made between those elements that are intrinsic to these religions and those that are by-products inspired by them. Lumping them all together causes the reader to be wary of Eastern religions in general and reduces the possibility of engaging in a serious dialogue with them. Even greater confusion is created when themes proper to these religions and very familiar to monks engaged in dialogue are subjected to criticism, such as the Buddhist notion of emptiness, God's presence in the depths of human existence, practices of meditation, or the theory of subtle energies and *chakras*. These are all rich themes, and when brought into an informed dialogue with the ancient traditions of Asia they can result in a fuller understanding of the mystery of the Trinity. The danger is that the scope of dialogue will be reduced by opposing these categories to a limited understanding of Christian thought. The risk is even greater in that monks engaged in dialogue were not consulted as the document was being developed. The only reference to monks occurs at the end of the document when they are invited to share their spiritual heritage with those who are searching. There is no mention of their long experience with Buddhism and Hinduism, and thus the document implicitly raises questions about the legitimacy of looking to the East for wisdom. *Jesus Christ, the Bearer of the Water of Life* makes reference to the *Letter on Christian Meditation* (1989) that was discussed in the previous chapter. One positive feature of the document is that it invites a critical response by calling attention to its provisional character and by asking Christians to make known their spiritual needs. I propose, therefore, to respond to this invitation by calling attention to four misunderstandings.

An egocentric practice. The document on New Age presents meditation as an egocentric activity that favors turning inward in order to come to an autonomous self-realization that gets in the way of a relationship to a personal God (JBWL 4). It is true that meditation practice can, in effect, become a refuge and foster lethargy and isolation, both of which are at odds with Christian values. However, the question raised by meditation is not limited to this risk. What is called meditation does not refer to a single method that guarantees the same outcome in every setting. Therefore it is simply not possible to speak of meditation in general, as if it were some monolithic reality, and contrast it with Christian prayer. Meditation practices are varied and complex. The only way one can grasp their full meaning is by taking into account the intention of the meditators, their faith, and the ascetic and philosophical milieux that have shaped them. The problem in question is not meditation itself but the way it is practiced. In the Zen tradition, for example, sitting meditation (zazen) is just the opposite of egocentrism. The point of zazen is to come to an immediate grasp of reality as it is, beyond thought, imagination, and feeling. It spurs those who meditate not to identify themselves with their natural inclinations, for they get in the way of awakening to the true and unqualified nature of the mind. The Zen tradition even warns against the temptation to become attached to sitting meditation, because zazen is about every moment and every activity.

What this means is that meditation is not a technique, but a way of living every moment, an awakened relationship with the world. The practice of meditation is individual, but it is not individualistic, and it does not encourage a turning inward on oneself. Each individual is responsible for his or her own self-knowledge, and no authentic spirituality will fail to provide the means to realize this requirement. But coming to self-knowledge does not mean cutting oneself off from the world. Just the opposite. Those who confront their own limitations in order to rise above them with wisdom and compassion are not lacking in hospitality. In fact, they grow in their capacity to be open and welcoming.

The negation of grace. The document on New Age presents meditation as an obstacle to our relationship with God by identifying it as a psychophysiological exercise stripped of any reference to grace (JBWL 3.1). This point of view supposes that meditation is understood at best as a preparation for Christian prayer, and that it has no relation to transcendence.

This is true if meditation is motivated by the intention and the desire to construct our own paradise. In Zen such an intention does not exist; all that counts is attention. Full awareness is, in itself, the absence of effort. Nothing is desired; awakening cannot be forced, since it is not the guaranteed result of a spiritual technique. *Satori* has nothing to do with the number of years one has practiced. The effort encouraged by the Buddhist tradition is not so much the negation of grace as the affirmation of personal responsibility on the way of liberation. That same Buddhist tradition also insists that enlightenment or awakening is not something we create or bring about. It is already present in each person, but hidden by ignorance. Certain Buddhist monks, in fact, affirm that a kind of grace is not a foreign concept to them (see Mitchell and Wiseman [2010], 218–25).

If liberation cannot be acquired by a spiritual technique it also cannot be acquired without our dedication, without faith in our own awakening (Dumoulin [1974], 86), and without making ourselves receptive to it. I believe this is what Jesus was referring to when he pleaded in vain with his disciples in the Garden of Eden to stay awake. Resisting sleep and keeping alert does not mean a rejection of grace, but an expression of our prayer to be more receptive to it: "You also must be ready, for the Son of Man is coming at an unexpected hour" (Luke 12:40). One thing is certain. In this debate facile comparisons and contrasts have to be avoided. Placing the Christian concept of grace in opposition to meditation practices in other traditions leaves too many questions unaccounted for, as a spiritual dialogue can easily show.

The praise of pantheism. By cautioning against the danger of identifying God with the world of phenomena or with the self, the document on New Age emphasizes the necessity of insisting on the absolute distance between the creator God and the created world (JBWL 4). It is altogether right to preserve divine transcendence and reject idolatry. But we have to be careful lest, in calling attention to this danger, we cast doubt on other religious traditions by accusing them of pantheism. This judgment is a heritage of the nineteenth century and comes from a condescending attitude that does not take into account the experience of the other and the inner logic of another religious tradition but is content to interpret it in the light of one's own categories. For example, the Hindu teaching found in the Upanishads on the identity of the "soul" (*atman*) and the Absolute (*Brahman*): "I am Brahman" (*aham brahma asmi*) does not allow us to conclude that this is a pantheistic—and therefore false—vision of reality. Even if this Hindu teaching is miles away from a Christian understanding of God, we cannot simply conclude that there is a fundamental opposition between these two perspectives and that it is impossible to arrive at mutual understanding. Griffiths and especially Le Saux have shown how rich and complex a dialogue conducted at this level can be.

The agony of emptiness. What has just been said about pantheism holds also for emptiness, a central teaching of Mahayana Buddhism (JBWL 4). The New Age document opposes it to the love that binds humans to God. But emptiness (*sunyata*) is not non-being, the nothing of the nihilist, or the absence of any thing, but rather the matrix of all possibility, the space par excellence of wisdom and compassion. As to the question of relationship, it can be said that emptiness points to the interdependence of all things, since they of themselves do not possess an essence that is proper to them and permanent. To be sure, emptiness is a category that belongs to a system that does not include the idea of a creator God or of a relationship of love with such a God. But once again, rather than rejecting this approach we should regard it as an occasion for fruitful dialogue.

The fear of Gnosticism. Any treatment of New Age must clearly distinguish it from Eastern spiritualities. This is important in order to provide a nuanced assessment of the philosophical and religious background of certain aspects of New Age and also for the purpose of encouraging dialogue with the great religions of Asia. Distinguishing the two right at the beginning makes it easier to assist people who are on a spiritual quest—which is exactly why the document was produced. Not making this distinction can create confusion in the minds of Christians who are not well informed and who might therefore think that all forms of meditation are basically the same or be suspicious of any tradition that speaks of emptiness or of the divine within the self. The risk of this happening is all the greater in that New Age does not designate a definite group with appointed leaders and official representatives, but rather a hodgepodge of opinions and practices. If someone recommends caution about New Age, many groups and currents of thought immediately presume they are being referred to. Neglecting to make the proper distinctions can have even more serious consequences, including casting doubt on the legitimacy of the great mystical tradition of Christianity. Fundamentally this debate is not so much between a Christian and a non-Christian view of the human-divine relationship as between two approaches to truth, one mystical, the other more dogmatic, both of which can be found within Christianity.

The debate about Eastern spiritualities is not new. In the preceding chapters we have seen that it causes anxiety and tension within the church, as monks involved in dialogue are well aware. We have only to call to mind the *Letter on Christian Meditation*, the controversial comments John Paul II made about Buddhism in his book *Crossing the Threshold of Hope*, or the equally controversial statements of Cardinal Ratzinger that appeared in *L'Express* on March 20, 1997, when he described

Eastern practices as a form of autoeroticism. We can also recall the disciplining of the German Benedictine Willigis Jäger—who was frequently cited in the MID *Bulletin* in the 1980s—for his teachings on Zen. If the intent of the document was to provide guidelines to Christians who were searching for the Absolute outside the confines of their own religion, it is also possible to detect another concern, one that is less obvious because it is so deeply embedded. I speak of the unresolved fear of Gnosticism within the Western church.

Since it is not possible to go into detail about this issue, as important as it is, let me simply say that issuing a blanket condemnation of Gnosticism makes it very difficult, if not impossible, to work out a spirituality of dialogue with Eastern religions. In order to understand Eastern religions it is necessary to become familiar with the "Gnostic" element that plays such a large part in them. At the same time, an encounter with these religions leads to a recognition and rediscovery of a properly Christian *gnosis*.

To get a better idea of what is involved in this controversy, it will be helpful to recall that the Greek word *gnosis* designates an intuitive knowledge of the essential nature of things that cannot be grasped by reasoning and is in itself liberating. It cannot be easily identified and can be applied to many different points of view and contexts. It is, however, necessary to distinguish a Christian *gnosis* and one that borrows elements from Christianity but does not respect the way these elements fit into the whole of Christian teaching.

The first kind of *gnosis* is a charismatic knowledge that involves all the dimensions of the human being; by it one comes little by little to a better grasp of the incomprehensible love of God. It is a contemplative way of knowing that is conferred by the Spirit of God (Eph 1:17; 1 Cor 2:11-12). Saint Paul exhorts Christians to grow in this kind of knowledge (Col 1:9-10; see also 2 Pet 3:16-18), which he attributes to the "spiritual" person in opposition to the "unspiritual" or "natural" person (1 Cor 2:14-16). While it is true that theology needs this kind of *gnosis* (Rahner [1970], 203), it needs to be distinguished from the

Gnostic movements that have threatened the integrity of the Christian faith from the beginning to the present day. These movements call themselves Christian but they are characterized by random beliefs that are at odds with Christian revelation. Among the most common are: the soul is a divine particle that has fallen into human flesh; the world is a prison from which we must free ourselves; the world is organized to reflect a radical dualism between absolute good and absolute evil; the teaching concerning salvation is twofold, one for the masses, the other only for initiates.

In the church both types of *gnosis* have elicited mistrust. Dissident groups made their appearance very early, for example those of Valentine, Basilides, Marcion, and Montanus. But there were also theologians faithful to the church, such as Clement of Alexandria and Evagrius of Pontus, who attempted to incorporate some of the profound and valuable elements of *gnosis* into their faith. The monastic tradition and the contemplative life it fosters were primarily responsible for keeping this legitimate form of *gnosis* alive in the church, principally in the Orthodox tradition. The more dogmatic Western church, however, has regularly regarded it as a menace to the integrity of the faith, especially since the sixteenth century.

What is it that is so disturbing about *gnosis* as an element of Christian contemplative life? Something described as "Gnostic" often refers to what is at the very heart of the Gospel experience, namely, the action of the Spirit, that fundamental divine power that secretly transforms hearts and leads them to their perfection. This deifying experience of God can be so strong it leads mystics to speak of becoming God, not in essence but by participation. Benoît Billot points us in this direction when he says, "I could no longer say the awe-inspiring word 'God,' or talk of God in the third person as if he were not me as well" (EMDI 7[28]). Even if contemplatives are not able to comprehend what God is, even less put their understanding into words, they are still able to taste the divine (*pati divina*), feel the fire of God, delight in the love of God. But many find this experience suspect, and for a number of reasons. It confers a certainty forged by the power of love, and this certainty becomes central, relegating dogma and hierarchy to their proper secondary role as signs pointing to union with God, which is the only thing that counts. There are those who are suspicious of any approach that cancels the distance between the Creator and the creature. When a contemplative says, as Le Saux did, "the real Christ for me is myself, myself risen again"[45] (see Keating [1992], 13), some people become uneasy, interpreting these words as indicative of pantheism. For others, however, they are a declaration of the immensity of God's love for human beings. The tradition of Christian mysticism shows us that believers only become fully aware of the distance between God and humans and of the relationship of love that binds them to one another when they participate with their whole being in the life of the Spirit, leaving behind the thought patterns of human wisdom and all images.

There are some who think the "nothing" (*nada*) of John of the Cross reduces God to a shadowy, indefinite concept. But is it not even more perilous to affirm, as does the document on New Age, that in Christian faith the idea of God is "very clear" (JBWL 4)? This fails to acknowledge what is beyond reasoned and written formulas, that is, the contemplative experience that witnesses to a God who draws close to us in the "night" of understanding (John of the Cross [2009], 69–70), and that the revelation of God's mystery, of the God who is mystery, is only offered to those who desire to encounter God and become submissive to the divine will. To say that God is mystery does not mean that God is inaccessible or completely beyond the possibility of being known to some degree. It is rather a way of saying that no language is capable of expressing the kind of experiential knowledge that the All Holy One offers us.

Being against Gnosticism is not something new in the church. Today it can be seen in the opposition to Eastern spiritualities that, in the context of dialogue, encourage Christians to rediscover the richness of mystical and apophatic literature of writers from the desert fathers and mothers down to our own times. These spiritualities should not be confused—though they often are—with the Gnostic heresies of New Age. In point of fact, spiritual dialogue with Buddhism and Hinduism is just what is needed to bypass this deceptive mishmash and arrive at a better understanding of these religions—and of Christianity as well. The Christian faith is not only love (*agape*); it is also knowledge (*gnosis*) of the divine mysteries, a knowledge that is experienced as liberating.

The Sri Lankan Jesuit Aloysius Pieris says that *gnosis* and *agape* are two inseparable and complementary ways to describe those intimate moments with the ultimate source of liberation. Contrary to what is usually said, they are present as much in Buddhism as in Christianity. Pieris shows that neither the position of most Christian theologians, who refuse to acknowledge an interior knowledge (*gnosis*), nor that of many Buddhist thinkers, who tend toward a denial of love (*agape*), is justifiable. We have to go beyond this artificial division, he says, and recognize that *gnosis* is not foreign to the Christian experience nor is *agape* to that of the Buddhist. Only in this way will we be able to engage in dialogue where heart speaks to heart.

The spirituality of dialogue that is being explored and developed by monks urges us to reconsider these questions without resorting to apologetics or to a priori arguments typical of defensive discourse. What is needed as we dialogue with other spiritualities is a new and deeper appreciation of interiority, the contemplative experience, the mystical and apophatic dimension of the Christian tradition, doing so not to betray the spirit of Christ but to enter more deeply into it. A properly Christian *gnosis* needs to be regained in order to have a right relationship to transcendence. In order for this to happen, a spirituality of dialogue is needed. But that there is a risk that this could lead to Gnosticism is all the more reason for a careful and informed response to it.

Spiritual Spaces and Contexts

The church in the West is faced with the challenge of reintegrating the contemplative way into its life of faith, of recognizing the value of an experiential knowledge of divine wisdom alongside the knowledge conveyed by dogma, and of finding ways to bring together the historical and mystical expressions of the kingdom. Interaction with Eastern spiritualities can provide invaluable assistance in accomplishing this task, as the fathers of dialogue have shown us. If such interaction is to bear fruit there needs to be an accurate understanding of the different ways of meditation—not reducing them, on the one hand, to methods to achieve physical and psychological well-being and, on the other hand, not simply engaging in a useless exercise of comparing them to one another. We need to let these ways of meditation elicit our respect for religious difference.

The document *Contemplation and Dialogue* proposes an attitude that is absolutely essential in an interreligious setting when it says that "we must never forget that, even when we only adopt spiritual methods, it is always *persons* that we receive. We encounter a tradition elaborated by generations of seekers of the Absolute" (Béthune [2002], 66). This awareness brings with it an obligation to understand Zen, yoga, and every other form of contemplative prayer in their respective ascetic, historical, linguistic, and philosophical spaces, that is to say, in the specific cultural and religious contexts in which they have been developed and practiced (Blée [2003b]). Once again the technical aspect of meditation is less important than the intention behind the practice and the outcome that can be expected. Thus in Zen we find different kinds of practice, depending on the intention of the practitioner. In *The Three Pillars of Zen*, Philip Kapleau speaks of *bompu zen* to refer to Zen practiced for health benefits; of *gedo zen* to refer to meditation-related activities such as Indian yoga or Christian contemplative prayer; of *shojo zen*, practiced by Buddhists of the Smaller Vehicle (*hinayana*) in order to arrive at self-liberation; of *daijo zen*, the Zen practiced by adherents of the Greater Vehicle (*mahayana*), who are dedicated to saving all living beings and achieving awakening; and of *saijojo zen*, a form of Zen that practices sitting meditation (zazen) as an end in itself since it is regarded as the manifestation or actualization of our true nature (Kapleau [1989], 46). The different intentions that shape the various forms of Zen depend on the specific milieu in which each has been developed; they are original and unique cultural products. Since these forms of meditation practice are provisional, conditioned, and contextualized, each leads to an original and specific experience of the Ultimate. One cannot therefore speak of a uniform religious experience that has no distinguishing features and is accessible to everyone, no matter what their culture or religion (see Panikkar [2002], 40–42).

For Buddhist and Christian monks the monastic way of life constitutes a common milieu in which they sense they are part of the same family. But this common milieu is only discovered through the specific milieu of the contemplative practices of each tradition. The monastic milieu indicates two different kinds of space. It is first of all the *center* or heart of the practice: the experience of awakening for Buddhists and of divine union for Christians, but also the profound sense of a mysterious unity among all believers. The monastic milieu is also the *environment* that surrounds practice, that is to say, the contextual elements that point it in a certain direction and shape the experience that will flow from it. These two dimensions are inseparable from the contemplative life and direct us not to separate the universal from the particular, unity from diversity.

We cannot pretend that all practices are equally valid, nor can we set up a scale of values to determine which ones are better than others. On the other hand it is possible to judge, at least to a certain degree, the *environmental* coherence of each practice, that is to say, the elements (rules, teacher, scriptures, asceticism, theology, etc.) that work together to bring one to the experience of transcendence, that shape the practice, and that show the depth of its meaning for our daily lives. The coherence of a spiritual practice becomes apparent to the degree that we are open to the experience of the Ultimate that sustains it and is its *center*. This is even more true in the context of dialogue. In a dialogic encounter with a member of another religion we can more clearly perceive the contours and internal structure of the two religious systems. We discover common points between the two religions as well as differences. From a dialogic perspective these convergences and divergences are not so much factors that bring us closer together or keep us farther apart, but indices that allow us to discern the inner coherence of each path and in this way facilitate mutual understanding.

For example, the perceived convergence between Christian contemplative prayer and Buddhist meditation does not mean they are identical. Each involves a different anthropology and a distinctive way of living that is in conformity with the inner logic of each system. By the same token, the divergence between divine grace and *karma*, for example, does not necessarily mean radical opposition, for in both cases—but following a different logic—the practitioner is asked to take responsibility for his or her own salvation. Convergences and divergences cannot be looked at in isolation from the specific coherence proper to each of the religious ways brought into dialogue. Contrary to common opinion, convergences and divergences do not indicate that religions are either identical or poles apart. Rather, since we are never totally the same or totally different, they are indicators of where the tension lies. This tension is what drives the Christian into the desert of otherness and thus gives rise to a spirituality of dialogue.

The Desert of Religious Otherness

The adoption of a contemplative path worked out in another religion is central to the development of the dialogue practiced by monks, for it permits them to experience the radical difference that arises from an encounter with someone whose faith is different before becoming aware of a real complicity. As we have seen above, it promotes access to what we have called the "desert of otherness." This expression might appear contradictory at first sight. The desert evokes isolation, aridity, the absence of life, while otherness suggestion conviviality, fullness, and fertility. Nonetheless, these two realities, the desert and others, go hand in hand, and for the better. Other people do not necessarily equal hell, though that well-known line from Sartre's *No Exit* can help to clarify the point I want to make. The other confronts us, is forever bound to us. Every individual is shaped by this interaction; no one can escape from it. Like it or not, we are involved with one another for better or worse. If we choose to ignore this fact, hell is not far off; if we accept it, then it is the desert that awaits us, that absolutely necessary space into which the Spirit drove Jesus right after his baptism (Matt 4:1). It is not a lifeless place or a place of punishment, but a place of exile on our journey to a fertile land (the kingdom) and the promise of a love beyond compare.

It has been said that the challenge of dialogue is not peace at any price, but an authentic opening to the other, and that is impossible without submission to the divine Spirit. When we accept that the Spirit dwells within us we allow that same Spirit to bring us closer to one another by weaving the bonds of love (*agape*) and communion (*koinonia*). Witnessing in this way to the uniqueness of the other and disallowing force of any kind, we make our way into the desert of otherness with all the risks that await us in the place of wandering (Heb 11:38). Monks engaged in dialogue show us the way into this desert and in so doing reveal an unusual dimension of the contemporary monastic vocation. Entering into relation with the other, the one whose deepest beliefs are radically different from ours, can be seen as the desert where the monastic vocation, both of monks and of lay people, is to be lived out.

To be more precise, we need to consider the following three points: (1) the desert of otherness is an expression of the need to return to the essential, especially now in these critical times; (2) the desert has significant features that can already be demonstrated; (3) the desert does not mean turning in on oneself, but going beyond oneself through wisdom and love.

Monasteries without Borders

If the monastic vocation appears outmoded in a world that so highly prizes activity and production, if it does not seem to be capable of saying anything to modern men and women, it should be remembered that throughout history it was often the monks who were at the vanguard in overcoming what seemed to be an impasse in times of societal and religious crisis. Today the followers of Saint Benedict are involved in groundbreaking activities that promise to be beneficial for the world at large. Merton is an especially powerful example, with his eloquent and fiery denunciations of racism, war, nuclear arms, and the consumer society. We can also think of John Main and Thomas Keating who, each in his own way, promoted contemplative prayer for lay people, even though contemplation had traditionally been thought of as a prayer that was suitable only for the most gifted of monks. Moreover, Benedictines and Cistercians were intent to show that there were elements of the monastic way of life that were applicable to all people, not just to those who lived in monasteries.

Monks are, par excellence, intense and determined people. Impelled by a strong desire to enter into communion with the reality beyond transitory appearances and phenomena, they make a deliberate choice to give up everything to realize this communion here and now by seeking the solitude that allows them to confront themselves. Over the course of history this return to the essential usually involved a separation from worldly affairs and a retreat into the desert, that privileged place of encounter with the divine. It was, in fact, in the Egyptian desert that Christian monasticism was born. The first to go there were the hermits (anchorites), but little communities of monks (cenobites) very soon began to form around *abbas*, monks who were renowned for their holiness.

From that time on there has been a difference of opinion about the way to practice solitude. The tension can already to be found in the gospel story of Martha and Mary (Luke 10:38-42), one of whom represents the necessity of retreating from the world to become holy and the other the importance of being engaged in the world in order to participate in the coming of the kingdom. The type of monastery that became common in rural Europe was indicative of an attempt to preserve both these ideals. The tension was intensified by the emergence in the thirteenth century of the first apostolic orders. In the sixteenth century Saint

John of the Cross and the reformed Carmelites would become victims of this tension. From that time on monasteries ceased to have pride of place in a society that was increasingly based on activity, progress, and equality.

Nonetheless, even in contemporary society the monastic vocation has not become outmoded, for the simple reason that the desert has not lost its meaning. It continues to call us back to the essential, to the necessity of confronting and conquering death. It does this even more in times of crisis. From the fourth to the sixth century the fathers of the desert were largely responsible for keeping the Christian faith alive and strong enough to survive the decline of the Roman Empire. The monks of Saint Columban in the sixth and seventh centuries and the Benedictines in the Middle Ages planted the Christian message throughout Western Europe, making it possible for Christianity to survive the barbarian invasions and lay the foundations of a new civilization.

As Christianity confronts the challenges of globalization, modernity, and religious pluralism it is once again fighting for its survival, at least in the West. In these critical times monks have once more come to the fore, first of all by widespread missionary activity in the 1960s and then by creating a movement dedicated to the encounter with other religions. It is within this context that they once more invite us into the desert, no longer presented as a geographical location or, in fact, as any place at all, but rather as a relational space in which we meet the other, particularly the other who does not believe as we do and who has therefore been traditionally regarded as the enemy of the Christian.

This desert has no physical boundaries; it is mobile because you can take it with you. But at the same time it is something physical, something embodied. It is not located in a barren wasteland or even in the structured organization of a monastery, but there where we are most truly ourselves, where we have our identity as beings-in-relation. Is it not true that the place "*where* you are, especially if you are *in love* matters less than *who* you are with?" (Freeman [2000], 116). This kind of desert reminds us of the importance of interiority in every spiritual journey. Just as God does not dwell in temples made by human hands (Acts 17:24), the pilgrimage of the mystic is not a journey to some external shrine, but to the sacred space within the self (MacInnes [2003], 187).

The desert shows us how urgent it is to follow the interior laws of the Spirit without, however, opting for a total and permanent separation from the affairs of the world as did the classic hermit or cenobite. As Merton insisted, the crisis that faces us today is about the actual survival of the human race. Comparing the situation of the fathers of the desert with our current crises, Merton wrote, "Our danger is far more desperate. Our time, perhaps, is shorter than we think" (Merton [1960], 23). In this setting the challenge of the contemplative is to find the solitude that is necessary for his spiritual quest not in isolation from society but at its center, in the cultural and psychological thickness of a relationship with the other and in the renunciation of those things that we are especially attached to. As demanding as it is, this aspect of the monastic vocation is what is best suited to the present situation: not abandoning structures and institutions but allowing them to be transformed through relationships that bring about a radical change of heart.

This idea is not new; Jesus and the prophets before him showed the way. It is useless to offer sacrifice if there is no change of heart (Jer 24:7; Mark 7:6). Jesus dedicated himself to a radical transformation of society by the simple fact that he gave himself fully to a relationship with the other by attending to outcasts, the poor, and even his enemies in the person of the Roman centurion, the publican, and the Samaritan, to those who professed a different belief (John 4:20-21).

In the history of the church a relationship to the poor was always a priority, since the kingdom of God is theirs (Matt 5:3; Jas 2:5). The same attention, however, has not been given to our relationship with the enemy, that is, those who believe, but believe differently. There are, to be sure, some outstanding examples, such as the meeting of Francis of Assisi with the Sultan Al-Kamil in Egypt in 1219. However, the main attitude toward those who do not share our beliefs has been one of mistrust and rejection, an attitude that took the form of extreme violence in the

Crusades, the Inquisition, and the dragonnades against the Huguenots. In our day love of other believers is just as important as love of the poor, because hatred and violence between religious communities inevitably increases misery, desolation, hunger, and instability. Combating poverty implies entering the desert of otherness so as not to engage in any activity that causes poverty. This is what the Cambodian Buddhist Maha Ghosananda was saying when he called on monks at the Gethsemani Encounter in 1966 to make battlefields and prisons their temples.

If this approach seems promising, does it not call into question the institutional structures of monasticism? In fact, the desert of otherness is not in any way opposed to monasticism. On the contrary, it can invigorate it by denouncing the existence of too much comfort and distraction, and by encouraging it to rededicate itself to the search for God along with all who are engaged in the quest for truth. The monk and the hermit continue to model the necessity of withdrawal if one is to have a spiritual life. It would be illusory to think one could dispense with solitude, even if it is only for short periods of time, for it is in the serenity of such separation that we can come face to face with ourselves. What is essential here is achieving an inner silence, that absence of judgment (Luke 6:37) that is the true foundation of divine love.

While the solitude of the desert of otherness is an optimum space for developing this silence and testing its integrity, it still remains true that some periods of physical separation are needed to insure that this interior silence becomes deeply and firmly established. That is one of the reasons why the possibility of a temporary commitment to monastic life needs further investigation. If solitude is, as the ancients believed, the condition *sine qua non* for arriving at the perfection of holiness, that means that today there will once again have to be a place for it in the workplace and within relationships. Not only will that provide a way to evaluate the progress made during periods of retreat, but it will also color ordinary relationships with the patience, the wisdom, and the love that are characteristic of the solitary. In this regard Christians who would like to explore this option further can benefit greatly from dialogue with Buddhism, which has a well-developed form of temporary monasticism.

Another question needs to be addressed. Is not the linking of contemplation and action what the apostolic orders are all about, in particular the Jesuits, whose founder, Ignatius of Loyola, said that we are to "find God in everything"? What, then, is the special contribution of monks involved in dialogue?

First of all, monks witness to the importance of the apophatic tradition, which is not highly regarded by apostolic religious. In addition, the desert of otherness is more than a spiritual exercise that makes it possible to exercise discernment in the midst of action. It is also, and par excellence, the space of permanent retreat, constant questioning, and deep communion. There is no method that one must follow; all that is needed is heartfelt openness in one's relationship to the other.

Finally, if love of the other and the hospitality that expresses the depth of that love are proper to the mission of Christianity, the other—especially the other who is poor—has often been seen as a person to be saved, and only rarely a person who confronts us and makes us question our way of thinking and style of life. It is here that we can see the distinctiveness of the desert of otherness. It shows us that our relationship to the other is, in itself, a form of asceticism.

The Asceticism of Dialogue

Relationship to the other can be described as a desert when it becomes a place of asceticism, that is to say, a discipline that contributes to spiritual growth. Three characteristics of religious otherness justify such a description.

In the first place, otherness calls attention to the strangeness of the other, those absolutely fundamental and unchangeable characteristics that make the other different from us. To enter into relationship, then, means coming face to face with adversity. We can certainly share with the other, find similarities, or develop a close understanding, but we will never be identical to the other, will never feel at home on his or her turf. As is the case with the desert, relational space is space we travel through; we do not stay there. The desert is not a place to set up a permanent encampment, because there is no place to lay one's head. The desert is a place of passage, of wandering, or even of exile where love is accompanied by the anguish rooted in our ultimate incompleteness, which, however, reveals our true nature. The difference of the other shows us the gap in our vision of ourselves, the world, and God. This kind of self-knowledge is never easy to accept, but it leads us from slavery to freedom.

Second, otherness does not refer to the other in a purely abstract and unembodied way. The other is always known in relationship to oneself, a relationship that is not neutral but transformative. Those who enter into a relationship make known their interdependence, that place of self-transcendence and also of suffering. "God is present when I confront you" (Buber [1970], 28). Drawing close to God means experiencing the adversity that is present in every authentic relationship. Like the desert, this relationship is a place of trial and temptation precisely because it is the road to liberty and the kingdom. In fact, the kingdom cannot be entered unless one abandons the other kingdom, that of power and self-sufficiency (Matt 4:1-11). In a relationship with the other this test is not met once and for all but has to be endured again and again. That necessity indicates that while the desert promises an encounter with God, the desert is also the space where we fail to meet the test and where we are invited to be reconciled with God (Hos 2:16). This invitation comes to us in the battle that pits our egoistic tendencies and old habits against our will to overcome them in order to be open to what is greater than us. The other puts us in touch with the fears and hopes that shape our personality. That is why encountering the other is a source of suffering, especially when the relationship is one of deep love. In this case the danger does not lie in undergoing suffering, as difficult as that may be, for suffering is part of every relationship, but of breaking off the relationship and refusing to love again. We do not love to achieve well-being or to fulfill a desire, but to establish a true communion of persons without expecting anything in return. The desert of otherness, therefore, is not a place of death—death in the sense of absence of life, death as the gate to hell—for death is the absence of love, the place of indifference and agreement-at-any-price. Death is the refusal to engage in combat with the angel, while the desert is the arena for a mutual rebirth in the Spirit.

In the third place, a relationship with the other endures beyond physical presence. This brings us back to the notion of interiorizing one's relationship with someone who believes differently, which is what interreligious dialogue is ultimately all about. We offer a space within ourselves to the other, who, though physically absent, continues to confront us from within, creating an internal dialogue that makes it possible for a subsequent encounter to be more enlightened and more positive. We come back once again to the idea developed by Panikkar and Le Saux, that for interreligious dialogue to be fruitful there has to be an internal dialogue. In other words, there is no constructive dialogue between believers of different religions without a willingness to know the religious experience of one's dialogue partner. This is one more necessary and demanding dimension of the desert of otherness.

Interreligious hospitality is not extended only halfway. It does not consist in having one foot in one's own religion and one foot in that of the other, but in being fully oneself and having both feet in the religious universe of one's partner in dialogue. This does not mean putting one's own faith in parentheses, but rather being fully engaged with it in the relationship with the other. This gives rise to a certain tension that can, at times, be excruciatingly painful, as was the case with Le Saux. But without this tension, dialogue does not exist. This tension denotes the desert. It heightens our sense of urgency with the conviction that our very survival is at stake, and that maintaining our equilibrium depends on our full acceptance of reality as it reveals itself to us in each moment. The tension we experience leads to profound self-questioning, not the kind that looks for ready-made and reassuring answers but the kind that leads to a stripping away of idols and false identities. Béthune says much the same thing when he speaks about interreligious encounter as a mutual impoverishment that leads to reciprocal enrichment (Béthune [2002], 35). Finally, it is precisely by accepting this inner tension that Christians enter the solitude of the desert, not by breaking with the world but by dwelling in its center, at the very heart of relationship with the other.

No One Is His or Her Own Temple

It might seem that the solitude induced by the intrareligious experience is a turning in on the self in order to seek refuge in a virtual dialogue that is cut off from the other and the other's concrete reality. It is true that when Christian monks engage in some Eastern practices—Zen, for example—they come to know and understand themselves and rediscover the profound meaning of the Christian message that we are the temple of God. This is not, however, an expression of egocentricity or self-sufficiency. On the contrary, being the temple of the Spirit means going beyond the limits of the "old self." One's gaze is not directed toward oneself, but toward otherness. Martin Buber says that the Spirit is not found *in* the "I," but *between* the "I" and the "You." He uses the following analogy to explain what he means: "It is not like the blood that circulates in you but like the air in which you breathe. . . . It is solely by virtue of his power to relate that man is able to live in the spirit" (Buber [1970], 89). All in all, to understand oneself as the temple of the Spirit is to discover oneself as a relational being.

We are not our own temple. We are always the temple of a third person, the Spirit, and it is in our relationship to the other that we find our own temple. Those who give the Spirit free rein do not isolate themselves but surpass themselves. They confront adversity and face up to their own egoistic tendencies in order the better to overcome them. Immediately after his baptism, the Spirit drove Jesus into the Judean desert and put him to the test. In an interreligious context the Spirit does much the same thing by leading the Christian into the desert of otherness, where it reveals itself in other ways and is at the origin of every authentic prayer, Christian or not.[46]

Developing a Spirituality of Dialogue   185

To clear up some possible ambiguities, it might be good to say something about the relationship between the symbolic meanings of "temple" and "desert." From a biblical point of view the desert is the place for returning to authenticity, and it is contrasted with the temple, the place of cult and symbol of religious hierarchy and legalism. At the same time the temple is also the dwelling place of the God of the patriarchs and the place for an altogether special encounter with God. In fact, there are two kinds of temple: the first is the temple of stone that God abandoned and Jesus said would be destroyed; the second is the new and risen person in whom dwells the living God and whom Jesus is committed to raising in three days. The foundations of this latter temple are established in the journey through the desert by the fact that all forms of power and security are surrendered.

To recognize oneself as the temple of the Spirit means following in the direction in which one may least expect to be led, and not seeking comfort by staying fixed where one is. Those who are open to the Spirit are driven to the heart of otherness, of the stranger, of difference, and brought to the paradoxical realization that that is where the image of God resides. It is in relation to the other that we understand who we really are. To make this relationship one's temple is not to abandon one's own faith or to make an idol of the other, or to want to lose one's identity in the other. On the contrary, relationship summons us to respect, to silence, and to listening to the way the Spirit communicates its gifts, which are channeled through the religious distinctiveness of the other.

God's existence for human beings is always incarnated, and even though the Almighty transcends every category, each one of the divine manifestations is accompanied by a particular cultural development that can never be completely ignored. If the other leads us to regard the image of God from a particular point of view, that is because of the psychological and cultural ways in which the other's faith and beliefs have come to expression. When Christian monks practice Zen in the spirit of dialogue they do not cease to be disciples of Jesus. On the contrary, they are welcomed as such by all those Buddhist teachers who, generation after generation, have worked out a specific way to become awakened to the true nature of things. By attending to their age-old experience, the Christian arrives at a deeper consciousness of the mystery of the Triune God, to God's way of communicating with human beings and bringing about the salvation of all.

If relationship with the other is this temple that inspires hope, this desert beyond every desert, this space for a new monastic vocation, who then is invited to enter? It is certainly not set aside for a particular group, for this or that organized community. This invitation to the desert is offered to all people of good will, but to be able to pass through it, they ought to begin with two qualities that are at the heart of the monastic life: the determination to know oneself and enduring love for God and the neighbor. Entering the temple of otherness is impossible without a commitment to solitude and introspection, and such a commitment, in turn, is impossible without living out the commandment of love given us by Jesus. As it is written, "Everyone who loves is born of God and knows God" (1 John 4:7). What is then needed are two seemingly disparate qualities: the courage and daring of a warrior to take up the battle against the fears and powers in our unconscious, and the vulnerability of the lover who always wants what is good for the beloved in spite of all the ways that other causes distress and worry. These two qualities come together to address the necessity of transcending our limitations in self-giving, and they do so by calling us to fidelity to the mystery that is present in each of us and is greater than our hearts. What then is the shape of this desert of otherness, this new type of monastery? What kind of structure is appropriate? That remains to be seen. One thing is sure, however: existing models do not have to be rejected. Collaboration with the institutional hermit and cenobite will create new solutions that will benefit everyone. Monks in dialogue have a prophetic role to play, and we need to listen to them. If the desert of otherness is the place where human beings can be more receptive to wisdom, access to it must be made more direct.

An Ecclesial Responsibility

The coming together of monastic traditions and the interreligious experience that goes with this rapprochement opens up new perspectives and possibilities. In their effort to articulate a spirituality of dialogue, monks promote the contemplative life and a mutual understanding of different religions. They are constructing the matrix of an authentic life together that will give support to the resolution of conflicts by preventing the forces of division and various kinds of traditionalism from taking over. This is a development that is still fragile, and whether its impact will last depends on everyone doing his or her part. While the contribution of monks to this development has been and is crucial, it will be in vain if support is not forthcoming from other ecclesial communities and groups. The question at the present time is whether we are ready to commit ourselves to the way of dialogue. Dialogue is an activity that has been officially recognized as the vocation of every Catholic, but that does not guarantee it will actually happen or will bear fruit. There is a great risk that dialogue will be taken over by the state, for example, and become a diplomatic exercise, especially at a time when religious agendas are so evident in many armed conflicts.

Dialogue means that every individual is called to create a network of informal relationships in daily life. That is what is referred to as the dialogue of life, and it sets the stage for all the other kinds of encounter. The depth of this form of dialogue comes from a Christian spirituality of dialogue that denounces indifference and defies intolerance by really listening to the other. One question then arises: Am I ready to allow myself to be challenged, redirected, and transformed through my relations with religious otherness? That was the question Sister Denyse [GilChrist] Lavigne asked herself at the foundational meeting at Petersham: "Do I have the courage to engage in a complete rethinking of monastic life and structures?" All Christians are invited to ask themselves this same question in their own terms and in their own particular life setting. It is a question that over the last few decades has triggered a debate within the church, not only among theologians but among bishops, priests, religious, contemplatives, and the laity as well. In this debate can be found a whole range of opinions, from the most liberal to the most conservative, and on its outcome depends, in large part, the future orientation of the church.

I highlight three points that reflect the church's responsibility to address the spiritual dialogue initiated by Benedictine monks. First, the dialogue of spiritual experience will gain greater recognition by being more widely accepted, especially by those who are already involved in some form of interreligious dialogue. Second, the dialogue of spiritual experience is an invitation to reclaim the specifically evangelical character of the Christian identity rather than affirming it through defensive or apologetic postures. Third, spiritual dialogue broadens our understanding of mission.

Recognition and Cooperation

Dialogue has certainly found its place among the followers of Saint Benedict, but it is still not fully recognized in the theological consideration of specific subjects, such as Eastern forms of meditation or New Age. If the next step is developing a spirituality of dialogue, then dialogue will have to become an essential activity in the life of the church. In order for this to happen, dialogue will have to be included in the theological formation of monks. The intensive course on monastic interreligious dialogue offered at Sant' Anselmo in Rome in September 2001 was one way of encouraging this development. In fact, a similar program was recommended in 1986 by the Abbot Primate, Victor Dammertz, who wanted a course on non-Christian monasticism to be offered at Sant'Anselmo. Even earlier, a desire to include the monastic dimension in the teaching of other religions was expressed at the 1977 meeting in Loppem.

Developing a spirituality of dialogue will also require all who are involved in such activities to support and cooperate with each other. This cooperation can take place on different levels, and the numerous joint efforts that have already taken place offer examples of how to proceed. We should note that the Benedictines and the Cistercians made history when they joined together to create the secretariat for mission (AIM), and they now jointly sponsor the secretariat for interreligious dialogue. Since its inception monastic dialogue has always received the support of the pope. Paul VI encouraged its development with his message to the conference at Bangkok (1968). John Paul II did the same when he invited different groups of Buddhists taking part in the Spiritual Exchange program sponsored by DIM to meet him in Rome. Support has also been forthcoming from the Pontifical Council for Interreligious Dialogue, first when its president, Sergio Pignedoli, and his secretary, Pietro Rosanno, asked the abbot primate to have monks take the lead in promoting dialogue between monastic traditions (1974), and later, in 1991 and 1999, when Francis Arinze asked monks to report on their experiences in dialogue.

Cooperation is also taking place between the different continental and linguistic commissions and between monastic men and women. It must be said that women have played a key role in the development of monastic dialogue. Their long-term involvement ensures the continuity of this important work. For example, Sister Pascaline Coff's contribution to the cause has been exceptional, especially in the period from 1978 to 1988 when she alone handled the different responsibilities of the American commission: editing the bulletin, managing the office, and keeping track of finances. Without her energetic leadership monastic dialogue in America would certainly be much less dynamic and confident. Because of all she did, especially in MID's formative years, she is gladly referred to as the founding mother of the American commission.[47] We can also point to Sister Mary Margaret Funk, who served as executive secretary from 1994 to 2005 and whose leadership brought dialogue to a level of social engagement and made possible such major events as the Gethsemani Encounter.

It is interesting to note that during the hospitality programs offered by American monasteries to Tibetan monks, the Tibetans were concerned that there be a balance between more senior monks and novices in the groups that came to the United States. The Americans, on the other hand, strove for a balance between men and women in the groups that traveled to India and Tibet. In Europe it was the Benedictine sisters in Vanves who offered office space and facilities to the secretariat for mission. The contribution made by Sister Pia Valéri was especially significant. We should also mention Sister Iona Misquitta, who for many years coordinated the interreligious activities of monastic communities in India, and Sister Marie-Bruno Colin, who, before her untimely death in 2006, was the coordinator of the European commissions and a consultor to the Pontifical Council for Interreligious Dialogue.

If the momentum of this movement is to be sustained, cooperation now needs to take place first of all with contemplative religious communities, and then with apostolic communities that are engaged in dialogue. Buddhist monks have already asked that their dialogue partners not be restricted to Benedictines and Cistercians but include contemplatives belonging to other orders and in this way parallel, to some degree, what had already taken place on their side. At the Gethsemani Encounter (1996), for example, there were Tibetans, Japanese, Sri Lankans, Cambodians, Thais, and Americans belonging to different traditions and schools. Likewise, monks of the Orthodox Church as well as Protestants and Anglicans who are favorable to interreligious dialogue could bring a certain spiritual ecumenism to the movement. There should also be closer collaboration between contemplative orders involved in dialogue and apostolic communities. We can think, for example, of the Oblates of Mary Immaculate and their interreligious involvement with Amerindian traditions in Canada. The work of Achiel Peelman is especially notable. The Jesuits are very active in interreligious dialogue and among them are some of the most important thinkers in the dialogue of spiritual experience, including Hugo M. Enomiya-Lassalle, Henrich Dumoulin, Kakishi Kadowaki, William Johnston, Ignatius Irudayam, Anthony De Mello, Michael Amaladoss, Aloysius Pieris, AMA (Arul Maria Arokiasamy) Samy, Robert Kennedy, and Bernard Sénécal. Collaboration with the Jesuits is all the more feasible since their establishment in 1995 of a center for interreligious and ecumenical affairs.[48] One thing is certain: collaboration is needed to counteract an all-too-common tendency of Christian groups to act independently, or even worse, to foster rivalry by multiplying programs that address the same issue but are in no way related to one another. In the area of dialogue such a way of proceeding is especially harmful because it acts as a counter-witness to the cause that is being promoted.

There is also need for cooperation with the laity.[49] It bears repeating that the relevance of monastic dialogue is that it is for the benefit of the entire community of believers because its basic concern is with the kingdom of God, from which no one is excluded. Monks develop the dialogue of experience, doing so in relation to the dialogue of life that involves everyone, especially lay people, who have the responsibility of making the benefits of the monastic experience available to all sectors of life, both private and public. Interaction with lay Christians is also important because many of them are involved in a spirituality of dialogue, sometimes without identifying it as such and without appropriate direction. Some, for example, have adopted the practice of Zen or yoga; others are in an interreligious marriage. Together, monks and lay people need to create space for sharing and reflection.

We can mention another kind of collaboration—that with science. The debate between science and religion is well developed, and there is an impressive number of scientific studies dealing with so-called mystical states. It is somewhat ironic that it is the scientists, particularly the neurologists, who attest to the authenticity of states of extreme lucidity recounted in mystical literature (D'Aquili and Newberg [1999], 205), states produced by meditation, certain rituals, or severe fasts. If theology wants to respond to the important questions raised by recent research it will have to do it by accepting the same starting point, namely, the actual human experience of the divine. Without doubt, theology will find its fulcrum in a spirituality of dialogue because science does not restrict its experiments to one religion alone (even though, *de facto*, these particular experiments most often involve Zen or Tibetan monks), but conducts them over the whole religious landscape in order to find a common denominator for these different peak experiences. D'Aquili and Newberg speak of megatheology. In this setting monks are regarded as credible subjects because their exploration of the interior spaces of the divine mystery spans several spiritual traditions.

One final remark on the partners in dialogue: There can be no doubt that Christian monks have had an altogether special relationship with Zen Buddhists and Tibetans, and to a lesser degree with Hindu swamis. At this point in history the encounter with Eastern religions has a specific and prophetic role to play, and many thinkers believe it will have a decisive impact on the course of history (Guardini [1996]; Levi-Strauss [1992]; Gira [1989]). Already in 1947 Teilhard de Chardin said in an essay entitled *"L'apport spirituel de l'Extrême-Orient"* (The Spiritual Contribution of the Far East),

> In every domain of thought, whether religious or scientific, it is only in union with all other men that each individual man can hope to reach what is most ultimate and profound in his own being. By this I do not mean that we have to be initiated into a higher form of the spirit, but rather that, forming a new resonant whole, we must add volume and richness to the new (the humano-Christian) mystical note rising from the West. Such, in a word, I believe to be the indispensable role and the essential function at the present moment of the Far East. (Teilhard de Chardin [1975], 146–47)

The time is ripe to engage in an in-depth encounter with the spiritual East, and monks involved in dialogue are well placed to lead the way. However, the role of Asian spiritualities is not to affirm their superiority or diminish the value of other religions. They have as much need of a Christianity that knows how to reaffirm its own spiritual depth as Christianity has of them. Christianity can help them rid themselves of the forms of obscurantism and injustice that affect them and help them relate to the modern and scientific way of thinking to which not even they are immune. We can recall that monks became interested

Developing a Spirituality of Dialogue 193

in Buddhism and Hinduism for historical reasons, namely the monastic missionary movement of the first half of the twentieth century, and also because they found there the most developed forms of monastic life outside Christianity. But we should also note that once they became independent, interreligious commissions expanded their dialogue to all religions and did not simply limit themselves to strictly monastic traditions.

In practice, however, dialogue works best with spiritualities that are sensitive to the mystical or contemplative dimension, and the monotheistic religions are often resistant to this aspect of the spiritual life. Nonetheless, there are contacts with Islam and Judaism, and monks have engaged in fruitful dialogue with Sufism and the cabalistic tradition. But apart from contact with these minorities, dialogue with the Abrahamic religions remains one of the great challenges to be met. The growth of this dialogue will certainly be helped by the spirituality of dialogue that has already been developed in a close relationship with the religions of Asia.

In this situation what we need to do is foster an interreligious dialogue that goes beyond the classical categorization that contrasts the monotheistic or prophetic religions with religions that are referred to as Eastern or non-dual. This partitioning is still in force and creates an obstacle to the development of a more inclusive spiritual dialogue. Here again monks are the innovators when they invite Buddhists, Hindus, Jews, and Muslims to come together around the mystery that grants them the experience of together forming a single body in which their differences are preserved and respected.

Christian Identity

Spiritual dialogue demands that those who engage in it question themselves about the way they understand Christian identity. What makes me a Christian? Are we not lacking in humility when we say that we are Christians without stopping to ask ourselves what that implies? Are we ready to exhibit more faith than Peter, who denied his master three times (Matt 26:69-75), and who started to sink when he went to meet him on the water (Matt 14:28-32)? Are we able to keep watch with Jesus in the Garden of Gethsemani where his disciples gave in to sleep (Mark 14:37-38)? Are we courageous enough to follow him beyond our preconceived notions and certainties by entering into dialogue with the poor, the outcast, or the one who does not think and believe as we do? To be a disciple of Jesus demands a total commitment, and this commitment is, in itself, a risk, not at the end of the quest, but at its beginning.

To walk in the footsteps of Jesus does not give us a privileged position or protect us against all suffering. It means becoming strong and growing in wisdom through a stripping away of self that lasts until death and resurrection. Christian identity is not defined by belonging to a given community, still less by heredity or the profession of an article of faith. These elements are important, but they alone do not distinguish the disciple of Christ from one who is not.

In his Vipassana meditation retreats N. F. Goenka tells the story of a woman who came to him and said she was a Christian because she believed Jesus to be the Son of God. His response was "So what?" Buddhism challenges Christians by obliging them to be sure they are not simply living by blind faith. Are they really convinced of what they believe, or are they mindlessly repeating a formula? Of what value is a belief if the reality it designates is nothing more than an idea, if it does not bring about total transformation? It is precisely in relation to this demand that we can see the importance of the contemplative life, not as the affair of a few enlightened ones but as the heart of all authentic spirituality. It invites Christians to lay aside everything they hold dear, not rely on any exterior signs, and accept Christ, who comes to them through the silent and transforming power of the Spirit.

Aware of the suspicion that has surrounded the contemplative or mystical life in the Western church, we would be right to ask if it has a future. If Rahner was right, tomorrow's church will be a church of mystics or it will be no church at all. Therefore it has no other choice than to esteem the experience of the divine embodied in an attitude of submission to the spiritual power that heals, transforms, and brings creation to its fullness. The church must become the instrument of God and not vice versa. If the turning of the church toward the contemplative life offers the world a way to find a solution for many of its problems, this manner of life must still be looked at carefully, not romanticized and not instrumentalized by those whose intention is fundamentally reactionary. Since the mystical life still has to find its place in the Western church, these cautions are all the more important.

Since the beginning of the modern age, the mystical life has been relegated to the margins of spirituality, looked on at times with condescension as a bourgeois pursuit of a few privileged people and identified with supernatural and bizarre graces, out of the reach of ordinary Christians and cut off from social concerns. Therefore, if there is to be a future for the mystical life, a rehabilitation will have to take place in a theology and a community that are still suspicious of it, and it will have to be reestablished at the center of a simple life that is filled with the presence of God in the most ordinary circumstances of everyday life. The work of John Main and Thomas Keating offers a sign that this rehabilitation is taking place. Both have promoted contemplative prayer as constant attentiveness to the work of the Spirit, who is present to everyone at every moment. Contemplative prayer, as they present it, is not opposed to devotion; it improves and deepens it. Finally, contemplative prayer is not identified with paranormal phenomena and ecstatic experiences. It is essentially based on love of the divine presence and its self-effacing manifestation in love of the neighbor.

Recapturing the importance of the mystical or contemplative life today by promoting an embodied and pluralistic spirituality demands an in-depth interaction with other religions. That, in brief, is the message of monks engaged in dialogue. However, we can still ask ourselves if we really need Eastern spirituality to bring about this renewal. Would it not be enough to engage in an ecumenical dialogue with the Orthodox Church, which has been able to preserve a sense of interiority? This dialogue should certainly be fostered. Nonetheless, it does not in any way diminish the importance of a spiritual encounter with Asia. There are at least five reasons why this is so.

1. Dialogue with Buddhism or Hinduism generally leads to a contemplative renewal and to the rediscovery of the Greek fathers, the fathers of the desert, and the authors of the Eastern church. In other words, the Eastern religions seem to play a positive role as intermediaries in bringing the two lungs of the church into harmony.

2. A relation with these age-old religions so different from Christianity makes it possible to develop a spirituality of dialogue that can cope with a major external religious influence for the purpose of mutual understanding, without giving in to relativism or adopting a defensive attitude.

3. Contact with Eastern religions offers Christians the chance to explore new spiritual paths. According to Le Saux it provides an opportunity to discover in the Gospel those riches that Christian piety had never dreamed existed (Baumer-Despeigne [1994], 22), and it does this by favoring the development of some of the Zen, Sufi, or Tantric aspects of Christianity. This is all the more true because, as some have recognized, Eastern practices have been worked out in greater detail (Merton [1975], 343; Béthune [2002], 34).

4. Paying attention to these ways is important for advancing the inculturation of the church in Asia, as we have seen in the first chapter.

5. In the West many Christians feel alienated from their parishes and take up the practice of yoga or other types of meditation, finding there a help for their spiritual life. This shows that Western society's openness to Eastern ways can offer such people a means for rediscovering their Christian roots.

But is there not a danger of compromising our Christian identity? There is if this identity is reduced to promoting a certain style of life, a spiritual technique, a particular way of behaving, or a body of rules. Identity in this case becomes a means of consolidating one's position and excluding the stranger. But the disciples of Jesus are those who break down partitions and free love from the narrowness that is characteristic of provincialism. Christians refuse false identities and anything that would create an obstacle to the presence of God or prevent their search for truth. Christian identity is not a fortress or a pretext for waving a banner, be that a creed, a community, a way of life, or even a theology. Identity is strengthened by openness to the other and dying to the self, not by pulling back to a defensive position. Vulnerability and a process of stripping away are what give identity its vigor and authenticity. The symbols of leaven (Matt 13:33; Gal 5:9) or of the grain that dies in order to bear fruit (John 12:24) capture this meaning perfectly.

What is implied here is that Christians do not create their identity; they receive it from the Spirit. To put it another way, they are given it in their encounter with God, just as Jacob received his identity as Israel in his combat with the angel (Gen 32:29). There is, therefore, no need to defend one's identity; it is something to be witnessed to through one's total commitment. To become the incarnation of the Spirit sent by the risen Jesus does not mean controlling the Spirit, but rather following it in all humility in the mystery of the Father, of whom no one can claim to have a clear idea, much less a monopoly. Christians do not reveal their distinctiveness by their attachment to dogmas, for the truth acquired by human knowledge is never complete; instead, they show their distinction by their courageous reception of the mystery that is ceaselessly manifested in ways known only to God. This reception takes place above all in a relationship with the other, in this case in the love of those who do not believe as we do. Those who love can be brought to the point of giving up their very lives, as was so powerfully shown by the Trappist monks of Tibhirine in Algeria. Seen from this perspective, Eastern forms of meditation do not threaten Christian identity; rather, they give support to our reception of the many manifestations of God. Since the demands of dialogue require Christians to be, first and foremost, well rooted in their own tradition, dialogue also invites them to a deeper knowledge of who they are and an attentiveness to the distinctiveness of their own identity.

Dialogue and Mission

As has been seen in previous chapters, European and American monks have gradually distanced themselves from the Asian church and its process of inculturation. Does this signify a rupture between dialogue and mission? In an unpublished text written in 1979, shortly after the creation of the subcommissions, Tholens wrote, "We have left behind the familiar way of apologetics and mission and a new horizon has opened up—not that of a new missionary approach, but that of living together with the members of other religions and sharing what we have in common!"

There had always been a refusal to engage in a coercive form of mission that oppressed religious liberty and worked out strategies for conversion, no matter how subtle they might have been. However, dialogue did not and does not supplant mission, nor is it identified with it. What is happening is that interreligious dialogue, while it identifies itself as a completely separate activity, is at the same time shaping a new way of understanding mission and engaging in missionary activity. Furthermore, although mission is now generally regarded as the responsibility of the local church, that does not prevent—in fact, it encourages—cooperation between the Christian monks of Asia and those of the West.

In a world that is being overrun by fundamentalism, dialogue becomes a key element in a new way of looking at mission, which, in turn, is the responsibility of all the baptized, as was stressed by the encyclical *Fidei Donum* of Pius XII and the decree *Ad Gentes* of Vatican II. The 1984 pontifical document on the link between dialogue and mission, *The Attitude of the Church Toward Followers of Other Religions: Reflections and Orientations on Dialogue and Mission* (DM), sees dialogue as the norm and ideal of the Christian attitude. This text is important for the issue we are considering because it was inspired in part by the monastic experience of dialogue. Marie-Robert de Floris, who headed the secretariat for mission, was a member of a committee from the European interreligious commission that helped prepare this text defining how mission and dialogue are related. In the document can be found matters that are important to a mission proper to monks involved in dialogue, even if the final version of the document blurs their influence somewhat. Mission tends to be redefined not in opposition to evangelization but in the light of a new way of understanding evangelization. This new approach, briefly described below, defines mission by its goal, its foundation, and its practice.

Monks who are involved in dialogue do not put aside the inculturation of the church or the conversion of non-Christians, but these are not the center of their attention. They are more concerned about the critical state of humanity and want to offer a solution. They have in view two goals that complement and condition one another. The first concerns peace: working for the common good, promoting justice, and advancing communion among all people. In order to do that it is necessary to show initiative and create new ways of doing things. In this matter monks involved in dialogue have much to offer and are fully in accord with the mandate given by Paul VI at the United Nations in 1965: "To think in a new way about human beings, about their life in common, and about the paths of history and the destiny of the world." The pope reiterated this sense of urgency when he said in his encyclical *Populorum progressio* (1967), "'Seek and you shall find.' Blaze the trails to mutual cooperation among men, to deeper knowledge and more widespread charity, to a way of life marked by true brotherhood, to a human society based on mutual harmony" (PP, 85).

The second goal refers to conversion, understood as a humble return to God with the desire to become totally submissive. Conversion can certainly involve changing one's religion, but what is most characteristic of it is self-transcendence, passing from death to new life under the action of divine grace (DM 37). What is involved is assisting the salvific process active in the heart of each person and thus responding to the call of Paul VI, namely, "to consolidate and expand their collaborative efforts to reduce man's immoderate self-love and haughty pride, to eliminate quarrels and rivalries . . . so that a more human way of living is opened to all, with each man helping others out of brotherly love" (PP, 82).

The basis of a broader understanding of mission is the Holy Spirit, who directs Christians toward two fundamental attitudes: love and humility with regard to the boundless gifts of God. From its dwelling place in the human heart the Spirit endows people with the fire of love, draws them into relationships, and makes it possible for them to overcome deepseated differences (DM 44). The Spirit is the bond between the unity of all beings germinating in the heart of every person and its future realization. This same Spirit "directs the carrying out of God's design in the history of the individual and of all humanity until the time when God's children who are dispersed by sin will be reunited as one (see John 11:52)" (DM 43).

In addition to guiding human beings toward communion, the Spirit discloses the infinite riches of the gifts of God. The Spirit, who is the source of every true prayer, also breathes in places unknown to the Christian and gives witness to the faith that truth—which is not something to be possessed—is constantly being discovered in relationship with other believers. Salvation, therefore, is not the responsibility of any particular group, but of all believers, Christians and others, who are together called to communion in the universal Spirit and to sharing their spiritual riches, which might be thought of as a great world heritage.

Finally, monks involved in dialogue honor their calling by a twofold approach. First of all, they follow and place themselves at the service of the Spirit, the one who brings about conversion, and not human beings (DM 39). This fidelity to the Spirit may call for the questioning of institutions that can get in the way of conversion. Thus the starting point for mission is not the other or the other's defects, but we ourselves and our own defects. This way of understanding mission demands that we remove the plank from our own eye before pointing to the speck in the eye of our partner in dialogue (Matt 7:3-5).

Le Saux did indeed speak of India as "a land that is not yet Christian," but he also criticized Christian institutions that are so dogmatically rigid they get in the way of openness to the breath and redemptive light of the Spirit. He believed that the crisis we face today has come about because institutionalized religions have cut themselves off from life (Le Saux [1981], 205) and thus become an obstacle between the believer and Christ, between the Christian and humanity.

The second approach by which monks involved in dialogue honor their calling is by becoming pilgrims, and, in virtue of being pilgrims, missionaries, which is the vocation of all the baptized (DM 10). Being a pilgrim means walking alongside other believers toward a common destiny. The only way one can plumb the depths of one's own self is through a relationship with the other. Dialogue in depth makes it possible to open oneself more completely to the divine mystery, a mystery that coincides with that of every being. Le Saux believed that the remedy for the current crisis is to be found by looking for it together (Le Saux [1981], 210), an idea seconded by Tholens and recalled at the meetings that took place at Petersham and Loppem.

All people of good will, all who are in search of truth, are called, whatever their religious affiliation, to share the riches that flow from their respective traditions, to draw closer to the source that unites them, and together to preserve a spiritual presence in the world. It is by the sharing of religious experience that the human race has progressed and will continue to progress toward a fuller grasp of the divine mystery.

This spiritual journey does not lead to relativism or, even less, the fusion of all traditions into some kind of super-religion. In sum, a broader conception of mission means dedicating oneself to the mutual transformation that comes about when each of the dialogue partners awakens to what is most essential in their own tradition. Rather than demanding that others submit to their teaching, Christian monks direct them to what is best in their own. But, to repeat, this does not mean that they remain silent about their own beliefs and deepest longings. On the contrary, it means manifesting their desire to share what is most precious to them in order to help their partners in dialogue discover the source of that treasure in their own hearts (Le Saux [1981], 210). It was out of fidelity to this spirit that the American subcommission entered into dialogue with Muslims during the first Gulf War. On April 20, 1991, Armand Veilleux wrote to Katherine Howard, executive secretary of the subcommission, "It is important to make known in the West the spiritual depth of Islam."

Conversion is, therefore, reciprocal; one's own religious experience is enriched and purified by interaction. The Christian is called to become a better Christian; the Buddhist, a better Buddhist; the Hindu, a better Hindu. True communion is found when Christians and non-Christians live together in full commitment to their own internal convictions (Le Saux [1981], 220). That is also the way proposed by the Constitution on the Church in the Modern World: "Every group must take into account the needs and legitimate aspirations of every other group, and still more of the human family as a whole" (*Gaudium et Spes*, 26).

When monks who are engaged in dialogue put this Christian ideal into practice they are doing what was already put forward in 1883 at the first Parliament of the World's Religions in Chicago by the amazing Hindu teacher, Vivekananda. According to him, "The Christian is not to become a Hindu or a Buddhist, nor is the Hindu or Buddhist to become Christian. But members of each religion must assimilate the spirit of the others and yet preserve their individuality and grow according to their own law of growth."[50]

In making this proposal Vivekananda, who was very much ahead of his time, expressed an important dimension of the mission of monks in dialogue, to which all the baptized are called. Each person has the responsibility to be receptive, to listen to the other, and to detect the gifts received from God. The other is not an emptiness to be filled but a fullness to be discovered. Following Jesus, Christians are committed to loving other believers by discerning the Spirit that breathes there. In addition, they are invited to know the religion of their dialogue partners by entering into it. By doing this they open themselves to new dimensions of the Trinitarian mystery, allow their Buddhist or

Hindu partners to appreciate their own deepest spiritual longings, and open the doors to the space of authentic encounter.

If over the course of past centuries the dominant model of mission served only to advance a church that was determined to submit the Spirit to a certain idea of God and of Christ, today the monk engaged in dialogue is showing the way to mission at the service of the world by inviting the church to move forward in its search for the Ultimate in submission to the Holy Spirit and the discernment of its many gifts.

Situating mission in a pluralist perspective also introduces the possibility of salvaging the spiritual heritages of humanity that, for various reasons, are increasingly in danger of disappearing. We can think, for example, of the Zen tradition in Japan or of Kashmir Shaivism in India. Whether the waning of these treasures is because of a failure to adapt to modernity, a lack of teachers, or a weakening of practice, it can be arrested by renewal that comes about through interaction. They will not be preserved by the simple repetition of what has always been done. Conservation of spiritual heritages implies both continuity and rupture. They need to be freed of every form of obscurantism and enriched with new insights.

Mission consists in affirming one's roots, but not out of fear of losing one's religious identity, for fear is what feeds narrow-minded and uncompromising traditionalism. The challenge to Christians is to take up again the riches of their own tradition in a spiritual dialogue that is not concerned with strategies for making converts and expanding the faith. By acting in a spirit of true dialogue Christians do not weaken the church, but they do make it vulnerable, as Jesus was vulnerable. Christians trust in the Spirit by letting it direct the results of all activity undertaken in its name. In this way they are free to encounter the other without any reservation and with the greatest attentiveness, conscious of their unique role in joining other believers to promote the "values of the Reign of God, namely justice and peace, freedom and brother- and sisterhood, faith and charity" (Dupuis [2001], 249). If mission consists of assisting the birth of the Spirit in each person by becoming conscious of the manifold gifts of the Spirit, if mission means making free, and if the future of the church and the world depends on this understanding of mission, does it not then make sense to join with monks in delving into a Christian spirituality of dialogue?

Notes

[1] Here and through the rest of the book the term "monk" will be used inclusively to refer to monastic women as well as men. As we shall see, monastic women have played an important role in monastic interreligious dialogue.

[2] "Dialogue is part of the mission of the church." *Documentation catholique* 10 (20 May 1984): 522.

[3] This council was known as the Secretariat for Non-Christian Religions from its creation in 1964 until 1988.

[4] See *The Attitude of the Church Toward Followers of Other Religions: Reflections and Orientations on Dialogue and Mission*, Secretariat for Non-Christians (Pentecost 1984), and *Dialogue and Proclamation. Reflection and Orientations on Interreligious Dialogue and the Proclamation of the Gospel of Jesus*, Pontifical Council for Interreligious Dialogue 77 (Pentecost 1991).

[5] I use the terms "spiritual" and "religious" to describe a particular given experience. I neither oppose them—as is often done today—nor do I make them synonymous. I distinguish them as follows: In a spiritual experience a person's entire beings senses the presence of the transcendent, but at the same time, since the transcendent, by definition, cannot be conceived, the presence remains hidden. Religious experience also designates a relation to the sacred, but as it is conditioned by a vision of the world, community structure, and a body of practices connected with a particular tradition and scriptural corpus. These definitions lead me to believe that it is possible to have a religious experience that is not spiritual, and vice versa.

[6] The term "religious" in this case does not refer to members of apostolic or contemplative religious institutes. It is used in the larger sense of a person whose contact with the divine is mediated by a particular religious tradition.

[7] The sliding back and forth between the terms "interreligious" and "intrareligious" is not fortuitous. The latter term implies the subjectivity or interiority of the spirituality of the person involved in the activity of dialogue. It

does not, therefore, refer to two different forms of dialogue. This distinction underlines the importance of not reducing dialogue to an objective study of religions without taking into account the existential dimension and the relationship to one's faith in the welcome offered to other believers. Thus, complementarity between the *interreligious* dimension of dialogue, which refers above all to the external relationship between the adherents of different religions, and also to the attempt to communicate in order the better to understand one another, and the *intrareligious* dimension that engages the partner in dialogue in an all-encompassing internal dialogue between two different ways of thinking and feeling and calls us to strive to make our own the religious experience of the other in our relation to the Ultimate.

[8] *L'Actualité religieuse dans le monde* 2 (Oct. 1993): 34.

[9] *Bulletin of Monastic Interreligious Dialogue* 48 (1993): 1.

[10] Thomas Merton (1915–1968) was born in France. His mother was from the United States, his father from New Zealand. He spent his youth in Europe and the United States before beginning his studies at Cambridge and then at Columbia University in New York. He was something of a party boy, but his search for meaning drew him in his young adult years toward mysticism and asceticism. His conviction that the gifts of contemplation were at the heart of the Christian life and his desire to put them into practice drew him to enter the Trappist abbey of Gethsemani in 1941. He was ordained a priest in 1949. Merton was a renowned and prolific author, and his vast output includes poetry, articles, essays on prayer, the monastic life, the liturgy, war, nuclear armament, racism, and Eastern religions. What gave unity to his work was his profound dedication to contemplation, which led him toward the end of his life to devote himself to the work of reconciliation of communities, societies, and religions. He was fascinated by Buddhism and Taoism and studied them intensely but did not become familiar with the settings in which they developed. The invitation of Jean Leclercq to participate in the 1968 congress in Bangkok made it possible for him to travel to Asia, where he met the Dalai Lama and wrote his *Asian Journal* before making his way to Bangkok. It was there that he died, accidentally electrocuted in his room.

[11] *North American Board for East-West Dialogue* 16 (1983): 3.

[12] Henri Le Saux (1910–1973) was born at Saint-Briac, a small coastal village in Brittany. Sensing a vocation to the priesthood early in life, he began his seminary studies in Rennes, entered the Benedictine monastery of Sainte-Anne de Kergonan in October 1929, and was ordained a priest in December 1935. His intellectual qualities were put to the service of the community as librarian and professor of church history and patristics. These same qualities also prepared him for more exotic undertakings. At the age of twenty-four Le Saux felt a call to India. He ardently desired to join Jules

Monchanin, a diocesan priest from Lyons who arrived in India as a missionary in 1939. His intention was to live as an Indian and in this way make it possible for Christianity to be expressed in a lifestyle and forms of prayer that were proper to that part of the world. Even though his initial request to leave the monastery was turned down by his superior, Le Saux did not lose hope and began studying Tamil. Finally he was granted his request and arrived in India on 15 August 1948. He never doubted that a most extraordinary adventure awaited him and, through him, the entire church.

[13] Alan Richard Griffiths (1906–1993) was born into a middle-class Anglican family and already gave evidence of strong spiritual leanings when he was a child. At the age of seventeen, when he was taking a walk, he was overcome by the beauty of the sunset and had a mystical experience of a sacred oneness with all of nature. Upon completion of his studies at Oxford he and some friends went off to live in a farmhouse without any of the material comforts he so strongly criticized. They intended to spend all their time with poetry and the reading of religious books. He did not call himself a Christian, but he showed a marked interest in spirituality. With the theologian C. S. Lewis, who was his teacher and friend at Oxford, he became interested in the place of transcendence in English literature. After a number of profound conversion experiences, one of which came after working in a London slum following his studies, Griffiths became a Catholic. The thought that he was no longer at the center of his own life led him to enter the Benedictine abbey of Prinknash near Gloucester, where he took the name Bede. Invited to go to India, he and the Trappist Francis Mahieu founded the monastery of Kurisumala in the mountains of Kerala for the purpose of undertaking as Christians the way of life of the *sannyasi*. Some years later, Henri Le Saux asked him to take over the direction of Shantivanam. He accepted and made India his second home, even though he had gone there with the thought of staying for only a short time.

[14] *North American Board for East-West Dialogue* 31 (1988): 2.

[15] We are indeed speaking about the "North American" subcommission, an organization that is by definition continental. In practice, however, it is only operative in the United States. This is not to say that Canada is excluded, but that, *de facto*, Canadian monks by and large have not become involved in the activities of monastic dialogue. Therefore I will generally refer simply to the "American" subcommission.

[16] *North American Board for East-West Dialogue* 10 (1981): 5.

[17] *North American Board for East-West Dialogue* 7 (1980): 3.

[18] It is convenient to use the word "monk" to refer to Christians, Buddhists, and Hindus because it immediately indicates a certain style of life. But we have to be attentive to the particular way each tradition thinks of the monastic life. We have to distinguish the *monachos* (alone, simple),

the *sadhu* (poor person), the *sannyasi* (renunciant), and the *yogi* (one who transcends opposites) in Hinduism, and the *bhikshu/bhikkhu* (mendicant) in Buddhism. While each approach has its particular characteristics, they all involve detachment from a transitory world, the quest for the Absolute, following a discipline and a master, a sharp awareness of death, poverty, and chastity, and the importance of silence. This same difficulty with terminology is found when we deal with other Christian concepts—"religion," for example—to describe other religious systems.

[19] See the letter of Cardinal Pignedoli in Marie-Robert de Floris, "Dialogue interreligieux monastique. Une nouvelle activité monastique de l'AIM," *Bulletin de l'AIM* 17 (1974): 61–63.

[20] Its American counterpart is known as Alliance for International Monasticism.

[21] *Actes du congrès de Kandy, Sri Lanka*, Vanves (1980): 23.

[22] *Bulletin of Monastic Interreligious Dialogue* 60 (1998): 9.

[23] *Dialogue Interreligieux Monastique. Bulletin de la Commission Francophone d'Europe* 8 (March 1993): 1.

[24] M. Freeman, "Monastic Interreligious Dialogue. Contact Persons Workshop. Christian-Hindu," 13–16 June 1994; report of the Abbey of Saint Procopius, Lisle, Illinois.

[25] "Lettre du Chairman du North American Board à l'AIM," addressed to M.-R. de Floris, Mistassini, 26 February 1980, in *Commission Monastique Interreligieuse*, Secrétariat DIM à Vanves, Circulaire 7 (Feb. 1980).

[26] About Robert Vachon see Joseph Baxer, *An Intercultural Life* (Bloomington IN: Xlibris, 2007).

[27] See "Correspondance entre H. De Lubac s.j. et Jacques Langlais c.s.c.," *Monchanin* 32 (Jan.-Feb. 1972): 2–12, and Robert Vachon, "L'A.I.M. et sa revue," *Interculture* 135 (Oct. 1998): 11.

[28] The conferences by Panikkar and the discussions that followed can be found in *Blessed Simplicity* (1982).

[29] An unpublished paper of Pierre de Béthune titled "Un avis personnel au sujet du NABEWD."

[30] The Alliance for International Monasticism (AIM) in the United States parallels the activities of Aide Inter-Monastères in Paris. Patrick Regan was a member of the board of directors of AIM in Europe, representing the American branch of AIM. The interreligious subcommissions in Europe (DIM) and America (NABEWD) were officially attached only to the office in Paris.

[31] See "Secrétariat D.I.M. à Vanves," Circulaire 2 (July 1978): 2.

[32] Henceforth this document will be referred to as *Letter on Christian Meditation* or simply *Letter*.

[33] See *Bulletin of Monastic Interreligious Dialogue* 52 (1995): 2.

[34] *Dialogue interreligieux monastique. Bulletin de la Commission francophone d'Europe* 9 (Nov. 1993): 8.

[35] "The Buddhist Point of View and the Christian Point of View Regarding Techniques of Meditation."

[36] "Contemplation and Interreligious Dialogue. Orientations and Perspectives Drawn from the Experience of Monks", *Secretariatus pro non christianis* 84 (1993, XXVIII/3): 250–70.

[37] Steve Gruber, Review of Panikkar's *Le dialogue intrareligieux* in *North American Board for East-West Dialogue* 15 (1982): 11.

[38] Mary Margaret Funk, former executive secretary of the American commission, told me in 1994 that many monastic men and women abandon the practice of contemplation for practical reasons such as working for the financial stability of the monastery.

[39] "Lettre aux présidents des Conférences épiscopales sur la spiritualité du dialogue," *Pontificium Consilium pro Dialogo inter Religiones* 101 (1999/2): 266–70.

[40] Patrick Henry, ed., *Benedict's Dharma. Buddhists Reflect on the Rule of Saint Benedict* (New York: Riverhead, 2001).

[41] Donald W. Mitchell and James A. Wiseman, eds., *Finding Peace in Troubled Times: Buddhist and Christian Monastics on Transforming Suffering* (New York: Lantern Books, 2010).

[42] Donald W. Mitchell and William Skudlarek, OSB, eds., *Green Monasticism: A Buddhist-Catholic Response to an Environmental Calamity* (New York: Lantern Books, 2010).

[43] We should be clear that, contrary to common opinion, the identifying marks of a saint are not perfection and virtue but an incomparable experience of God (Joseph Beaude, *La mystique* [Paris: Cerf, 1990], 13; Yves Raguin, *L'attention au mystère. Une entrée dans la vie spirituelle* [Paris: Desclée, 1979], 155), an experience that can be described as "the intellectual, affective, and sensual grasp of a reality that surpasses the ordinary sphere of human experience, and that takes place in ordinary circumstances" (Raguin, *L'attention*, 134).

[44] The term "mystical," as it is used here, does not refer to parapsychological phenomena that can be brought about by spiritual practice, but to the essence of the contemplative life, that is to say, the knowledge or wisdom gained by the person who goes beyond thought and imagination and in wordless silence enters the domain where only faith has meaning and nothing stands in the way of the agonizing and salutary welcoming of divine love.

[45] See the film by Patrice Chagnard, *Swamiji, un voyage intérieur*, C.F.R.T., TF1, 1984. The English version is titled *Abhishiktananda, An Interior Journey*.

[46] Speaking of the Day of Prayer for Peace held in Assisi on 27 October 1986, Pope John Paul II affirmed that "every authentic prayer is inspired by the Holy Spirit, who is mysteriously present in the heart of each person."

Speech to the Cardinals of the Roman Curia, 22 December 1986. *Bulletin du Secrétariat pour les nonchrétiens* 64 (1987): 69.

[47] See *Bulletin of Monastic Interreligious Dialogue* 60 (1998): 8.

[48] See *Documents of the Thirty-Fourth General Congregation of the Society of Jesus* (Saint Louis: The Institute of Jesuit Sources, 1995), 80.

[49] While monks are lay people and not clerics, the renunciation and contemplation that characterize their way of life distinguish them from the believer who is involved in worldly affairs. It used to be thought that their way of life made it possible for monks to attain the highest levels of the contemplative life while lay people, because they continued to be involved in the affairs of the world, could hope for salvation but not a high degree of union with God.

[50] *North American Board for East-West Dialogue* 46 (1993): 10; *Bulletin of Monastic Interreligious Dialogue* 48 (1993): 2.

Bibliography

1. Books and articles cited; listed by author

AMALADOSS, Michael
1994 *Towards Fullness. Searching for an Integral Spirituality*. Bangalore, NBCLC.
1997 *À la rencontre des cultures. Comment conjuguer unité et pluralité dans les Églises?* Paris, Éd. de l'Atelier.

ÅMELL, Katrin
1998 *Contemplation et dialogue. Quelques exemples de dialogue entre spiritualités après le concile Vatican II*. Uppsala, The Swedish Institute of Missionary Research.

ARINZE, Francis
1992 "Letter of Cardinal Francis Arinze on Interreligious Monastic Dialogue." *North American Board for East-West Dialogue* 43, 15–16.
1997 "Spirituality in Dialogue." *Bulletin. Pontificium Consilium pro Dialogo inter Religiones* 96 (1997/3), 371–76.

BALTHASAR, Hans Urs von
1977 "Meditation als Verrat." *Geist und Leben. Zeitschrift für Azese und Mystik* 50, 260–69.
1983 *Des bords du Gange aux rives du Jourdain*. Paris, Saint Paul.

BASSET, Jean-Claude
1996 *Le Dialogue interreligieux. Histoire et avenir*. Paris, Cerf.

BATCHELOR, Stephen
1994 *The Awakening of the West. The Encounter of Buddhism and Western Culture*. Berkeley, Parallax Press.

BAUMER-DESPEIGNE, Odette
1983 "The Spiritual Journey of Henri Le Saux–Abhishiktananda." *Cistercian Studies* 18, 310–29.
1990 "Cheminement spirituel d'Henri Le Saux (Textes inédits)." *La Vie spirituelle* 144, 531–43.
1993 "The Spiritual Way of Henri Le Saux—Swami Abhishiktananda." *Bulletin of Monastic Interreligious Dialogue* 48, 20–25.
1994 "Abhishiktananda." *Bulletin of Monastic Interreligious Dialogue* 51, 17–24.

BEAUDE, Joseph
1990 *La mystique*. Paris, Cerf.

BÉTHUNE, Pierre de
1981 "The Opening Stage of Dialogue with Non-Christian Monks." *North American Board for East-West Dialogue* 12, 9–11.
1998 "The Bond of Peace. A Few Theological Reflections about Interreligious Prayer." *Pontificum Consilium pro Dialogo InterReligiones* 98/2, 159–65.
2002 *By faith and hospitality: the monastic tradition as a model for interreligious encounter*. Leominster, Gracewing.
2003 "De la peur à l'ouverture." *Actualité des religions* 49 (May-June), 37–39.

BLÉE, Fabrice
1996a "Les enjeux du dialogue intrareligieux. Des repères pour une nouvelle spiritualité chrétienne à l'heure du pluralisme religieux." In Camil MÉNARD and Florent VILLENEUVE, eds., *Spiritualité contemporaine. Défis culturels et théologiques*. Montréal, Fides, coll. Héritage et Projet 56, 253–69.
1996b "Une rencontre historique. La rencontre de Gethsémani." *Présence magazine* (November), 5.
1998 "Pour un dialogue entre l'Orient et l'Occident. Mort et Réincarnation chez Lobsang Rampa et chez Sogyal Rinpoche." In Bertrand OUELLET and Richard BERGERON, eds., *Croyances et sociétés*. Montréal, Fides, coll. Héritage et Projet 59, 433–59.
1999a "Aux frontières du silence. Exploration du dialogue interreligieux monastique." *Théologiques* 7/2, 79–94.
1999b "Dialogue et renouveau monastique." *La Vie spirituelle* 731 (June), 257–70.

1999c *Le dialogue interreligieux monastique. L'expérience nordaméricaine. Histoire et analyse*. PhD dissertation, Montréal, Université de Montréal.

2000 "Quelle voie chrétienne-bouddhiste? Pour une articulation de la double appartenance religieuse." In Dennis GIRA and Jacques SCHEUER, eds., *Vivre de plusieurs religions. Promesse ou illusion?* Paris, Atelier, coll. Questions ouvertes, 151–60.

2003a "Le milieu de la pratique Zen. Pour une spiritualité du dialogue." *Origins* 3–4, 23–34.

2003b "Double appartenance religieuse et dialogue interreligieux monastique." *Mission* 10, 9–32.

BUBER, Martin
1970 *I and Thou*. New York, Charles Scribner's Sons.

COFF, Pascaline
1994 "Bede Griffiths: The Man, The Monk, The Mystic." *Bulletin of Monastic Interreligious Dialogue* 51, 24–29.

COMBY, Jean
1992 *Deux mille ans d'évangélisation. Histoire de l'expansion chrétienne.* Paris, Desclée.

CORLESS, Roger
1989 *The Vision of Buddhism*. New York, Paragon House.

CRONIN, Kevin M.
1992 *Kenosis. Emptying Self and the Path of Christian Service*. Rockport, Element.

DALAI-LAMA
1996 *The Good Heart. A Buddhist Perspective on the Teachings of Jesus*. Somerville MA, Wisdom Publications.

D'AQUILI, Eugene, and Andrew B. NEWBERG
1999 *The Mystical Mind. Probing the Biology of Religious Experience*. Minneapolis, Fortress Press.

DINGES, William
1978 "Parliament of World Religions—1893—US Forerunner of Present East-West Encounter." *North American Board for East-West Dialogue* 3, 4–5.

DREVET, Camille, ed.
1967 *Massignon et Gandhi. La contagion de la vérité.* Paris, Cerf.

DUMOULIN, Heinrich
1974 *Christianity Meets Buddhism.* Lasalle, Open Court.

DUPUIS, Jacques
2001 *Christianity and the Religions: From Confrontation to Dialogue.* New York, Orbis Books.

FLORIS, Marie-Robert de
1977 "Abbots' Congress—Rome, September 1997. Dom M. Robert de Floris: Report on A.I.M. Secretariat." *A.I.M. Bulletin* 23.

FREEMAN, Laurence
2000 *Jesus, the Teacher Within.* New York, Continuum.

GADILLE, Jacques
1983 *La mutation des modèles missionnaires au XXe siècle. Expériences d'inculturation chrétienne.* Les cahiers de l'Institut catholique de Lyon 12.

GERRY, Joseph
1997 "Gethsemani—U.S.A.: Gethsemani Buddhist-Christian Encounter on Spiritual Life, Prayer, and Meditation, 22–27 July 1996." *Pontificium Consilium pro Dialogo inter Religiones* 95 (1997/2), 216–19.

GIRA, Dennis
1989 *Comprendre le bouddhisme.* Paris, Centurion.
1991 *Les Religions.* Paris, Centurion.

GIRA, Dennis, and Jacques SCHEUER, eds.
2000 *Vivre de plusieurs religions. Promesse ou illusion?* Paris, Atelier, coll. Questions ouvertes.

GORDAN, Paul
1979 "Interreligious Dialogue and the A.I.M.." *A.I.M. Bulletin* 27, 43–45.

GREGORIOS, Paulos M.
2000 *Religion and Dialogue.* Delhi, ISPCK.

GRIFFITHS, Bede
1982 *The Marriage of East and West: A Sequel to the Golden String.* London, Collins.
1992 *The New Creation in Christ.* Springfield, Templegate.

GUARDINI, Romano
1996 *The Lord*. Washington DC, Regnery.

JOHN OF THE CROSS
2009 *The Ascent of Mount Carmel*. Charleston SC, Bibliolife LLC.

JOHNSTON, William
1995 *Mystical Theology. The Science of Love*. Maryknoll, NY, Orbis Books.

KAPLEAU, Philip
1989 *The Three Pillars of Zen*. New York, Doubleday Anchor.

KEATING, Thomas
1992 *Open Mind Open Heart. The Contemplative Dimension of the Gospel*. Rockport, Element.
1993 "The Christian Contemplative Tradition." *North American Board for East-West Dialogue* 46, 11.

KEATING, Thomas, Basil PENNINGTON, and Thomas E. CLARKE
1978 *Finding Grace at the Center*. Petersham, St. Bede's Publications.

KUTTIANIMATTATHIL, Jose
1995 *Practice and Theology of Interreligious Dialogue: A Critical Study of the Indian Christian Attempts Since Vatican II*. Bangalore, Kristu Jyoti Publications.

LAVIGNE, Denyse
1978 "Petersham . . . a threshold." *North American Board for East- West Dialogue* 2, 4–5.

LECLERCQ, Jean
1986 *Nouvelle page d'histoire monastique. Histoire de l'A.I.M. 1960–1985*. Paris, Publication de l'A.I.M.

LEVI-STRAUSS, Claude
1992 *Tristes Tropiques*. Paris, Union générale des Éditeurs.

LE SAUX, Henri (Swami Abhishiktananda)
1965 *La rencontre de l'hindouisme et du christianisme*. Paris, Seuil.
1967 *Prayer*. Delhi, ISPCK.
1981 "The Depth-Dimension of Religious Dialogue." *Vidyajyoti* 45, 202–21.
1998 *Ascent to the Depth of the Heart. The Spiritual Diary of Swami Abhishiktananda (1948–1973)*. Delhi, ISPCK.

LIPSKI, Alexander
1983 *Thomas Merton and Asia: His Quest for Utopia*. Kalamazoo, Cistercian Publications.

MACINNES, Elaine
2003 *Zen Contemplation for Christians*. Oxford, Sheed and Ward.

MASSEIN, Pierre
1979 "Le Point de vue bouddhiste et le point de vue chrétien sur les techniques de méditation." *Bulletin de l'A.I.M.* 27, 50–55.

MATUS, Thomas
1984 *Yoga and the Jesus Prayer Tradition. An Experiment in Faith*. Ramsey NJ, Paulist Press.

MERTON, Thomas
1960 *The Wisdom of the Desert*. New York, New Directions.
1972 *New Seeds of Contemplation*. New York, New Directions.
1975 *The Asian Journal of Thomas Merton*. New York, New Directions.
1995 *Thoughts on the East*. New York, New Directions.

MITCHELL, Donald W., and James WISEMAN
2010 *The Spiritual Life: A Dialogue of Buddhist and Christian Monastics*. New York: Lantern Books.

MOFFITT, John
1979 "Memories of Thomas Merton." *Cistercian Studies* 14.

O'HANLON, Daniel
1974 "Les Moines d'Asie découvrent l'Asie." *Bulletin de l'A.I.M.* 16, 7–27.

O'HARA, Mary L.
1977 "Report of the Meeting on Inter-Religious Dialogue held at Maria Assumpta Academy, Petersham, Mass. U.S.A., 4–13 June 1977." Unpublished report.

PANIKKAR, Raimon
1982 *Blessed Simplicity: The Monk as Universal Archetype*. New York, Seabury.
1999 *The Intrareligious Dialogue*. New York, Paulist Press.
2006 *The Experience of God: Icons of the Mystery*. Minneapolis, Fortress Press.

PAUL VI
1963 "Discours de S.S. Paul VI lors de l'ouverture de la deuxième session du Concile." In Paul-Aimé MARTIN, ed., *Vatican II. Les enseignements conciliaires. Texte intégral*. Montréal, Fides, 2001, 673–82.

PENNINGTON, Basil
1978a "The Petersham Meeting: Spirituality for a World Culture." *Bulletin de l'A.I.M.* The English Edition 24 (1988) 47–53.
1978b "Centering Prayer." In *Finding Grace at the Center*. Petersham, St. Bede's Publications, 5–6.

PIERIS, Aloysius
1988 "East in the West: resolving a spiritual crisis." *Monastic Studies* 18 (1988), 79–90.

RAGUIN, Yves
1979 *L'attention au mystère. Une entrée dans la vie spirituelle*. Paris, Desclée.

RAHNER, Karl, and Herbert VORGRIMMLER
1970 *Petit dictionnaire de théologie catholique*. Paris, Seuil.

RATZINGER, Joseph
1989 Letter to the Bishops of the Catholic Church on some Aspects of Christian Meditation. Available online at http://www.cin.org/users/james/files/meditation.htm (accessed 28 April 2010).

ROSSANO, Pietro
1981 "Dialog between Christian and non-Christian Monks: Opportunities and Difficulties." *North American Board for East-West Dialogue*. 10.

ST-ROMAIN, Philip
1991 *Kundalini Energy and Christian Spirituality*. New York, Crossroad.

STUART, James
2000 *Swami Abhishiktananda. His Life Told through His Letters*. Delhi, ISPCK.

TEILHARD DE CHARDIN, Pierre
1975 *Toward the Future*. New York and London, Helen and Kurt Wolff Book, Harcourt Brace Jovanovich.

THEISEN, Jerome
1995 "Abbot Primate Announces New General Secretariat." *Bulletin of Monastic Interreligious Dialogue* 52, 2.

THOLENS, Cornelius
1975 "Une Enquête auprès des monastères d'Occident pour la poursuite du dialogue inter-religieux." *Bulletin de l'A.I.M.* 19, 49–53.
1979 "Vibration of Love and the Pastoral Dimensions of Contemplation." *North American Board for East-West Dialogue* 5, 3–6.

THURSTON, Bonnie
1994 "Why Merton Looked East." *Bulletin of Monastic Interreligious Dialogue* 49, 20–24.

VEILLEUX, Armand
1980 "Lettre du Chairman du North American Board à l'A.I.M." Addressed to M.-R. de Floris, Mistassini, 26 February 1980. In *Commission Monastique Interreligieuse*. Secrétariat D.I.M. à Vanves, Circulaire 7 (February).

2. Documents cited, in alphabetical order by title or by the commonly used abbreviations

(Note: Most Vatican and papal documents are available in English on the Vatican website: www.vatican.va. They can most easily be accessed by going to the website and then to the appropriate link: "Papal Archive," "Roman Curia," or "Resource Library" [II Vatican Council]. However, the specific web address for each document available in English is also provided.)

Ad Gentes: On the Mission Activity of the Church (Vatican II) http://www.vatican.va/archive/hist_councils/ii_vatican_council/documents/vat-ii_decree_19651207_ad-gentes_en.html

DP—*Dialogue and Proclamation: Reflection And Orientations On Interreligious Dialogue and The Proclamation Of The Gospel Of Jesus Christ* (Pontifical Council for Inter-religious Dialogue) http://www.vatican.va/roman_curia/pontifical_councils/interelg/documents/rc_pc_interelg_doc_19051991_dialogue-and-proclamatio_en.html

Bibliography 219

DM— "Attitude de l'Église catholique devant les croyants des autres religions. Réflexions et orientations concernant le dialogue et la mission. " *Secretariatus pro non christianis* (Pentecost 1984). The only version available on the Vatican website is in Portuguese: http://www.vatican.va/roman_curia/pontifical_councils/interelg/documents/rc_pc_interelg_doc_19840610_dialogo-missione_po.html

EMDI—«Expériences monastiques de dialogue interreligieux». *Bulletin international des commissions pour le dialogue interreligieux monastique*, numéro spécial (F. 14), 63 pages. The English version appears in the *Bulletin of Monastic Interreligious Dialogue*, 70 (March 2003) 21–60.

FD—PIUS XII *Fidei Donum: On the Present Condition of the Catholic Missions, Especially in Africa* (Encyclical) http://www.vatican.va/holy_father/pius_xii/encyclicals/documents/hf_p-xii_enc_21041957_fidei-donum_en.html

Gaudium et Spes: Pastoral Constitution on the Church in the Modern World (Vatican II) http://www.vatican.va/archive/hist_councils/ii_vatican_council/documents/vat-ii_const_19651207_gaudium-et-spes_en.html

JPBW—*Jesus Christ the Bearer of the Water of Life: A Christian Reflection on the "New Age"* (Pontifical Council for Inter-religious Dialogue) http://www.vatican.va/roman_curia/pontifical_councils/interelg/documents/rc_pc_interelg_doc_20030203_new-age_en.html

Nostra Aetate: The Relation of the Church to Non-Christian Religions (Vatican II) http://www.vatican.va/archive/hist_councils/ii_vatican_council/documents/vat-ii_decl_19651028_nostra-aetate_en.html

PP—PAUL VI, *Populorum progressio: On the Development of Peoples* (Encyclical) http://www.vatican.va/holy_father/paul_vi/encyclicals/documents/hf_p-vi_enc_26031967_populorum_en.html

RE—PAUL VI, "Constitution apostolique *Regimini Ecclesiæ universæ* sur la Curie romaine." *Documentation catholique* 1500 (3 September 1967), 1441–73. Available in Italian and Latin on the Vatican website at http://www.vatican.va/holy_father/paul_vi/apost_constitutions/index.htm

RM—JOHN PAUL II, *Redemptoris missio: On the Permanent Validity of the Church's Missionary Mandate* (Encyclical) http://www.vatican.va/edocs/ENG0219/_INDEX.HTM

Index

Names

Abhishiktananda, 33, 42 (*See* Le Saux, Henri)
Amaladoss, Michael, 26, 190
Åmell, Katrin, 50, 129
Aitken, Robert, 41
Alvarez Velasco, Ramon, 148
Arinze, Francis, 122ff., 138, 147f., 189

Balthasar, Hans Urs von, 116f., 122
Basilides, 170
Basset, Jean-Claude, 18
Batchelor, Stephen, 8, 67, 77
Baumer-Despeigne, Odette, 65, 131, 155, 196
Benedict, Saint, 7, 10, 13, 30f., 44, 53, 55, 80, 137, 177, 188
Bernard of Clairvaux, Saint, 8
Béthune, Pierre-François de, 67f., 81, 87, 90, 98, 105f., 110f., 115, 121f., 124ff., 130ff., 134f., 142, 145, 151, 154, 157f., 173, 183f., 196
Billot, Benoît, 15f., 170
Blavatsky, Helena, 77
Blée, Fabrice, 4, 6, 67, 82, 118, 138, 141, 163, 173

Buber, Martin, 182, 184
Buddha, 41, 75, 161
Burnouf, Eugene, 77

Chaduc, Marc, 47, 155
Cicognani, Amleto Giovanni, 27
Clark, Thomas, 120
Clement of Alexandria, Saint, 170
Coff, Pascaline, 37, 44, 86, 99, 112, 119, 131, 189
Colin, Marie-Bruno, 190
Columban, Saint, 13, 178
Confucius, 39
Congar, Yves, 18
Corless, Roger, 57
Cuttat, Jacques-Albert, 19

Daine, Christine, 153
Dalai Lama, 29, 43, 83, 99, 109, 141ff., 206
Dammertz, Victor, 56, 105, 188
D'Aquili, Eugene, 191f.
De Mello, Anthony, 190
Dennis the Areopagite, 115
Desideri, Ippolito, 20
Dinges, William, 77
Dreuille, Mayeul de, 25, 66, 87, 91, 95f., 112
D'Souza, Eugene, 37

Index 221

D'Souza, Patrick, 26
Dumoulin, Heinrich, 40, 166, 190
Dupuche, John, 147
Dupuis, Jacques, 148f., 203
Dürckheim, C. G., 125

Eckhart, 115
Enomiya-Lassalle, Hugo M., 33, 95, 190
Evagrius of Pontus, 170

Floris, Marie-Robert de, 35, 56, 63, 84f., 95, 199
Francis of Assisi, Saint, 179
Freeman, Laurence, 147, 152, 156, 178
Funk, Mary Margaret, 99, 189

Gadille, Jacques, 19
Gandhi, 29
Gira, Dennis, 6, 138, 192
Gnanananda, 47
Goenka, N. F., 194
Gordan, Paul, 66, 90
Gregorios, Mar, 26
Gregory the Great, Saint, 29
Griffiths, Bede, 9, 29, 33, 38, 42ff., 47f., 59, 64, 66f., 73, 77, 96, 108, 120, 140, 147, 156, 167
Gruber, Steve, 130
Guardini, Romano, 192
Guigo the Carthusian, 126

Howard, Katherine, 105, 110, 202
Hunt, Kevin, 81
Huxley, Aldous, 40

Ignatius of Loyola, Saint, 181
Irudayam, Ignatius, 190

Jacob, 197
Jäger, Willigis, 169
John XXIII, 3
John of the Cross, Saint, 115f., 157, 171, 178
John Paul II, 2, 83, 118, 168, 189
Johnston, William, 9, 33, 155, 190
Jung, Karl, 68

Kadowaki, Kakishi, 190
Kapleau, Philip, 173
Keating, Thomas, 90f., 103, 111, 120, 125, 156f., 171, 177, 195
Kelly, Timothy, 99, 109, 142
Kennedy, Robert, 190
Kuttianimattathil, Jose, 19

Langlais, Jacques, 87
Lao Tzu, 39
Lavigne, GilChrist (Denyse) 52, 96, 100, 187
Leclercq, Jean, 17, 24, 26ff., 30ff., 42, 57, 62, 70f., 75, 77, 81, 85f., 89, 94ff., 206
Le Saux, Henri, 9, 18, 21, 33f., 37f., 42–48, 59, 64f., 72f., 93, 115, 126, 128f., 131f., 140, 144f., 147, 153–57, 167, 171, 183, 196, 201f.
Levi-Strauss, Claude, 192
Lipski, Alexander, 39, 41
Lubac, Henri de, 18f., 87
Luther, Martin, 8

MacInnes, Elaine, 39, 179
Maha Ghosananda, 100, 180
Mahieu, Francis (Acharya), 33, 66
Main, John, 125, 177, 195
Marcion, 170

Massein, Pierre, 117f.
Matus, Thomas, 147, 156
Meninger, Willing, 90
Merton, Thomas, 8, 27–30, 33ff., 38–43, 47f., 54, 68, 74, 76, 81, 94, 117, 127, 140ff., 151, 156, 177, 179, 196, 206
Misquitta, Iona, 190
Mitchell, Donald, 131, 142, 166
Moffitt, John, 26, 30, 33
Monchanin, Jules, 19, 21, 44, 47, 64, 87
Montanus, 170
Mother Angelica, 91
Mother Theresa, 29
Müller, Robert, 53, 89

Newberg, Andrew B., 191f.
Nobili, Roberto de, 20
Novalis, F., 77

O'Hanlon, Daniel, 53
O'Hara, Mary L., 54, 67, 72, 96
Oshida, Shigeto, 33

Panikkar, Raimon, 4, 21, 30, 67, 87f., 93, 109, 124f., 128–31, 149, 152, 174, 183
Pantajali, 41
Paul, Saint, 169
Paul VI, 20, 27, 31, 118, 189, 199
Peelman, Achiel, 190
Pennington, Basil, 54, 58, 86, 90, 134
Pieris, Aloysius, 68, 172, 190
Pignedoli, Sergio, 58–61, 122, 189
Pius XI, 15

Radcliffe, Timothy, 153

Rahner, Karl, 7, 18, 169, 194
Ramana Maharshi, 32, 47
Ratzinger, Joseph, 113, 116, 118ff., 122, 128, 168
Regan, Patrick, 91, 103, 111f.
Ricci, Matteo, 20
Rogers, Murray, 19
Rossano, Pietro, 58–61

Samy, Ama, 119, 190
Sénécal, Bernard, 190
Simeon the New Theologian, 149
Somdet Phra Ariavong Sankarat, 27, 93
Soos, Marie-Bernard de, 105
Steindl-Rast, David, 41, 81, 86
St-Romain, Philip, 155ff.
Stuart, James, 19, 154, 157
Suzuki, Daisetz, 40

Tai Situ Rinpoche, 108
Teilhard de Chardin, Pierre, 192
Theisen, Jerome, 55, 107
Tholens, Cornelius, 15–18, 23, 25, 50, 54, 61ff., 75, 81f., 86, 88f., 94, 96, 109, 198, 201
Thurston, Bonnie, 39f.
Tonini, Simone, 98, 102f.

Vachon, Robert, 87
Valentine, 170
Valéri, Pia, 190
Veilleux, Armand, 84f., 96, 110, 129, 202
Vivekananda, 202
Voltaire, 77

Weakland, Rembert, 32, 56, 61, 93

Zago, Marcello, 75f.

Subjects

Abbot Primate, 32, 55f., 58, 61, 66f., 85, 93, 97, 102, 104f., 107f., 111, 188f.
Ad Gentes, 22, 36, 198
Africa, 15–18, 21, 23f., 108
Agape, 172, 176 (*See* Love)
Aide à l'implantation monastique, 16, 23, 65 (*See* AIM)
Aide inter-monastères, 65 (*See* AIM)
AIM, 16, 23f., 28, 31, 35, 38, 50f., 56f., 60–63, 65ff., 70, 75, 85–89, 90, 92, 101–8, 117, 123f., 126, 189
Alliance for International Monasticism, 105 (*See* AIM)
America, American (North), 34, 37, 39, 42, 50, 55, 56f., 63ff., 66f., 70, 73, 81, 82–86, 88–92, 99, 102–12, 119f., 123f., 129ff., 137, 141, 156, 160, 189f., 198, 202 (*See* United States)
Anchorites, 177
Anglicans, 190
Anthropology, 79, 154f., 175
Antichrist, 117
Apatheia, 75
Asceticism, ascetical, ascetic, 14, 35, 37, 40f., 43ff., 47f., 57, 69, 73, 75, 78, 80, 82, 102, 118, 121, 126, 133, 157, 159, 162, 165, 173f., 181
Ashram, 19, 25, 42, 44, 45f., 61, 64f., 89, 93
Asia, Asian, 1, 7, 9f., 14, 19, 23–28, 30–33, 35–38, 41–45, 47f., 50f., 55ff., 59, 61ff., 65–69, 72–77, 79f., 82f., 91, 93ff., 102, 108, 113, 115f., 122f., 126, 129, 141, 156, 160, 164, 168, 192f., 196, 198
Assisi, 106, 138, 140, 143
Atman, 167
Australian Monastic Encounter (AME), 108

Bangalore, 24ff., 28, 30, 32f., 35f., 53, 56f., 53, 56f., 59, 61, 70, 81, 96, 117, 122
Bangkok, 24f., 27f., 30–33, 35, 38, 57, 59, 61, 67, 81, 93ff., 117, 122, 129, 142, 189
Benedictine/s, 5ff., 13f., 15, 17, 23ff., 27f., 32f., 43, 45f., 48, 51, 53, 55f., 58, 60ff., 66, 68, 72, 83, 87, 97, 101ff., 104f., 107f., 110, 115–18, 123, 127f., 130, 147f., 169, 177f., 188ff.
Benedictine Interfaith Dialogue (BID), 108
Brahman, 167
Brahmins, 64
Buddhism, Buddhist, 5f., 8, 11, 14, 24–29, 32, 34f., 38–43, 48, 53, 56f., 59, 62, 67, 69, 71ff., 75f., 80, 82f., 89, 108f., 115f., 120f., 124, 126, 129, 133f., 137f., 141f., 144, 149, 159ff., 163f., 166ff., 172–75, 180f., 186, 189f., 192ff., 196, 202

Cabalistic, 193 (*See* Judaism)
Carmelites, 178
Celibacy, 79
Centering Prayer, 50, 90f., 119ff., 125
Centre Monchanin in Montreal, 87

Chakras, 155, 164
Christ, 16ff., 22, 29f., 48, 60, 65, 78, 114, 134, 137, 140, 146, 149f., 153, 164, 171f., 194, 201, 203; Jesus Christ, 3, 80; Jesus, 114, 146, 149, 152, 164, 166, 176, 179, 184ff., 194, 197, 202f.
Church, 1f., 5–9, 11, 15–18, 20, 22ff., 31, 36f., 39, 44, 48–51, 55f., 58ff., 62f., 65, 70, 77f., 80, 83f., 86, 89f., 101, 113, 115ff., 121ff., 125f., 129, 132, 135, 138f., 143, 146, 148ff., 161ff., 168–72, 179, 187f., 190, 194ff., 198f., 202ff.
Cistercians, 14, 56, 177, 189f.
Cloud of Unknowing, The, 90
Communion of saints, 148, 150f.
Confucianism, 41
Congregation for the Doctrine of the Faith, 102, 113, 122f.
Contemplation, 3, 8, 11, 15, 21f., 31, 41, 45, 70, 74, 115, 120, 123–27, 137, 141, 145, 154, 156f., 159, 173, 177, 181; Contemplative/s, 5, 11, 22f., 42, 46, 52, 68, 80, 84, 145f., 170f., 179, 188, 190; Contemplative life/prayer/practice/etc., 6, 15, 21ff., 25, 27, 30ff., 36f., 39, 46, 51, 61, 69, 76, 90, 91, 117, 119–21, 125ff., 130–33, 139f., 145, 153, 155f., 159, 169–75, 176, 187, 190, 193–96; *Contemplation et dialogue*, 123, 137, 154; Contemplative Outreach, 90
Creation, 147, 149, 154, 195
Crusades, 8, 180

Dharamsala, 41
Dharmakaya, 41f.
Death, 149, 162, 178, 183, 194, 199
Desert, 7, 9, 139, 175–79, 182–85; Desert of otherness, 139, 175f., 180–84, 186
Dialogue Interreligieux Monastique (DIM), 28, 50, 71, 97f., 103–8, 110f., 124, 189
Dialogue and Mission, 5, 127, 145, 198
Dialogue and Proclamation, 3, 145
Dialogue of life, 3, 187, 191
Discernment, 23, 74, 122, 127, 145, 181, 203
Dzochen, 35

Eastern Church, 196
Ecumenical, 140, 191, 195
Emptiness, 35, 39, 42, 114, 153, 164, 167f., 202 (*See sunyata*)
Europe, European, 5, 7, 9, 13, 15f., 31, 45, 50, 55, 63–67, 70, 75f., 79, 82f., 85, 89, 97f., 102–12, 116, 123f., 137, 141, 160, 177f., 190, 198f.
Evangelization, 3,7, 13, 22, 33, 36, 199

Faith, 3ff., 10, 16–20, 26, 29, 31, 33, 35, 41, 54, 77, 81, 84, 87, 90, 130f., 134, 137f., 140, 145, 147–50, 158, 160, 164, 165f., 170ff., 175, 178, 183, 185, 193f., 200, 203
Fathers of the desert, 34, 120, 178f., 196
Fathers of dialogue, 33, 37f., 73, 126, 128, 173
Fidei Donum, 16f., 23, 198

Ganges, 128, 157
Gaudium et Spes, 26, 117
Gethsemani Abbey, 40f., 109; Gethsemani Encounter I, 99f., 131, 138, 141–44, 180, 189f.; Gethsemani Encounter II, 144; Gethsemani Encounter III, 144; Garden of Gethsemani, 194
Gnosis, 169–72
Gnostic, Gnosticism, 113, 152, 160, 168–72
God, 1, 3, 9, 15ff., 22f., 37, 39, 41, 43, 46f., 76, 78, 80, 113ff., 117f., 120, 134f., 137, 140, 148ff., 158, 161, 164ff., 167–71, 178, 180ff., 184ff., 194f., 197, 199f., 202f.; Experience of God, 26, 29ff., 45, 48, 158
Göttweig, 106, 108, 124
Grace, 23, 29, 38, 47, 114, 145, 149, 151, 157f., 166f., 175, 195, 199
Greek fathers, 196
Guha, 43
Gulf War, 202
Guru, 45, 47, 65

Hara, 158
Hell, 175f., 183
Hinayana, 173
Hindu, Hinduism, 5, 11, 14, 21, 24ff., 28f., 32, 34f., 38, 41, 43–46, 48, 53, 56f., 59, 62, 64f., 67, 69, 71ff., 75f., 80, 87, 89, 108, 115, 121, 124, 126, 128f., 133f., 137f., 149, 153ff., 159ff., 163f., 167, 172, 192f., 196, 202f.
Hippies, 25, 70
Holy Spirit, 25, 47, 54, 80, 114, 130, 147, 153ff., 157, 200, 203

Index   225

Holyoke, 57, 67, 84, 88, 103
Homo religiosus, 59
Hospitality, 4ff., 14, 45, 52, 80–83, 99, 133, 151, 166, 181, 183, 189

Identity, 2, 26, 51, 56, 66, 76, 113, 127, 134, 138, 150, 167, 178, 185, 188, 193–98, 203
Idolatry, 167
Inculturation, 26, 44, 56, 60, 62, 64, 125, 196, 198f.
India, 1, 7, 19f., 26, 28f., 42–45, 47f., 57, 64f., 68, 70, 73, 77, 82f., 108ff., 119, 131, 155, 173, 190, 201, 203
Inner dialogue, 4, 21 (*See* Intrareligious dialogue)
Inquisition, 180
Institut Catholique in Paris, 117
International Monastic Interreligious Dialogue (DIMMID), 28
Interreligious marriage, 191
Intrareligious dialogue, 10f., 21, 125, 127–33, 152, 163, 184 (*See* inner dialogue)
Islam, 6, 17, 41, 53, 124, 134, 193, 202 (*See* Sufi)

Japan, Japanese, 5, 39f., 82f., 86, 97f., 116, 190, 203
Jesus, (*see* Christ)
Judaism, 6, 124, 193 (*See* Cabalistic)

Kandy, 30, 65
Karma, 175
Kashmir Shaivism, 203
Kingdom of God, 68, 140f., 144–48, 152, 179, 191, 203

Kundalini, 155ff.

Latin America 14 (*See* South America)
Liturgy, 15, 80, 86
Loppem, 50, 52f., 58, 70, 72, 75f., 78ff., 83, 85, 97, 117, 156, 188, 201
Love, 8, 22, 26, 37, 54, 73, 81, 84, 114, 117, 140, 144f., 148f., 167–72, 176, 178, 180–83, 186, 195, 197, 200 (*See Agape*)

Mahayana, 167, 173
Mantra, 46, 120
Maurists, 8
Meditation, 5, 9ff., 14, 25, 34–38, 40f., 43–49, 51f., 57, 59, 69f., 72–76, 78ff., 89, 102, 112–23, 125–28, 139, 141, 143, 147, 154ff., 159–68, 173ff., 188, 191, 194, 196f.
Mission, missionary, 2, 11, 13–69 *passim*, 80, 88, 104ff., 108, 150, 178, 181, 188ff., 193, 198–204
Moksha, 126
Monk as universal archetype, 57, 59, 83, 88
Mysticism, 30, 40ff., 59, 121, 158, 171

Naropa Institute, 73
Negotiation, 55, 108, 144f.
Neurology, 158
New Age, 91, 155, 158, 160, 163–72, 188
Nirvana, 126
Non-duality (*advaita*), 35, 43, 47f., 64, 74

North American Board for East-West Dialogue (NABEWD), 50, 90f., 103, 105, 110f.
Nostra Aetate, 50, 135

Orthodox Church, 170, 190, 195

Pantheism, 167, 171
Parliament of the World's Religions, 109, 141, 202
Pati divina, 170
Patience, 23, 84, 145, 149f., 180
Pentecost, 25, 51f.
Petersham, 50, 52–55, 63, 70, 72, 75f., 82f., 85ff., 89, 91, 96, 117, 129, 187, 201
Pontifical Council for Interreligious Dialogue, 3, 75, 104, 107, 118, 121ff., 127, 131, 138, 164, 189, 190 (*See* Secretariat for Non-Christians)
Populorum progressio, 199
Protestants, 86, 190

Redemptoris Missio, 2
Regimini Ecclesiae Universae, 20
Relativism, 36, 134, 196, 201
Resurrection, 147, 194
Rickenbach Center, 85
Rule of Benedict, 23, 55, 81, 144

Saccidananda, 45
Sacrament/al, 79f., 86
Saint Benedict's Monastery, 110
Sannyasa, sannyasi, 44, 47, 64, 128
Sant'Anselmo, 188
Satori, 126, 166
Science, 161, 191
Secretariat for Non-Christians, 20, 58f., 61 (*See* Pontifical

Council for Interreligious Dialogue)
Self-knowledge, 26, 153, 166, 182
Shakti, 46, 153, 155, 157
Shantivanam, 19, 42–47, 61, 64f.
Shariram, 155
Sherab Ling, 108
Silence, 6, 8f., 13, 22f., 36, 41, 45ff., 51, 120, 126f., 129f., 133, 139f., 145, 151, 157f., 162, 180, 185
Solitude, 6, 45, 139, 177, 179f., 184, 186
South America, 7, 108 (*See* Latin America)
Spencer Abbey, 120
Spiritual Exchange program, 5, 97f., 116, 189
Spirituality of dialogue, 11f., 19, 135, 136–204 *passim*
Sri Lanka, 7, 30, 41, 68, 108, 172, 190
Sufi, 5, 193, 196 (*See* Islam)
Sunyata, 35, 167 (*See* Emptiness)

Tantric, 196
Taoism, 41, 138
Temple, 153, 178, 180, 184ff.
Theology, 19, 78ff., 82, 114, 129, 147, 154, 157f., 169, 174, 191, 195, 197; megatheology, 192
Theravada Buddhism, 35
Tibhirine, 197
Tibet, Tibetan Buddhism, 20, 29, 35, 41f., 48, 68, 82f., 108, 162, 189f., 192

Transcendental Meditation, 115f., 120
Transfiguration, 155
Trappist/ine, 15, 39f., 52, 81, 90, 141, 197

Umbralatilem, 15
United Nations, 53, 89, 199
United States, 7, 70f., 82, 85, 91f., 105, 110f., 120, 138, 141, 190 (*See* America, American)
Unity, 9, 47, 53f., 77, 80, 139–42, 148, 151, 174, 200
Upanishad, 46, 167

Vanves, 16, 85, 103, 190
Vatican II/Second Vatican Council, 3, 18f., 22, 27, 34, 36f., 45, 101, 136, 148, 198
Vedanta, 43, 37
Vipassana, 9, 35, 159, 162, 194
Voies de l'Orient, 138

World Community for Christian Meditation, 147

Yoga, 9, 11, 35f., 41ff., 46f., 69, 74, 116, 119f., 125, 154f., 159f., 173, 191, 196

Zazen, 35, 153ff., 165, 173
Zen, 5, 9, 11, 35, 38–43, 48, 74, 82, 116, 119ff., 125, 153ff., 158ff., 162, 165f., 169, 173, 184f., 191f., 196, 203

www.ingramcontent.com/pod-product-compliance
Lightning Source LLC
Chambersburg PA
CBHW051940290426
44110CB00015B/2051